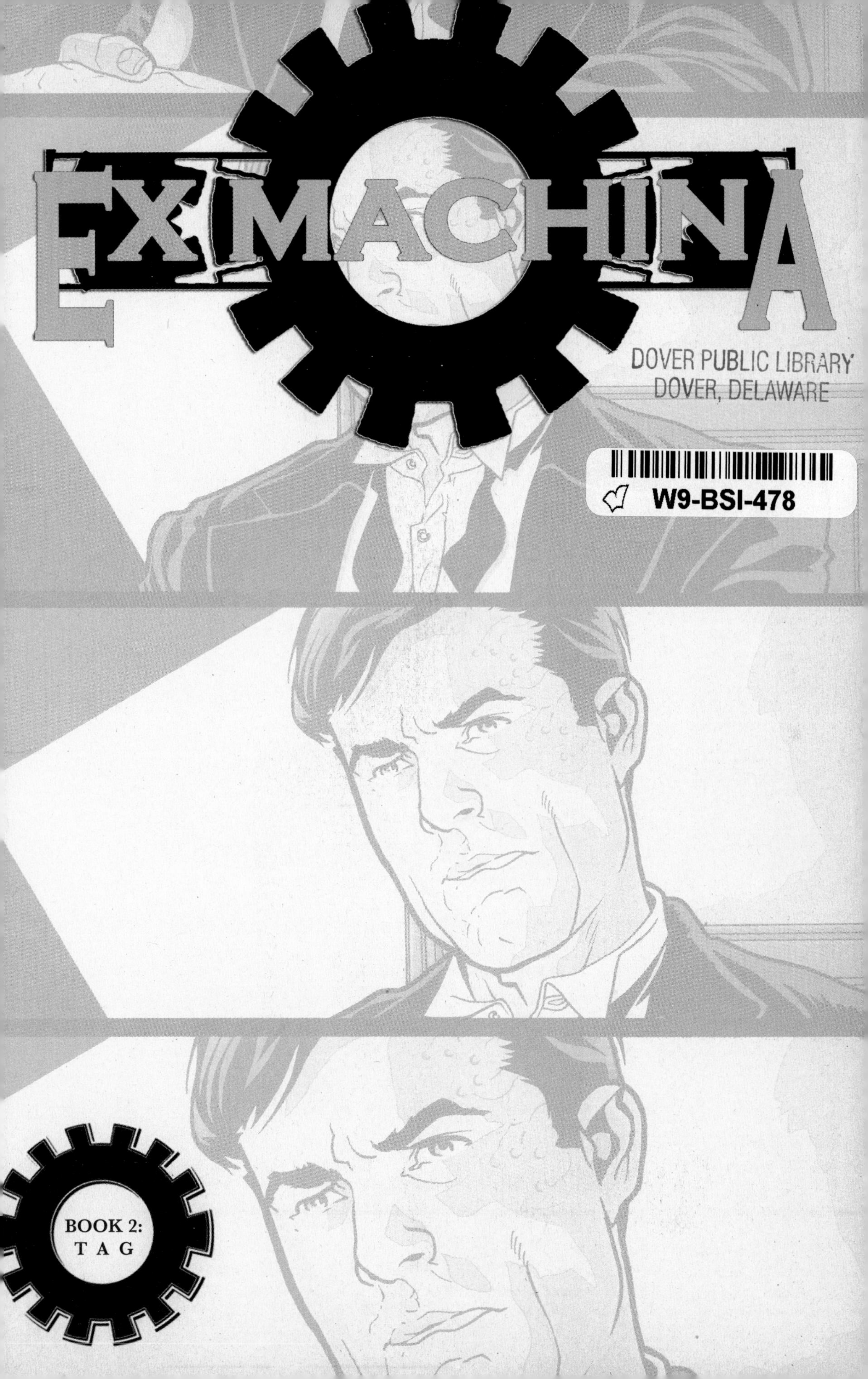
EX MACHINA
BOOK 2:
TAG

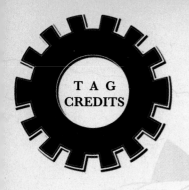

TAG CREDITS

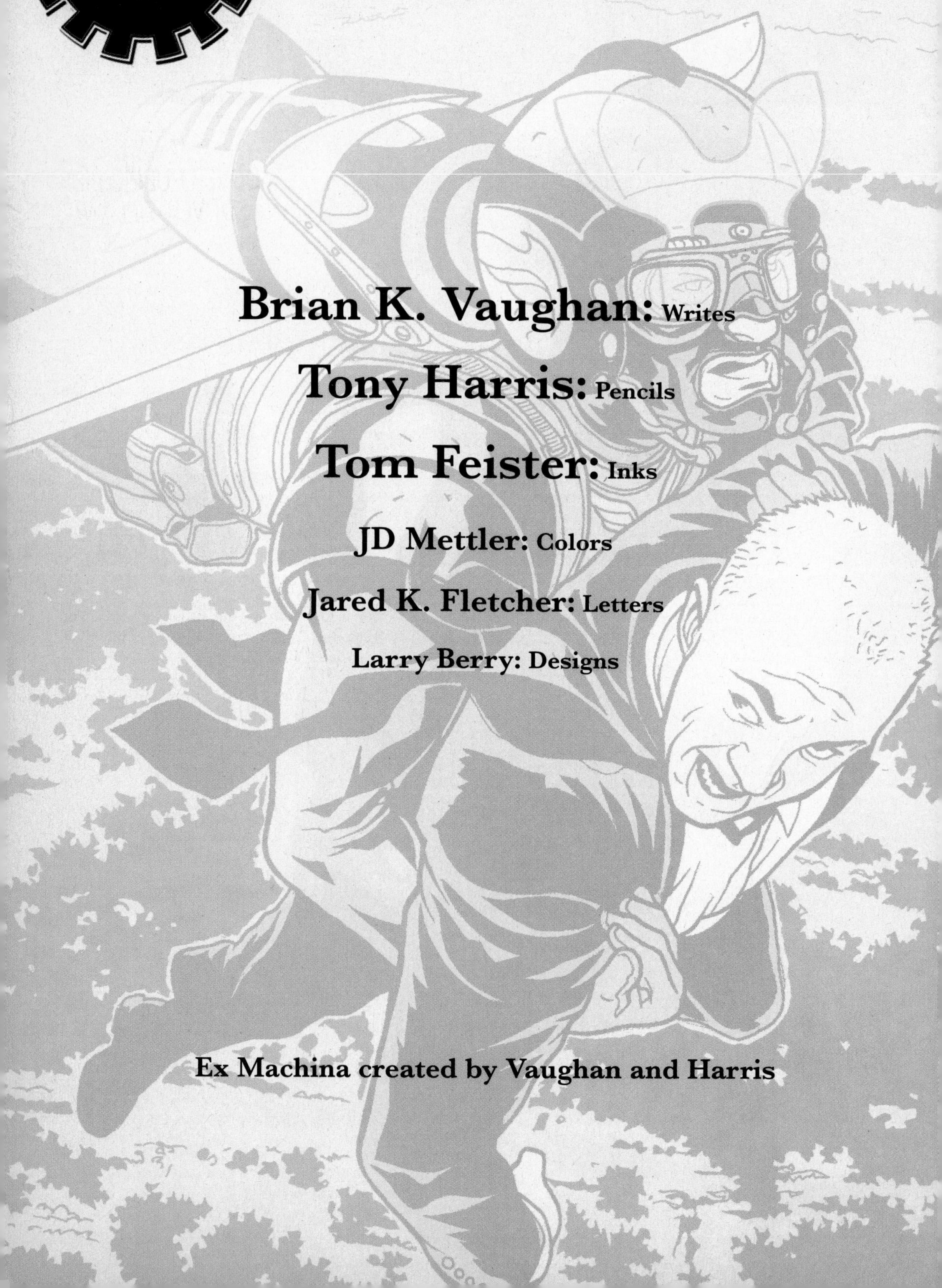

**Brian K. Vaughan:** Writes

**Tony Harris:** Pencils

**Tom Feister:** Inks

**JD Mettler:** Colors

**Jared K. Fletcher:** Letters

**Larry Berry:** Designs

**Ex Machina created by Vaughan and Harris**

EX MACHINA: TAG. Published by WildStorm Productions, an imprint of DC Comics. 888 Prospect St. #240, La Jolla, CA
92037. Cover, introduction, compilation copyright © 2005 Brian K. Vaughan and Tony Harris. All Rights Reserved. EX
MACHINA is ™ Brian K. Vaughan and Tony Harris. Originally published in single magazine form as EX MACHINA #6-10
© 2005 Brian K. Vaughan and Tony Harris.

WildStorm Signature Series is a trademark of DC Comics. The stories, characters, and incidents mentioned in this magazine
are entirely fictional. Printed on recyclable paper. WildStorm does not read or accept unsolicited submissions of ideas,
stories or artwork. PRINTED IN CANADA

DC Comics, a Warner Bros. Entertainment Company.

**TAG INTRO**

We're not terribly good at this sort of thing but we thought we should do it...because even though we have never met him, we are in love with Brian K. Vaughan. And we have been from the moment we picked up the first issue of Y: THE LAST MAN and started giggling when everything with a Y-chromosome suddenly exploded like a cat in a microwave–giggling not in a disturbing, sociopathic way, but in a completely delighted way as the sheer audaciousness of a new story-teller startled us awake from the sleep-walking world of comics where "fresh" and "original" are usually synonyms for "costume change." We left the comic shop that day with little hearts in our eyes...and ever since, we have faithfully bought every comic with Brian K. Vaughan's name on it.

However, as Sappho suggested, what is once sweet often turns bitter.

We had, on occasion, talked about the fact that if a real super-hero existed he or she would be a shoo-in for any political election. Let's face it, California elected someone just because he used to pretend he was a super-hero. The moral quagmire of politics seemed to us an ideal world to set a new kind of super-hero story. We kept the idea safe in our back pocket, figuring there were only a handful of writers who would dare defy one of the Establishment's favorite creeds: thou shalt not mix Art and Politics.

So, without any inkling whatsoever, we picked up the first issue of EX MACHINA and immediately the valentine-colored eyes with which we usually read a Brian K. Vaughan comic turned a Hulk-shaded green. How does one describe the feeling a writer has when they discover one of their ideas in the arms of another? Shock. Outrage. Panic. Lots of huffing and puffing followed by a slow deflation into resignation with mumbled, begrudging respect designed to mask petty, bitter jealousy.

It took a while for us to be big enough to buy the second issue but we're glad we did. The book is absolutely terrific. Tony Harris and Tom Feister's clean-lined, expressive artwork seamlessly weaves the "real" world of politics into the normal fabric of comics. And as for Brian's impeccable storytelling, well, what can we say? We love him.

**– The Wachowski Brothers**

Not only are they the insanely talented filmmakers behind the *Matrix Trilogy* and the forth-coming *V for Vendetta*, the Wachoswki Brothers also write and publish comic books under their *Burlyman* Entertainment line, including such great titles as *Doc Frankenstein* with Steve Skroce and *Shaolin Cowboy* by Geof Darrow.

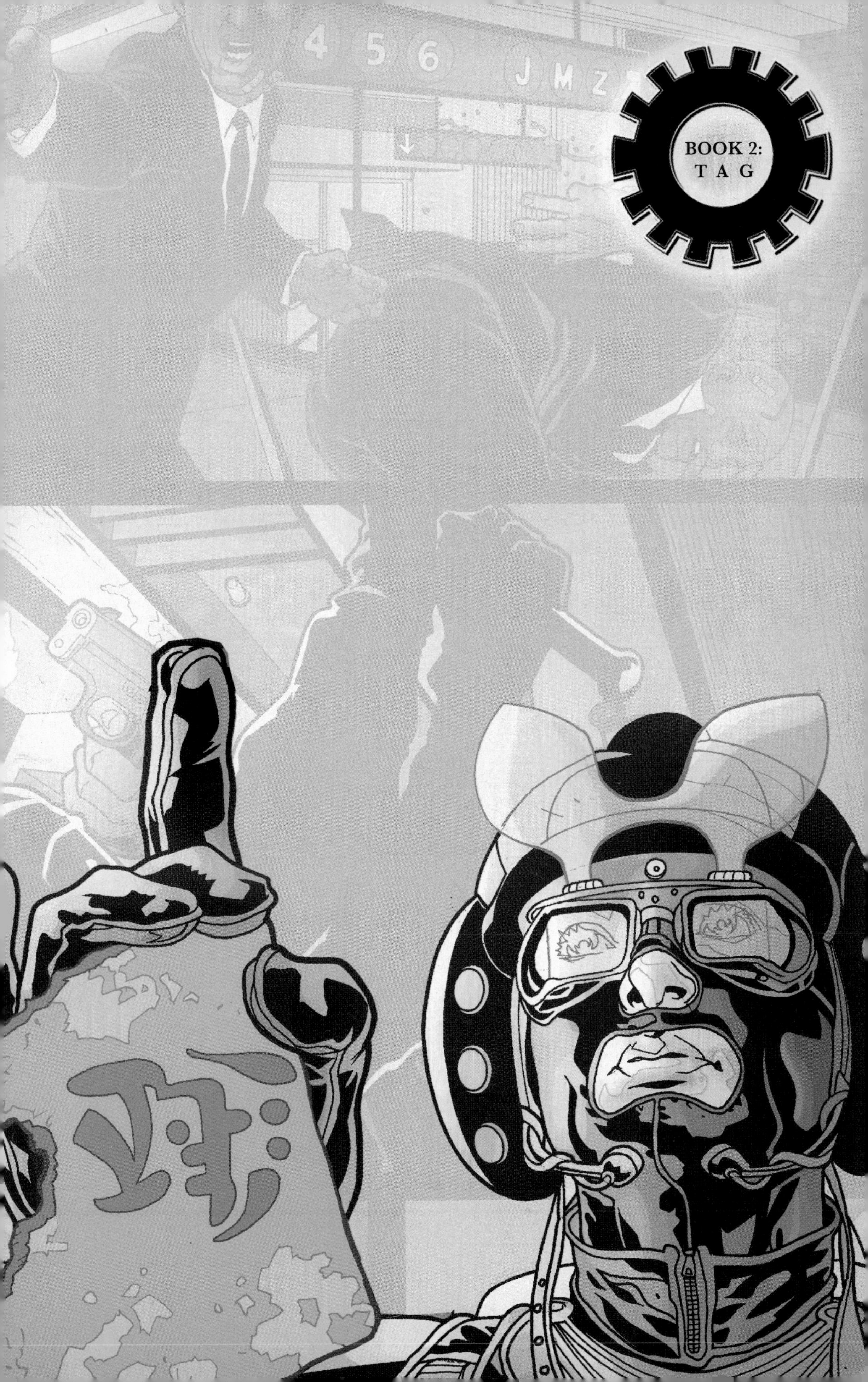
4 5 6
J M Z
BOOK 2:
T A G

PTER

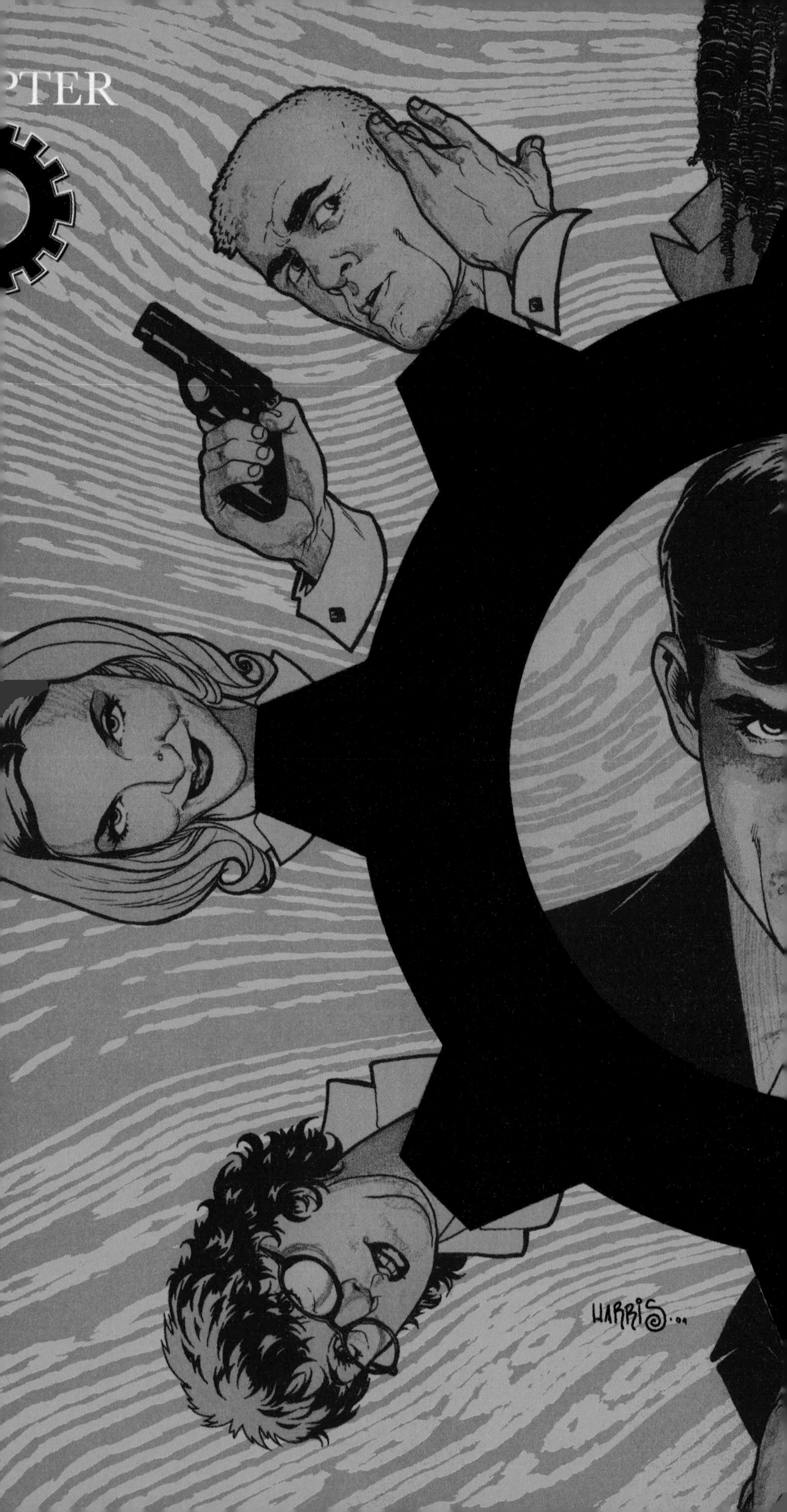
HARRIS

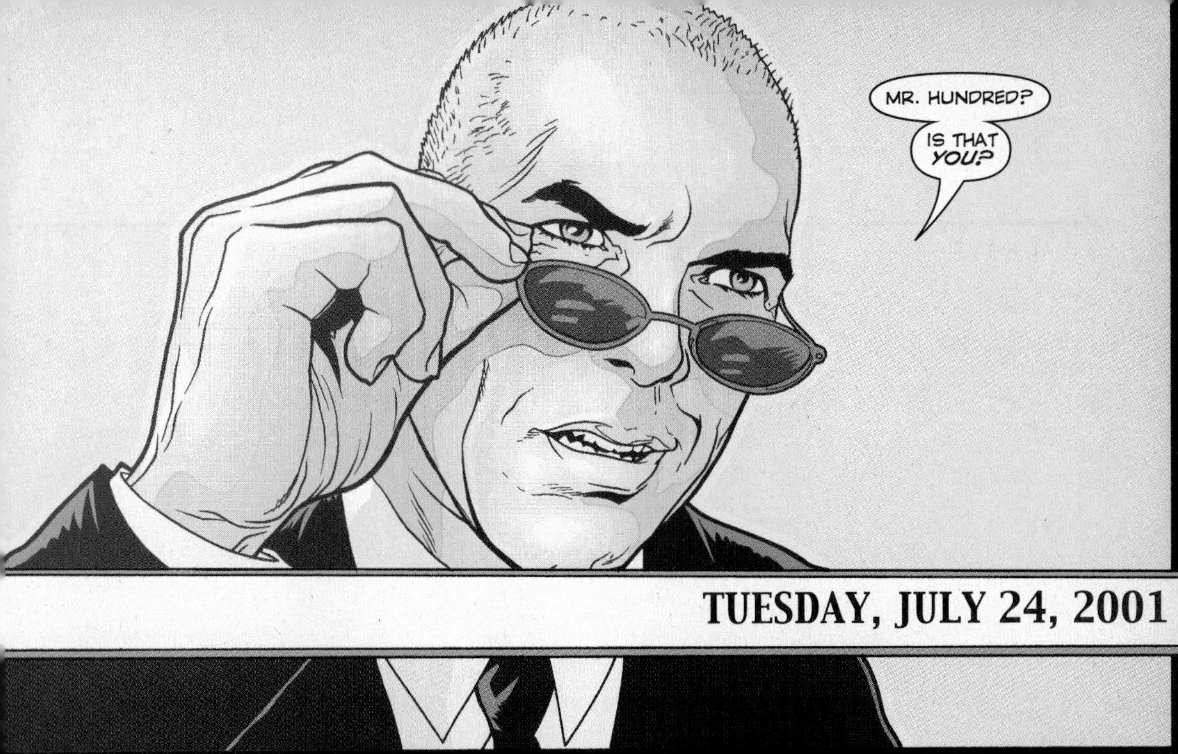
MR. HUNDRED?
IS THAT YOU?
TUESDAY, JULY 24, 2001

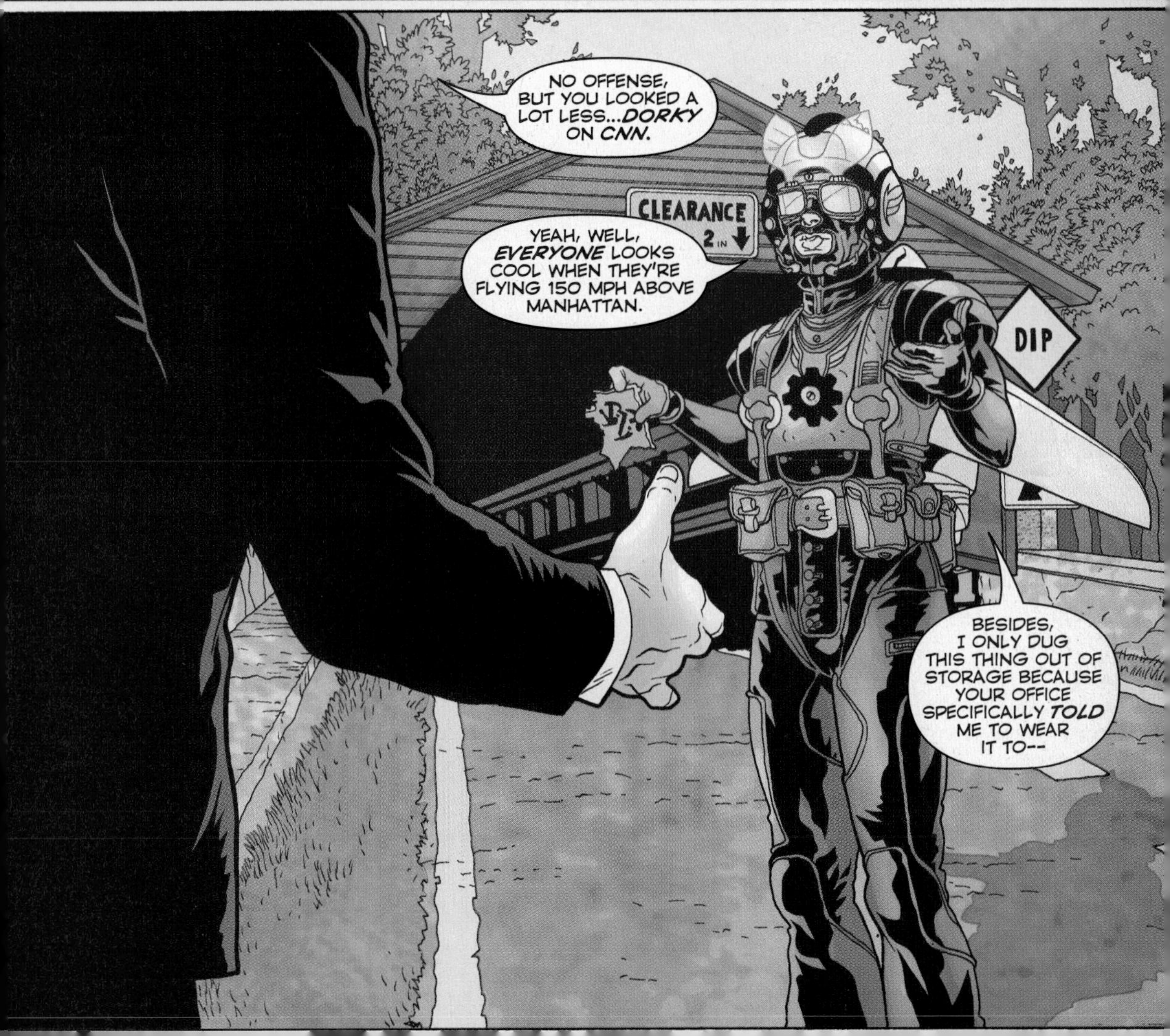
NO OFFENSE, BUT YOU LOOKED A LOT LESS...DORKY ON CNN.
CLEARANCE 2 IN
YEAH, WELL, EVERYONE LOOKS COOL WHEN THEY'RE FLYING 150 MPH ABOVE MANHATTAN.
DIP
BESIDES, I ONLY DUG THIS THING OUT OF STORAGE BECAUSE YOUR OFFICE SPECIFICALLY TOLD ME TO WEAR IT TO--

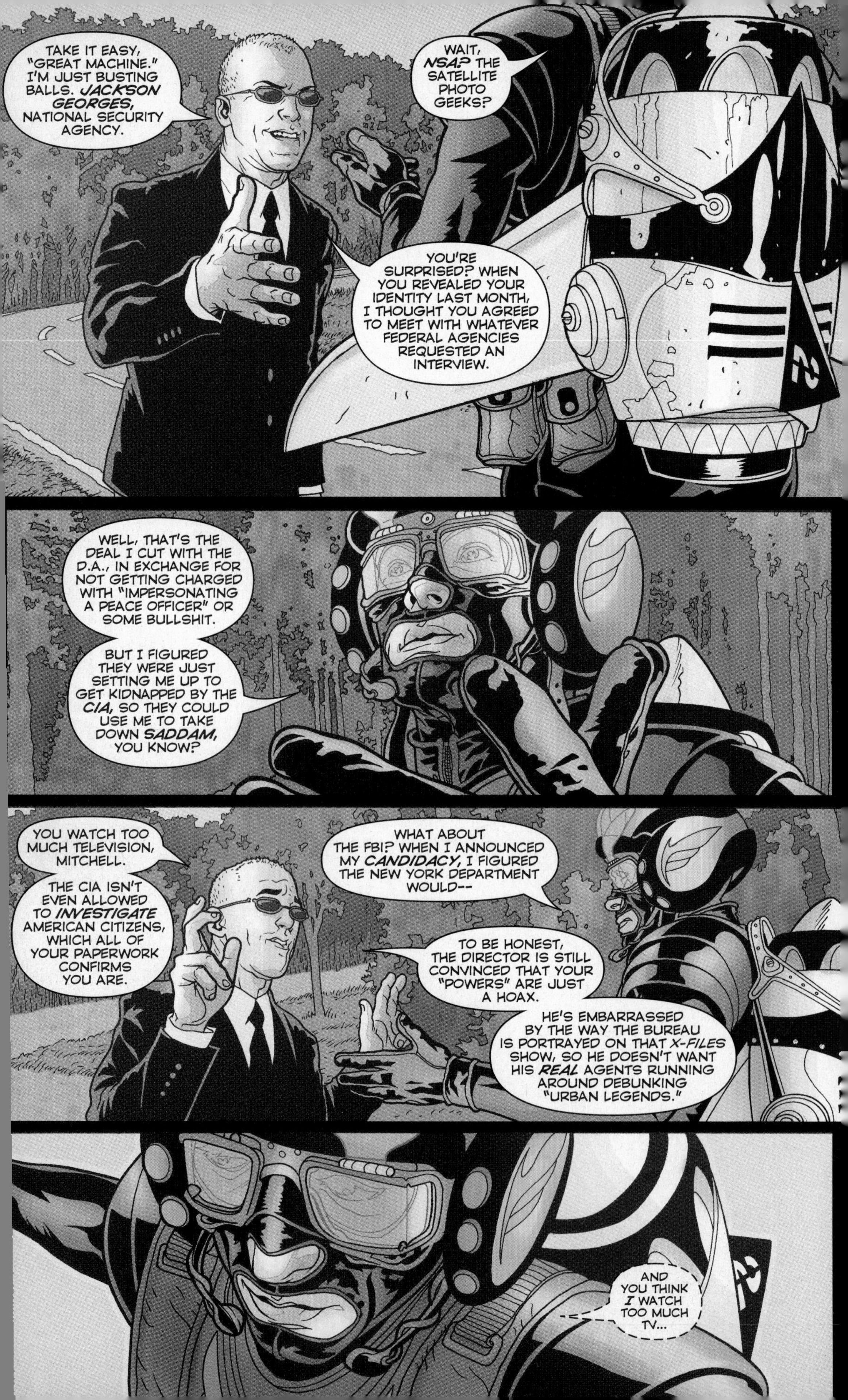
TAKE IT EASY, "GREAT MACHINE." I'M JUST BUSTING BALLS. *JACKSON GEORGES,* NATIONAL SECURITY AGENCY.
WAIT, *NSA?* THE SATELLITE PHOTO GEEKS?
YOU'RE SURPRISED? WHEN YOU REVEALED YOUR IDENTITY LAST MONTH, I THOUGHT YOU AGREED TO MEET WITH WHATEVER FEDERAL AGENCIES REQUESTED AN INTERVIEW.
WELL, THAT'S THE DEAL I CUT WITH THE D.A., IN EXCHANGE FOR NOT GETTING CHARGED WITH "IMPERSONATING A PEACE OFFICER" OR SOME BULLSHIT.
BUT I FIGURED THEY WERE JUST SETTING ME UP TO GET KIDNAPPED BY THE *CIA,* SO THEY COULD USE ME TO TAKE DOWN *SADDAM,* YOU KNOW?
YOU WATCH TOO MUCH TELEVISION, MITCHELL.
THE CIA ISN'T EVEN ALLOWED TO *INVESTIGATE* AMERICAN CITIZENS, WHICH ALL OF YOUR PAPERWORK CONFIRMS YOU ARE.
WHAT ABOUT THE FBI? WHEN I ANNOUNCED MY *CANDIDACY,* I FIGURED THE NEW YORK DEPARTMENT WOULD--
TO BE HONEST, THE DIRECTOR IS STILL CONVINCED THAT YOUR "POWERS" ARE JUST A HOAX.
HE'S EMBARRASSED BY THE WAY THE BUREAU IS PORTRAYED ON THAT *X-FILES* SHOW, SO HE DOESN'T WANT HIS *REAL* AGENTS RUNNING AROUND DEBUNKING "URBAN LEGENDS."
AND YOU THINK *I* WATCH TOO MUCH TV...

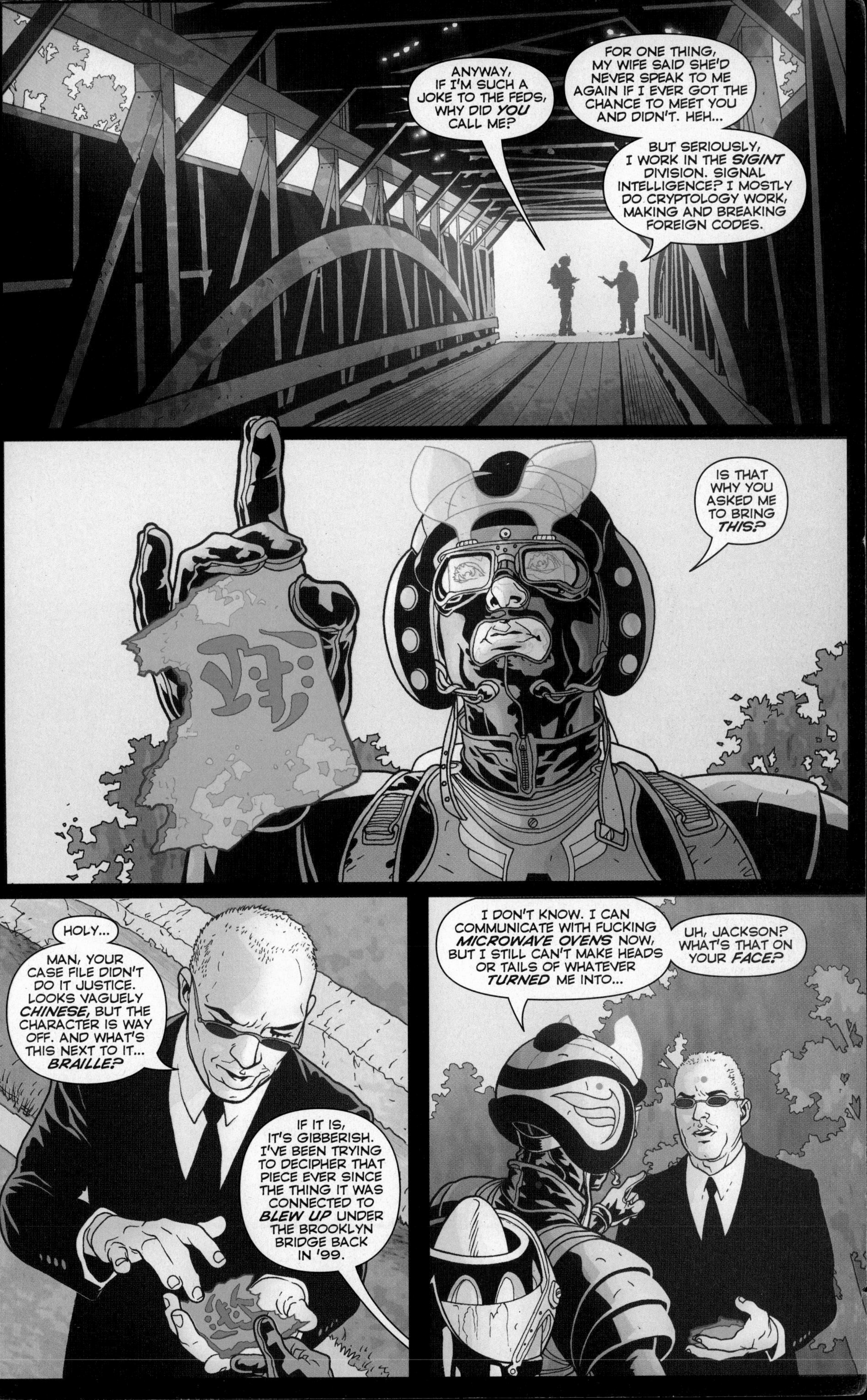
ANYWAY, IF I'M SUCH A JOKE TO THE FEDS, WHY DID *YOU* CALL ME?
FOR ONE THING, MY WIFE SAID SHE'D NEVER SPEAK TO ME AGAIN IF I EVER GOT THE CHANCE TO MEET YOU AND DIDN'T. HEH...
BUT SERIOUSLY, I WORK IN THE *SIGINT* DIVISION. SIGNAL INTELLIGENCE? I MOSTLY DO CRYPTOLOGY WORK, MAKING AND BREAKING FOREIGN CODES.
IS THAT WHY YOU ASKED ME TO BRING *THIS?*
HOLY...
MAN, YOUR CASE FILE DIDN'T DO IT JUSTICE. LOOKS VAGUELY *CHINESE,* BUT THE CHARACTER IS WAY OFF. AND WHAT'S THIS NEXT TO IT... *BRAILLE?*
IF IT IS, IT'S GIBBERISH. I'VE BEEN TRYING TO DECIPHER THAT PIECE EVER SINCE THE THING IT WAS CONNECTED TO *BLEW UP* UNDER THE BROOKLYN BRIDGE BACK IN '99.
I DON'T KNOW. I CAN COMMUNICATE WITH FUCKING *MICROWAVE OVENS* NOW, BUT I STILL CAN'T MAKE HEADS OR TAILS OF WHATEVER *TURNED* ME INTO...
UH, JACKSON? WHAT'S THAT ON YOUR *FACE?*

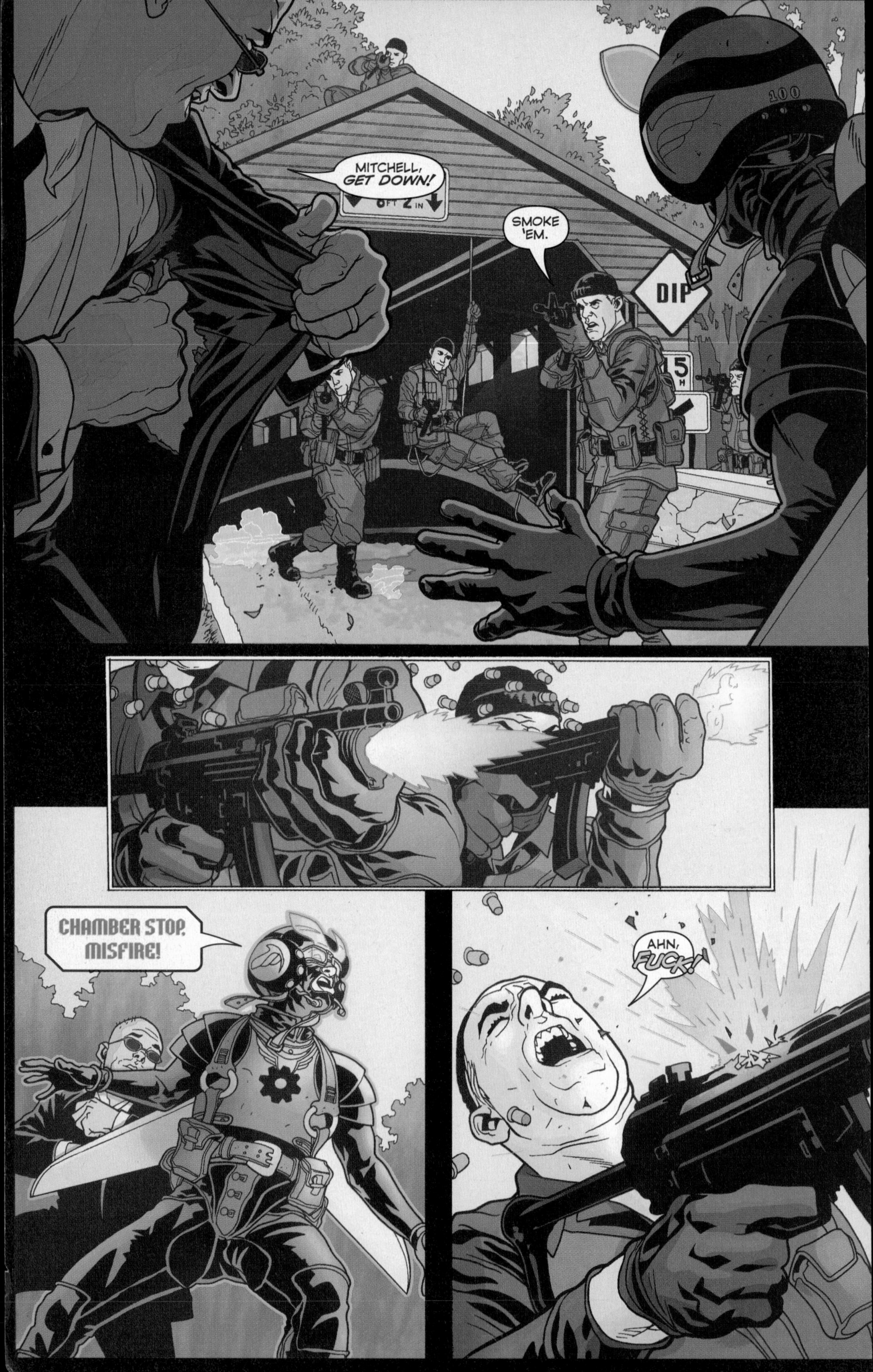
MITCHELL, GET DOWN!
6FT 2IN
SMOKE 'EM.
DIP
CHAMBER STOP. MISFIRE!
AHN, FUCK!

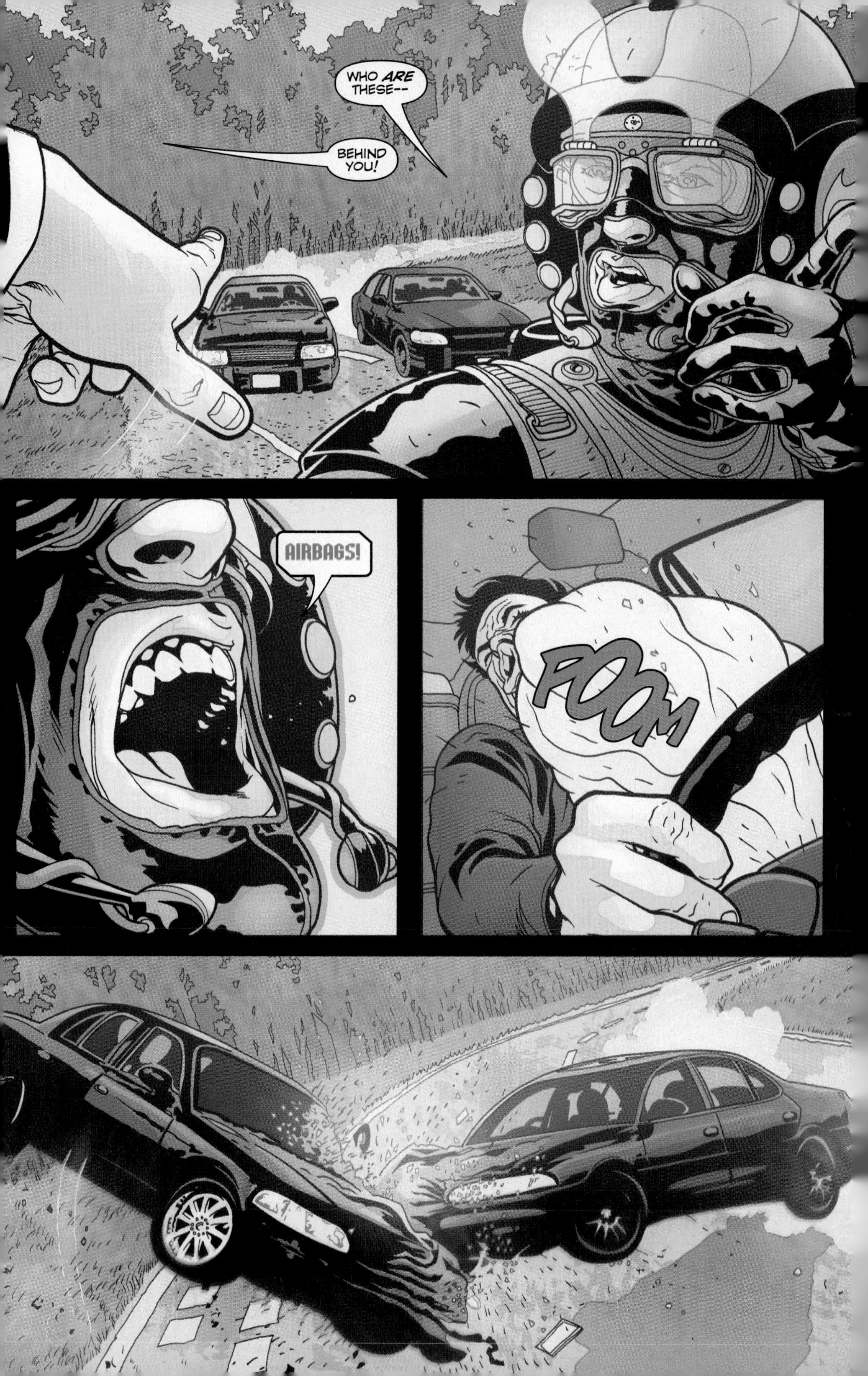
WHO *ARE* THESE--
BEHIND YOU!
AIRBAGS!
POOM

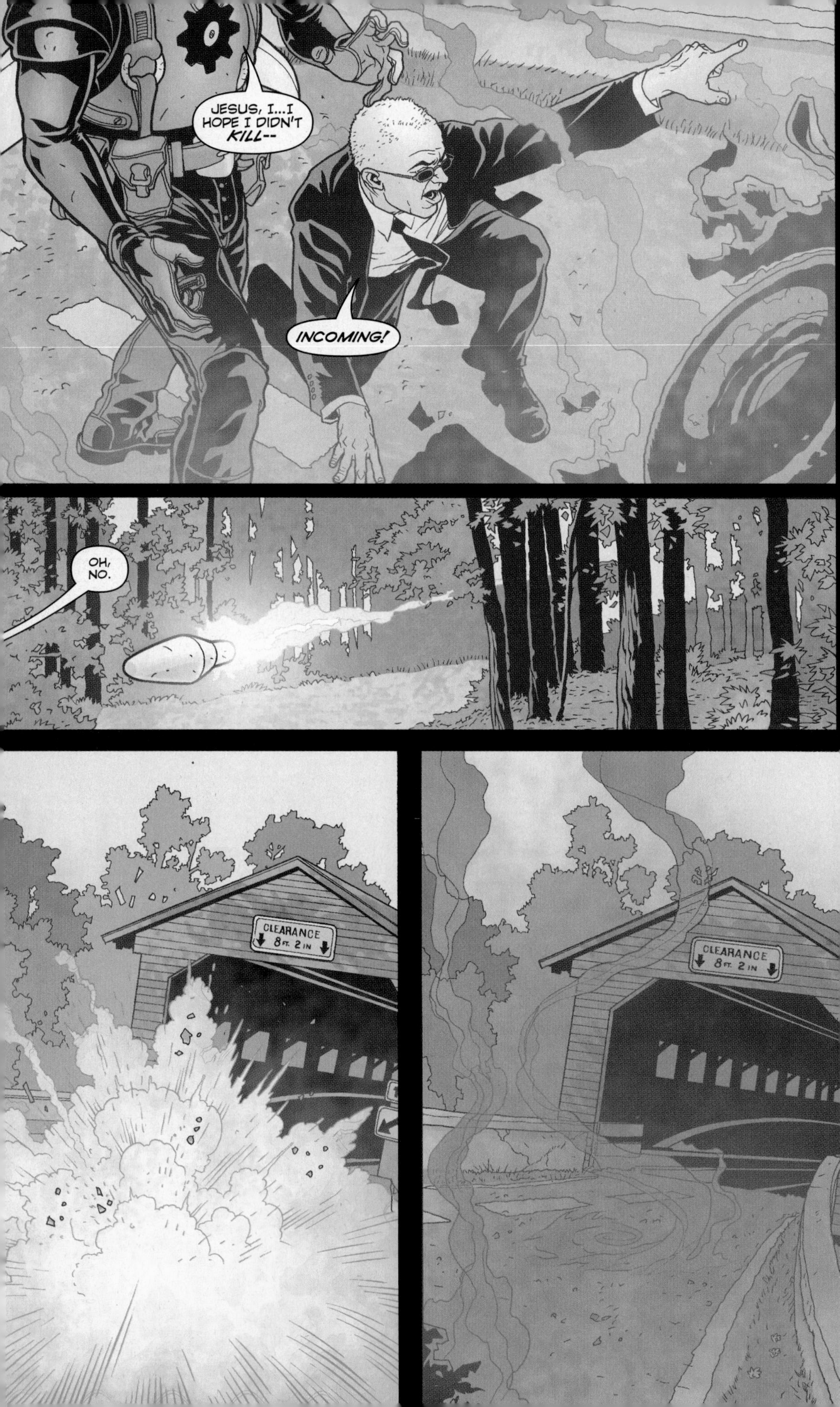
JESUS, I...I HOPE I DIDN'T *KILL*--
*INCOMING!*
OH, NO.
CLEARANCE 8 FT. 2 IN
CLEARANCE 8 FT. 2 IN

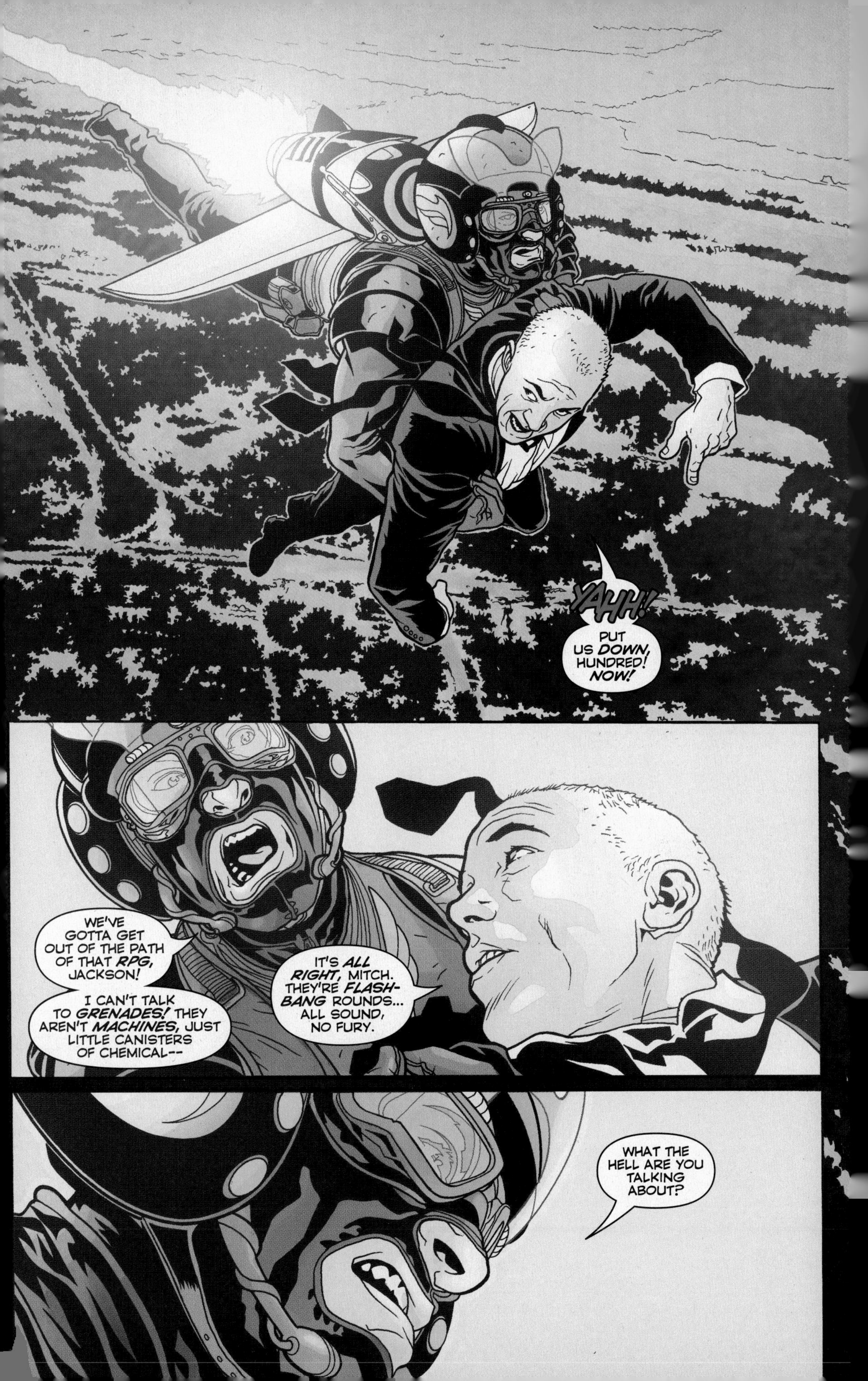

YAHH!
PUT US DOWN, HUNDRED! NOW!
WE'VE GOTTA GET OUT OF THE PATH OF THAT RPG, JACKSON!
I CAN'T TALK TO GRENADES! THEY AREN'T MACHINES, JUST LITTLE CANISTERS OF CHEMICAL--
IT'S ALL RIGHT, MITCH. THEY'RE FLASH-BANG ROUNDS... ALL SOUND, NO FURY.
WHAT THE HELL ARE YOU TALKING ABOUT?

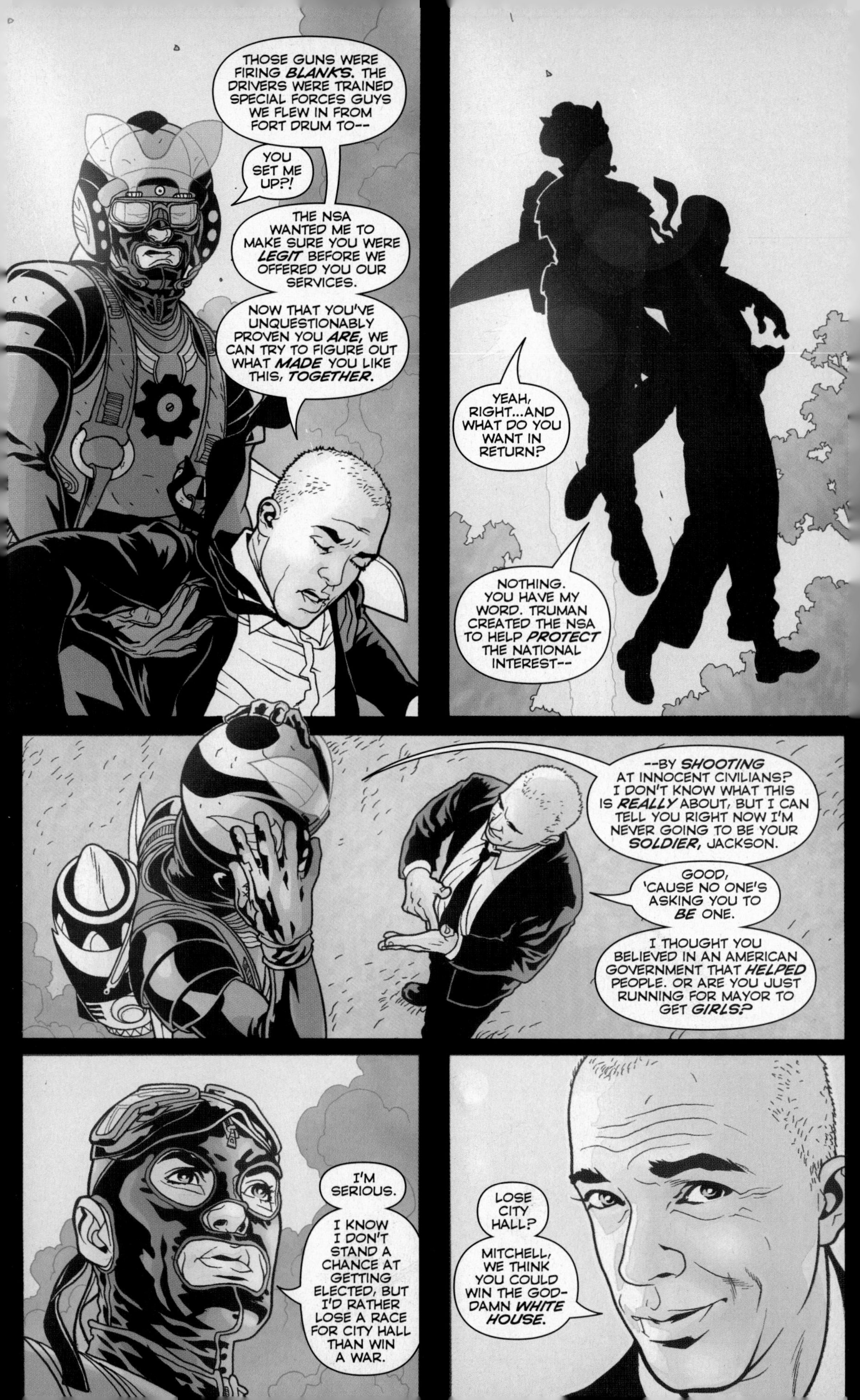

THOSE GUNS WERE FIRING BLANKS. THE DRIVERS WERE TRAINED SPECIAL FORCES GUYS WE FLEW IN FROM FORT DRUM TO--
YOU SET ME UP?!
THE NSA WANTED ME TO MAKE SURE YOU WERE LEGIT BEFORE WE OFFERED YOU OUR SERVICES.
NOW THAT YOU'VE UNQUESTIONABLY PROVEN YOU ARE, WE CAN TRY TO FIGURE OUT WHAT MADE YOU LIKE THIS, TOGETHER.
YEAH, RIGHT...AND WHAT DO YOU WANT IN RETURN?
NOTHING. YOU HAVE MY WORD. TRUMAN CREATED THE NSA TO HELP PROTECT THE NATIONAL INTEREST--
--BY SHOOTING AT INNOCENT CIVILIANS? I DON'T KNOW WHAT THIS IS REALLY ABOUT, BUT I CAN TELL YOU RIGHT NOW I'M NEVER GOING TO BE YOUR SOLDIER, JACKSON.
GOOD, 'CAUSE NO ONE'S ASKING YOU TO BE ONE.
I THOUGHT YOU BELIEVED IN AN AMERICAN GOVERNMENT THAT HELPED PEOPLE. OR ARE YOU JUST RUNNING FOR MAYOR TO GET GIRLS?
I'M SERIOUS.
I KNOW I DON'T STAND A CHANCE AT GETTING ELECTED, BUT I'D RATHER LOSE A RACE FOR CITY HALL THAN WIN A WAR.
LOSE CITY HALL?
MITCHELL, WE THINK YOU COULD WIN THE GOD-DAMN WHITE HOUSE.

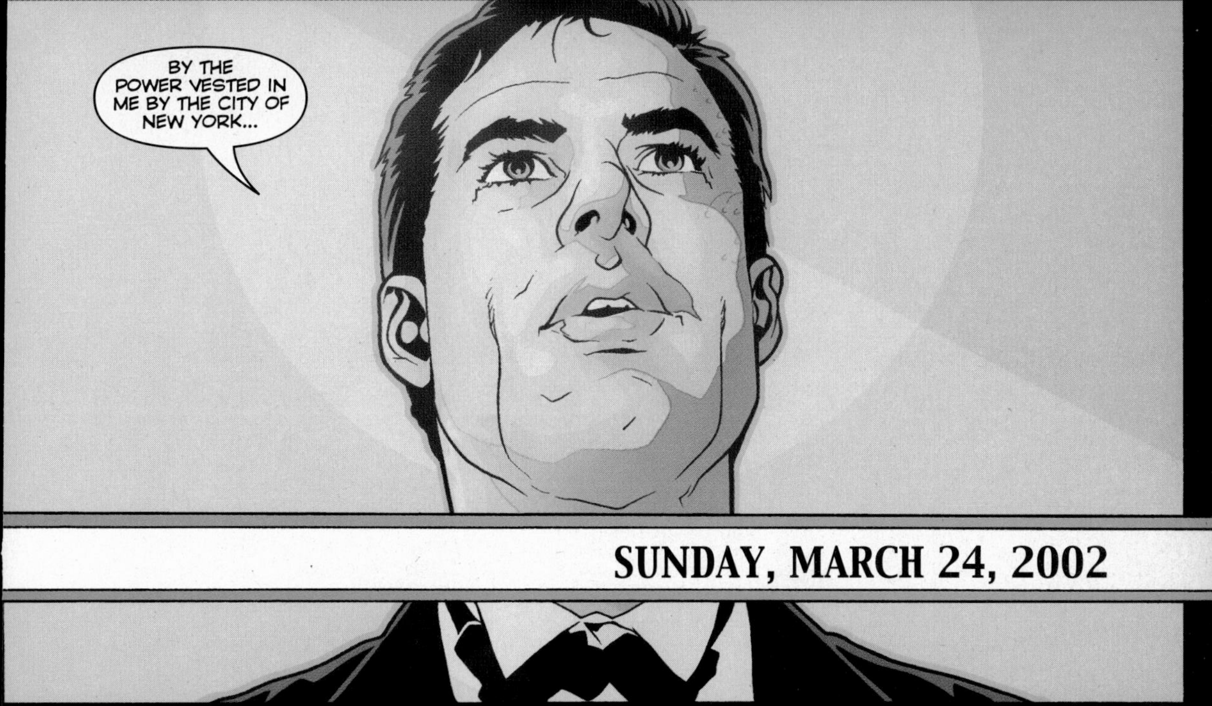
BY THE POWER VESTED IN ME BY THE CITY OF NEW YORK...
SUNDAY, MARCH 24, 2002

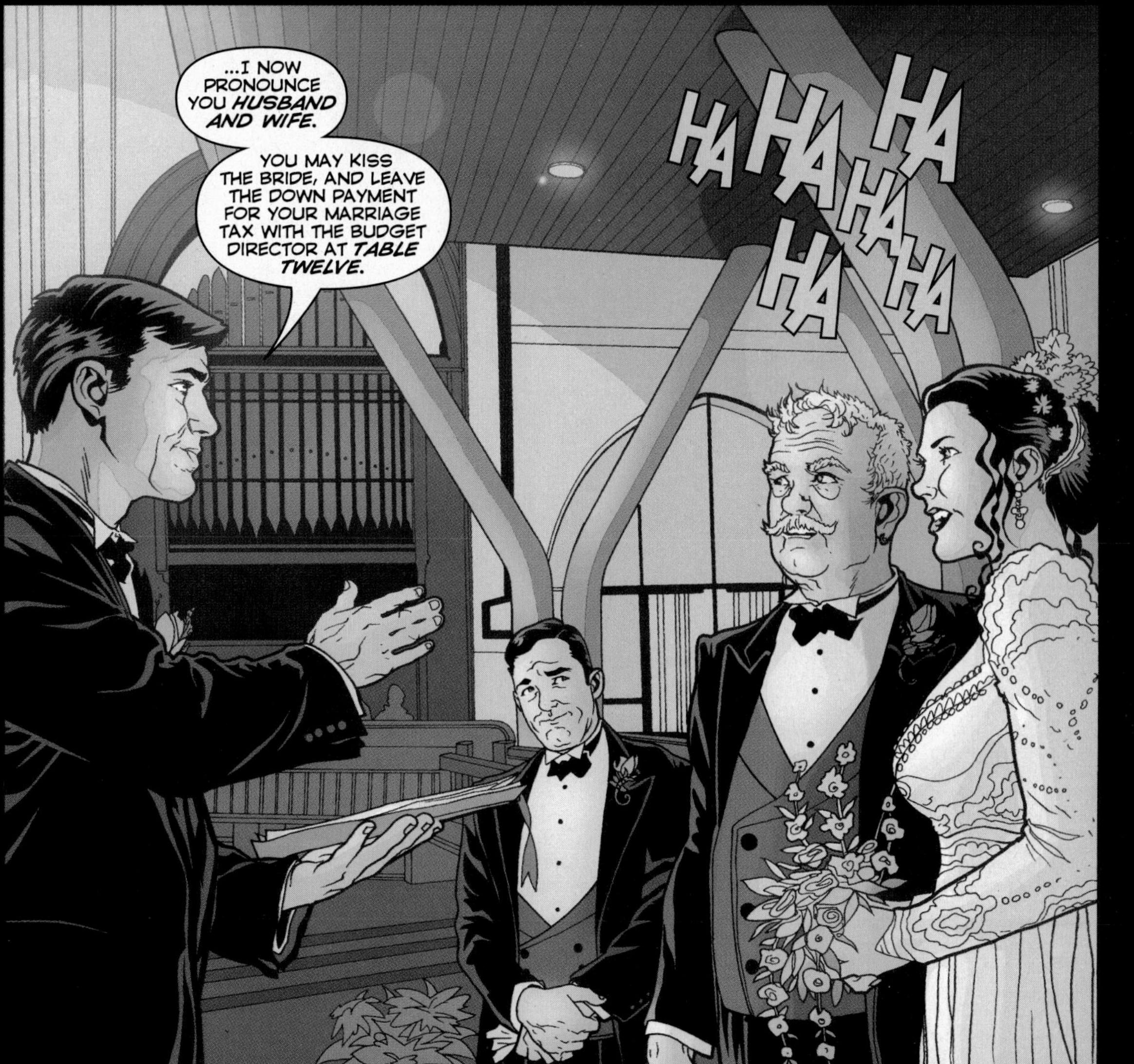
...I NOW PRONOUNCE YOU *HUSBAND AND WIFE*.
YOU MAY KISS THE BRIDE, AND LEAVE THE DOWN PAYMENT FOR YOUR MARRIAGE TAX WITH THE BUDGET DIRECTOR AT *TABLE TWELVE*.
HA HA HA HA HA HA HA HA

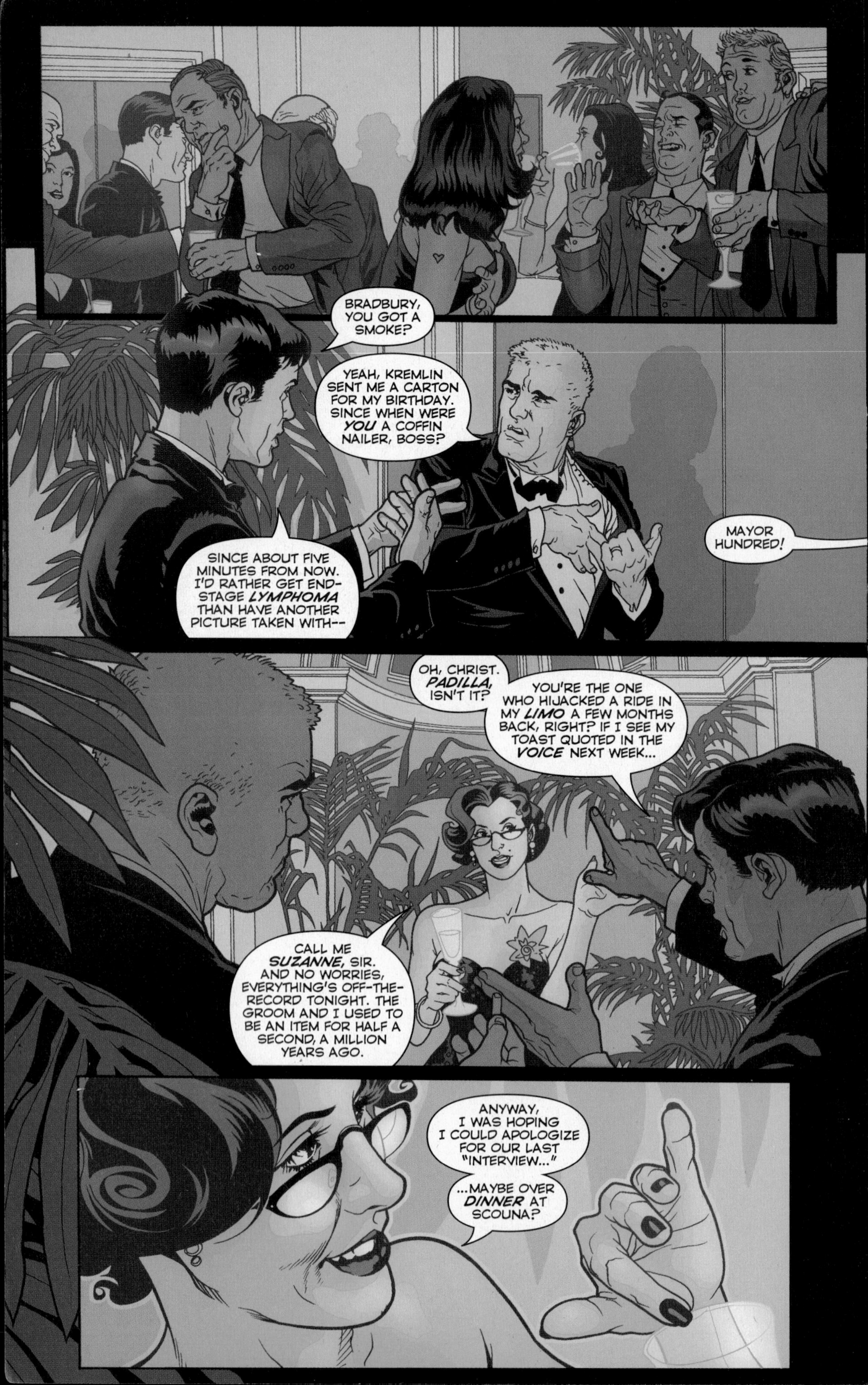
BRADBURY, YOU GOT A SMOKE?
YEAH, KREMLIN SENT ME A CARTON FOR MY BIRTHDAY. SINCE WHEN WERE *YOU* A COFFIN NAILER, BOSS?
SINCE ABOUT FIVE MINUTES FROM NOW. I'D RATHER GET END-STAGE *LYMPHOMA* THAN HAVE ANOTHER PICTURE TAKEN WITH--
MAYOR HUNDRED!
OH, CHRIST. *PADILLA,* ISN'T IT?
YOU'RE THE ONE WHO HIJACKED A RIDE IN MY *LIMO* A FEW MONTHS BACK, RIGHT? IF I SEE MY TOAST QUOTED IN THE *VOICE* NEXT WEEK...
CALL ME *SUZANNE,* SIR. AND NO WORRIES, EVERYTHING'S OFF-THE-RECORD TONIGHT. THE GROOM AND I USED TO BE AN ITEM FOR HALF A SECOND, A MILLION YEARS AGO.
ANYWAY, I WAS HOPING I COULD APOLOGIZE FOR OUR LAST "INTERVIEW..."
...MAYBE OVER *DINNER* AT SCOUNA?

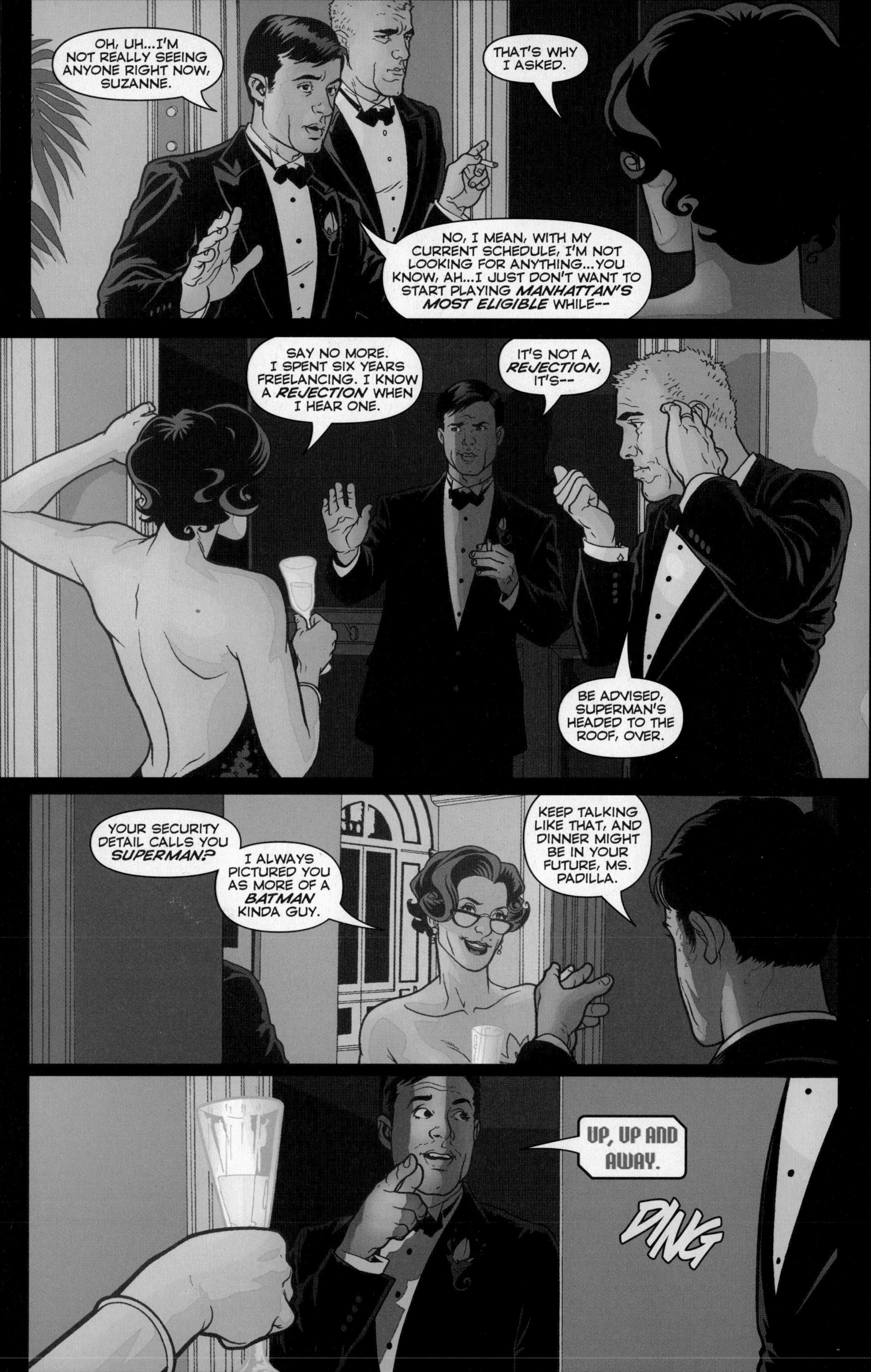
OH, UH...I'M NOT REALLY SEEING ANYONE RIGHT NOW, SUZANNE.
THAT'S WHY I ASKED.
NO, I MEAN, WITH MY CURRENT SCHEDULE, I'M NOT LOOKING FOR ANYTHING...YOU KNOW, AH...I JUST DON'T WANT TO START PLAYING MANHATTAN'S MOST ELIGIBLE WHILE--
SAY NO MORE. I SPENT SIX YEARS FREELANCING. I KNOW A REJECTION WHEN I HEAR ONE.
IT'S NOT A REJECTION, IT'S--
BE ADVISED, SUPERMAN'S HEADED TO THE ROOF, OVER.
YOUR SECURITY DETAIL CALLS YOU SUPERMAN?
I ALWAYS PICTURED YOU AS MORE OF A BATMAN KINDA GUY.
KEEP TALKING LIKE THAT, AND DINNER MIGHT BE IN YOUR FUTURE, MS. PADILLA.
UP, UP AND AWAY.
DING

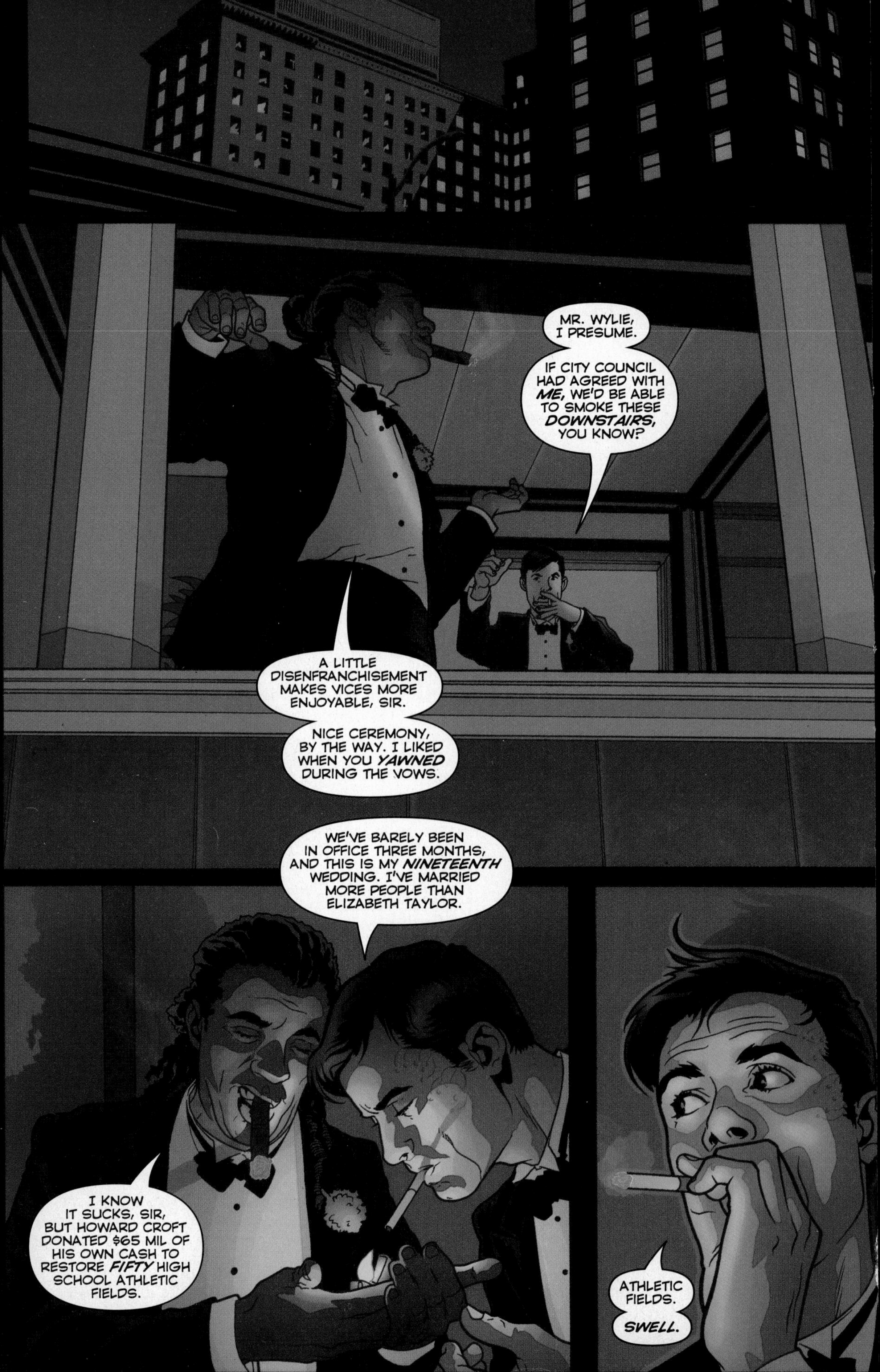

MR. WYLIE, I PRESUME.
IF CITY COUNCIL HAD AGREED WITH *ME,* WE'D BE ABLE TO SMOKE THESE *DOWNSTAIRS,* YOU KNOW?
A LITTLE DISENFRANCHISEMENT MAKES VICES MORE ENJOYABLE, SIR.
NICE CEREMONY, BY THE WAY. I LIKED WHEN YOU *YAWNED* DURING THE VOWS.
WE'VE BARELY BEEN IN OFFICE THREE MONTHS, AND THIS IS MY *NINETEENTH* WEDDING. I'VE MARRIED MORE PEOPLE THAN ELIZABETH TAYLOR.
I KNOW IT SUCKS, SIR, BUT HOWARD CROFT DONATED $65 MIL OF HIS OWN CASH TO RESTORE *FIFTY* HIGH SCHOOL ATHLETIC FIELDS.
ATHLETIC FIELDS.
*SWELL.*

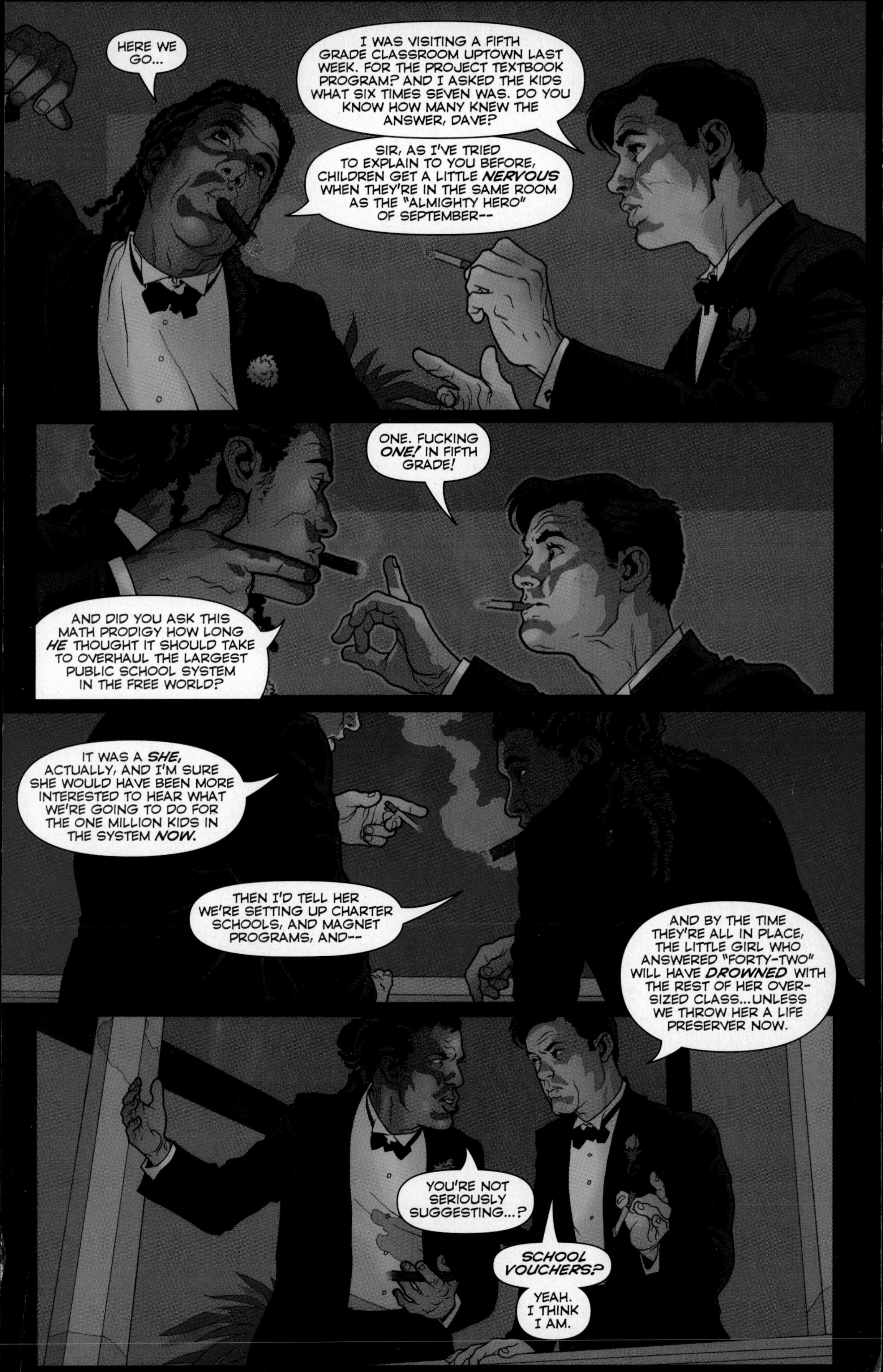
HERE WE GO...
I WAS VISITING A FIFTH GRADE CLASSROOM UPTOWN LAST WEEK. FOR THE PROJECT TEXTBOOK PROGRAM? AND I ASKED THE KIDS WHAT SIX TIMES SEVEN WAS. DO YOU KNOW HOW MANY KNEW THE ANSWER, DAVE?
SIR, AS I'VE TRIED TO EXPLAIN TO YOU BEFORE, CHILDREN GET A LITTLE NERVOUS WHEN THEY'RE IN THE SAME ROOM AS THE "ALMIGHTY HERO" OF SEPTEMBER--
ONE. FUCKING ONE! IN FIFTH GRADE!
AND DID YOU ASK THIS MATH PRODIGY HOW LONG HE THOUGHT IT SHOULD TAKE TO OVERHAUL THE LARGEST PUBLIC SCHOOL SYSTEM IN THE FREE WORLD?
IT WAS A SHE, ACTUALLY, AND I'M SURE SHE WOULD HAVE BEEN MORE INTERESTED TO HEAR WHAT WE'RE GOING TO DO FOR THE ONE MILLION KIDS IN THE SYSTEM NOW.
THEN I'D TELL HER WE'RE SETTING UP CHARTER SCHOOLS, AND MAGNET PROGRAMS, AND--
AND BY THE TIME THEY'RE ALL IN PLACE, THE LITTLE GIRL WHO ANSWERED "FORTY-TWO" WILL HAVE DROWNED WITH THE REST OF HER OVER-SIZED CLASS...UNLESS WE THROW HER A LIFE PRESERVER NOW.
YOU'RE NOT SERIOUSLY SUGGESTING...?
SCHOOL VOUCHERS?
YEAH. I THINK I AM.

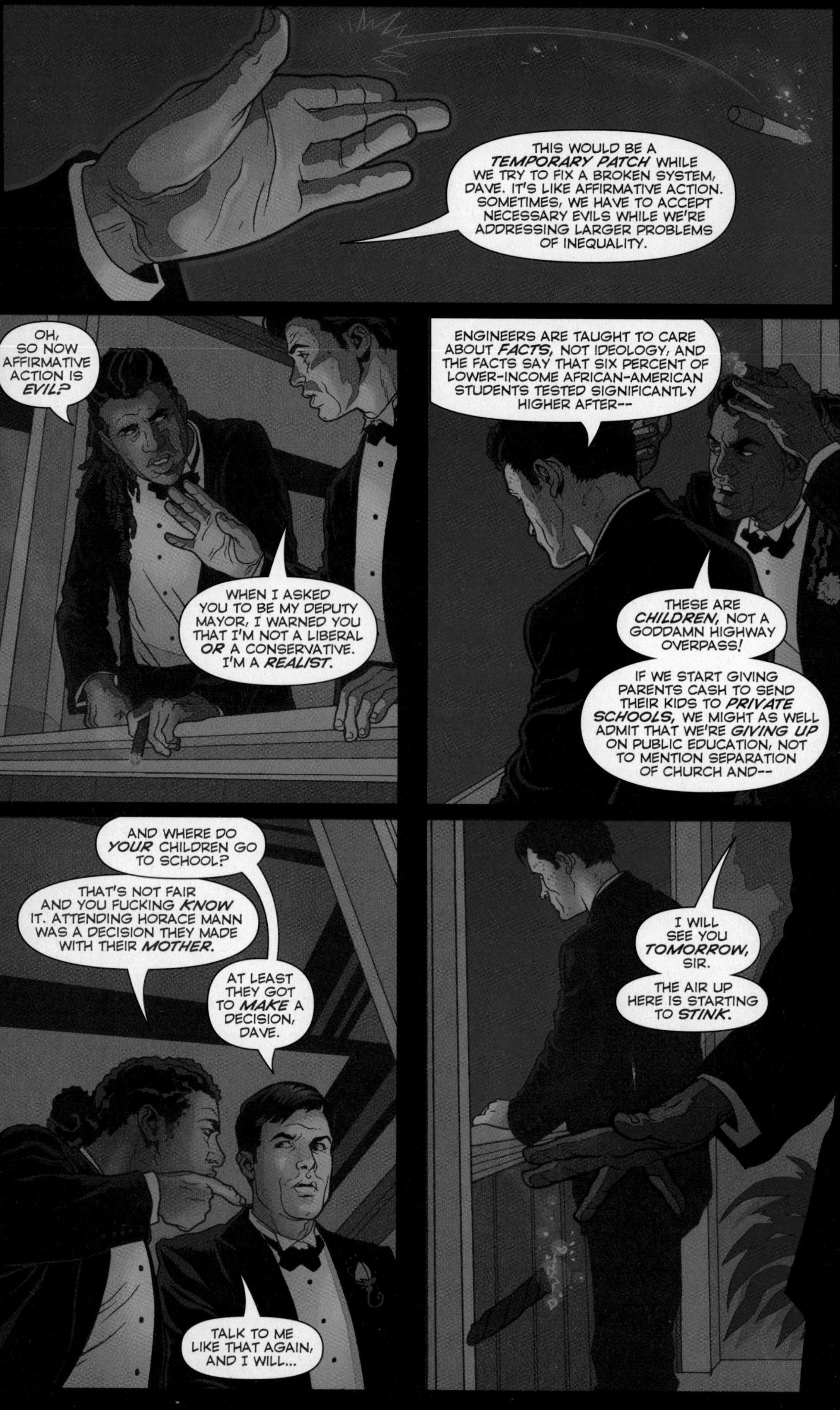
THIS WOULD BE A TEMPORARY PATCH WHILE WE TRY TO FIX A BROKEN SYSTEM, DAVE. IT'S LIKE AFFIRMATIVE ACTION. SOMETIMES, WE HAVE TO ACCEPT NECESSARY EVILS WHILE WE'RE ADDRESSING LARGER PROBLEMS OF INEQUALITY.
OH, SO NOW AFFIRMATIVE ACTION IS EVIL?
WHEN I ASKED YOU TO BE MY DEPUTY MAYOR, I WARNED YOU THAT I'M NOT A LIBERAL OR A CONSERVATIVE. I'M A REALIST.
ENGINEERS ARE TAUGHT TO CARE ABOUT FACTS, NOT IDEOLOGY, AND THE FACTS SAY THAT SIX PERCENT OF LOWER-INCOME AFRICAN-AMERICAN STUDENTS TESTED SIGNIFICANTLY HIGHER AFTER--
THESE ARE CHILDREN, NOT A GODDAMN HIGHWAY OVERPASS!
IF WE START GIVING PARENTS CASH TO SEND THEIR KIDS TO PRIVATE SCHOOLS, WE MIGHT AS WELL ADMIT THAT WE'RE GIVING UP ON PUBLIC EDUCATION, NOT TO MENTION SEPARATION OF CHURCH AND--
AND WHERE DO YOUR CHILDREN GO TO SCHOOL?
THAT'S NOT FAIR AND YOU FUCKING KNOW IT. ATTENDING HORACE MANN WAS A DECISION THEY MADE WITH THEIR MOTHER.
AT LEAST THEY GOT TO MAKE A DECISION, DAVE.
TALK TO ME LIKE THAT AGAIN, AND I WILL...
I WILL SEE YOU TOMORROW, SIR.
THE AIR UP HERE IS STARTING TO STINK.

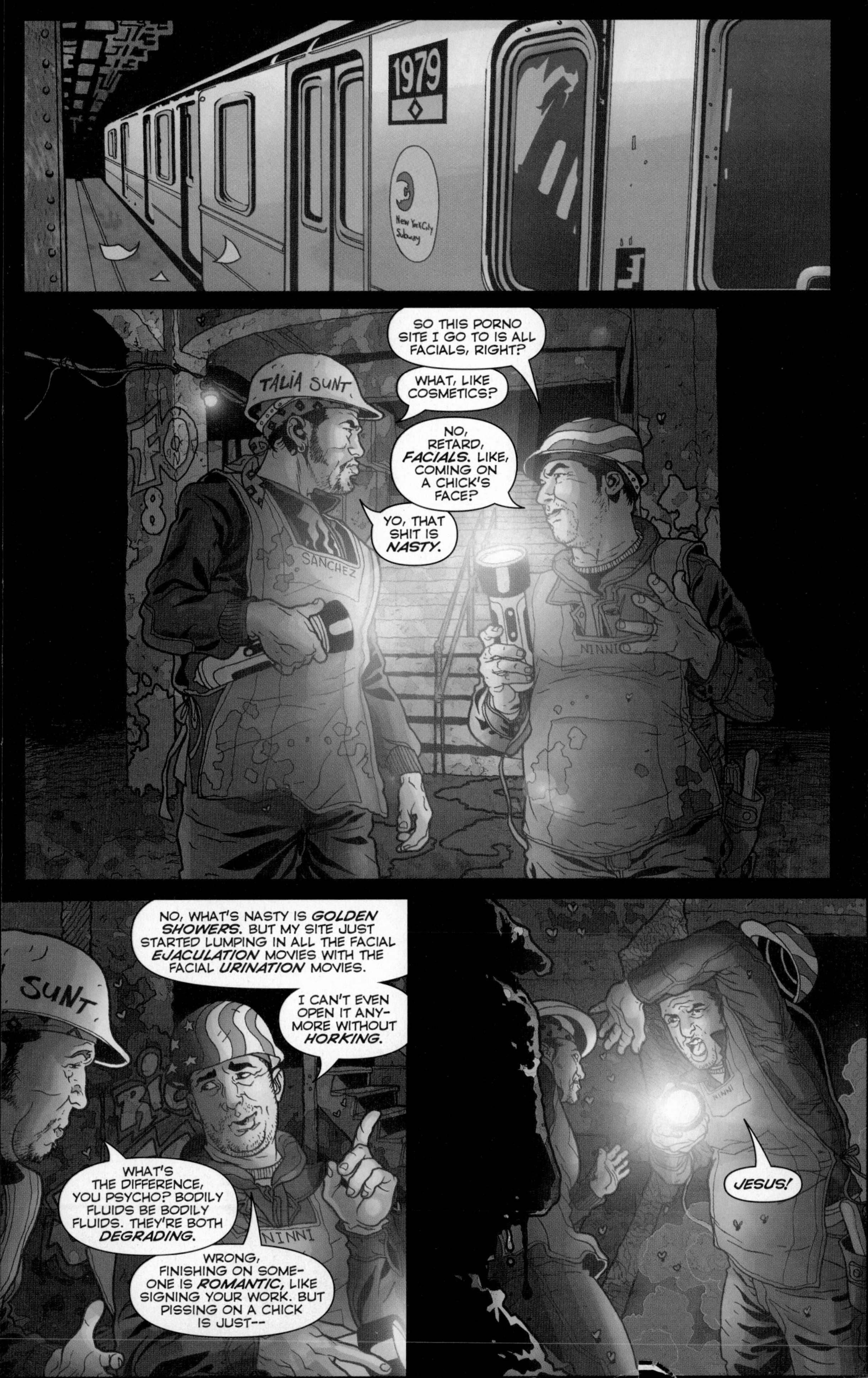
1979
New York City Subway
SO THIS PORNO SITE I GO TO IS ALL FACIALS, RIGHT?
WHAT, LIKE COSMETICS?
NO, RETARD, FACIALS. LIKE, COMING ON A CHICK'S FACE?
YO, THAT SHIT IS NASTY.
TALIA SUNT
SANCHEZ
NINNI
NO, WHAT'S NASTY IS GOLDEN SHOWERS. BUT MY SITE JUST STARTED LUMPING IN ALL THE FACIAL EJACULATION MOVIES WITH THE FACIAL URINATION MOVIES.
I CAN'T EVEN OPEN IT ANYMORE WITHOUT HORKING.
WHAT'S THE DIFFERENCE, YOU PSYCHO? BODILY FLUIDS BE BODILY FLUIDS. THEY'RE BOTH DEGRADING.
WRONG, FINISHING ON SOMEONE IS ROMANTIC, LIKE SIGNING YOUR WORK. BUT PISSING ON A CHICK IS JUST--
JESUS!

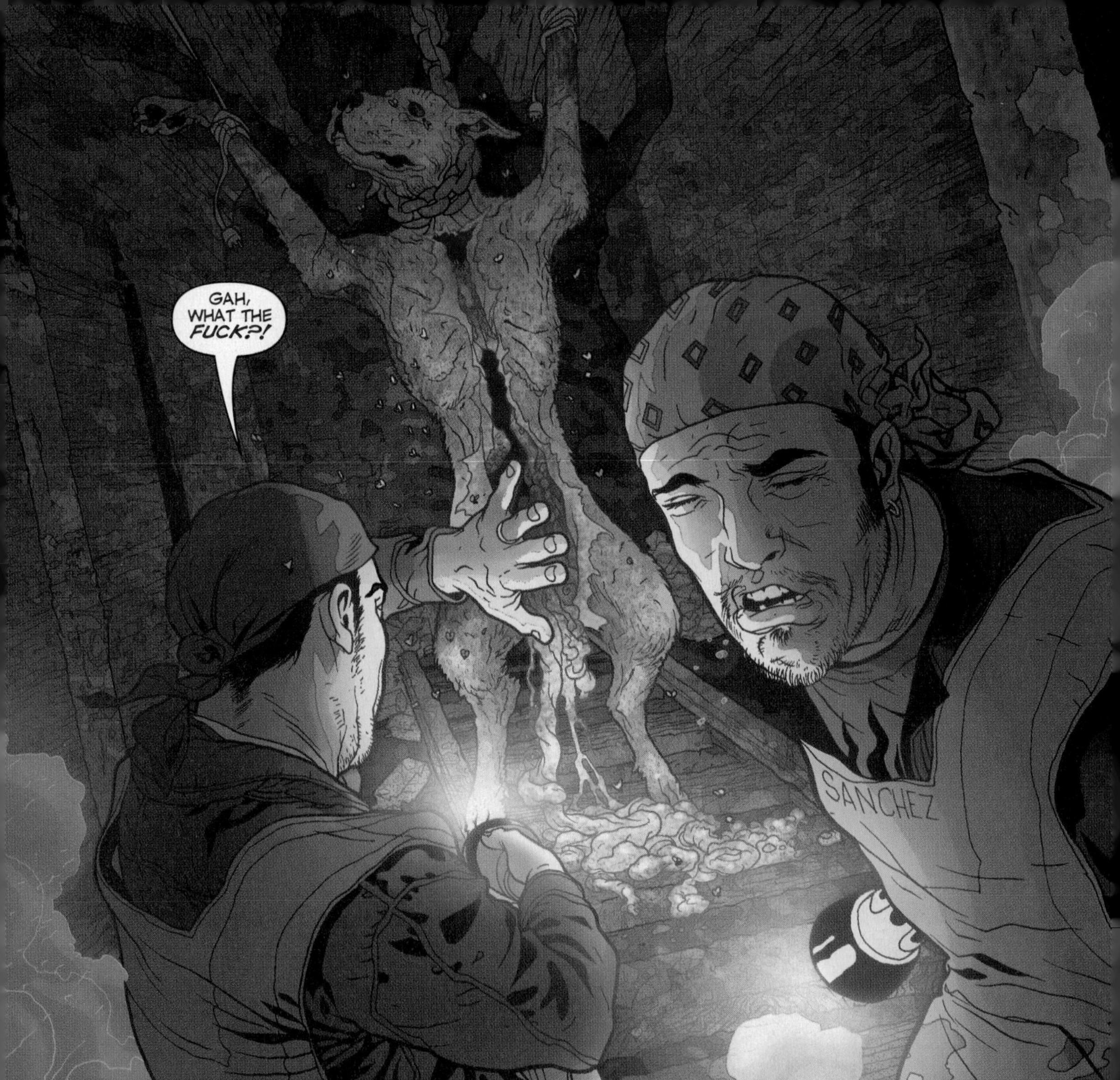
GAH, WHAT THE FUCK?!
SANCHEZ

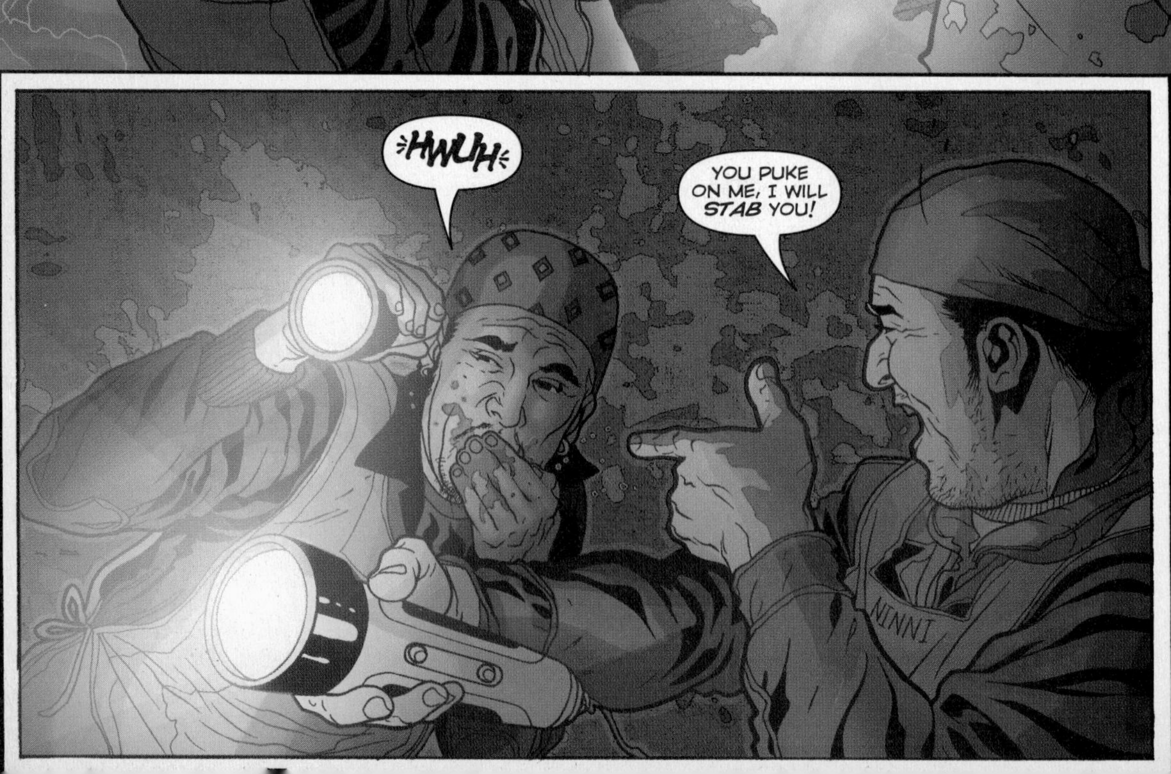
HWUH
YOU PUKE ON ME, I WILL STAB YOU!
NINNI

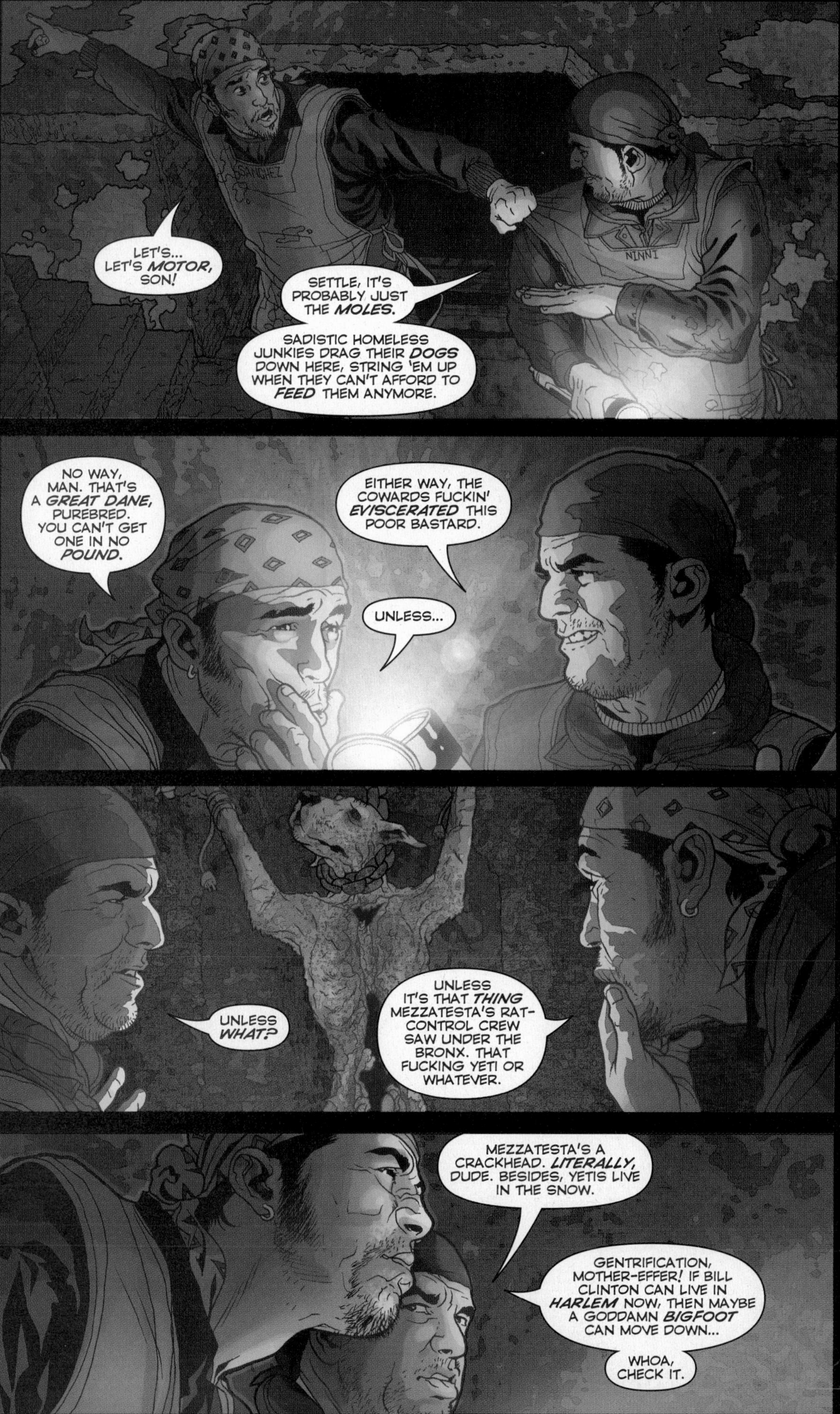
SANCHEZ
NINNI
LET'S... LET'S MOTOR, SON!
SETTLE, IT'S PROBABLY JUST THE MOLES.
SADISTIC HOMELESS JUNKIES DRAG THEIR DOGS DOWN HERE, STRING 'EM UP WHEN THEY CAN'T AFFORD TO FEED THEM ANYMORE.
NO WAY, MAN. THAT'S A GREAT DANE, PUREBRED. YOU CAN'T GET ONE IN NO POUND.
EITHER WAY, THE COWARDS FUCKIN' EVISCERATED THIS POOR BASTARD.
UNLESS...
UNLESS WHAT?
UNLESS IT'S THAT THING MEZZATESTA'S RAT-CONTROL CREW SAW UNDER THE BRONX. THAT FUCKING YETI OR WHATEVER.
MEZZATESTA'S A CRACKHEAD. LITERALLY, DUDE. BESIDES, YETIS LIVE IN THE SNOW.
GENTRIFICATION, MOTHER-EFFER! IF BILL CLINTON CAN LIVE IN HARLEM NOW, THEN MAYBE A GODDAMN BIGFOOT CAN MOVE DOWN...
WHOA, CHECK IT.

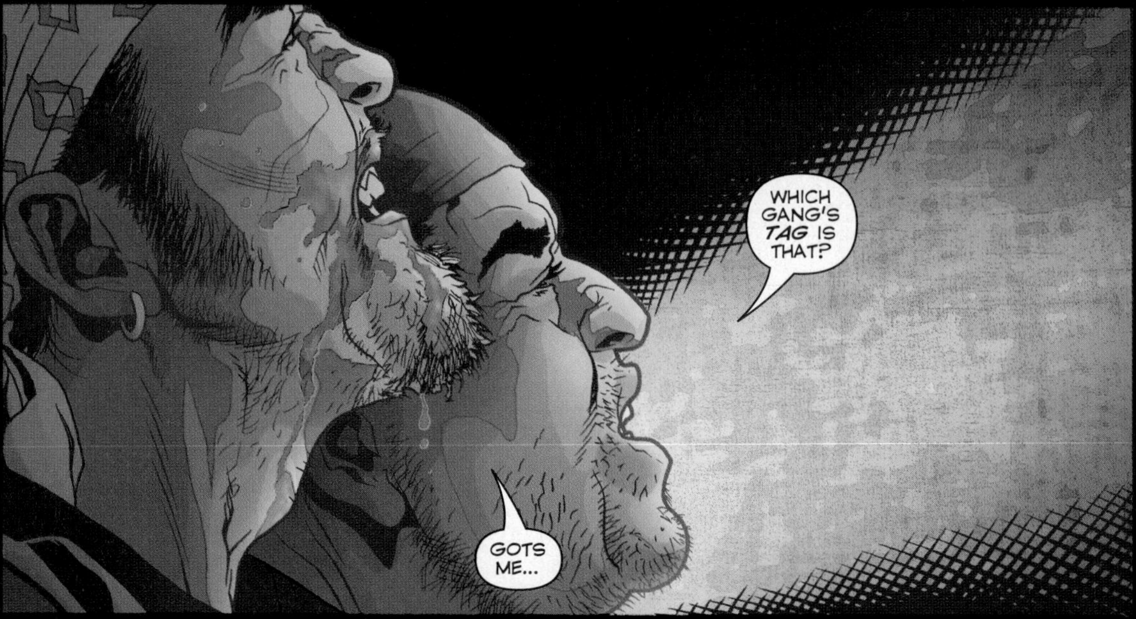

WHICH GANG'S *TAG* IS THAT?
GOTS ME...

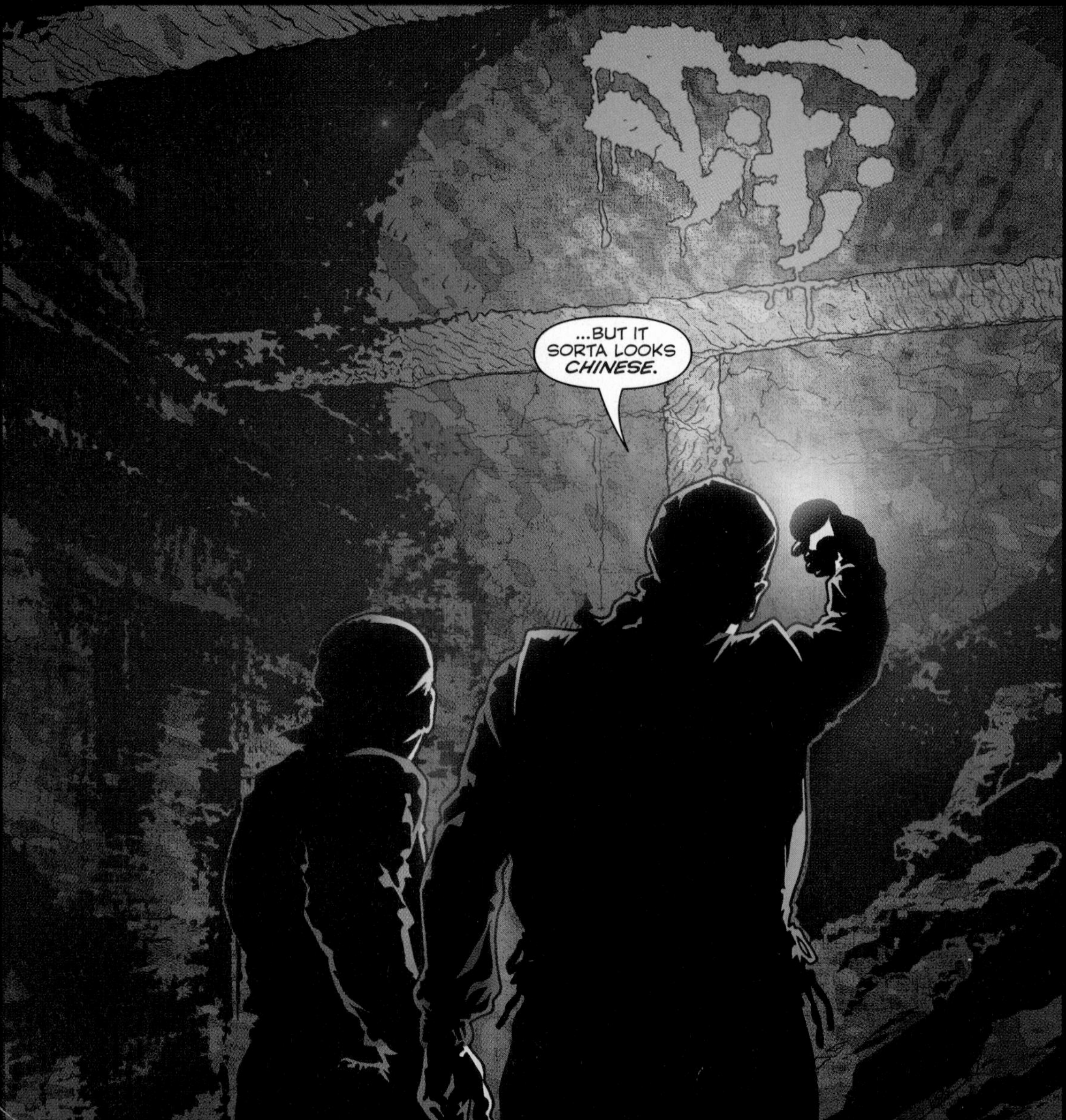

...BUT IT SORTA LOOKS *CHINESE*.

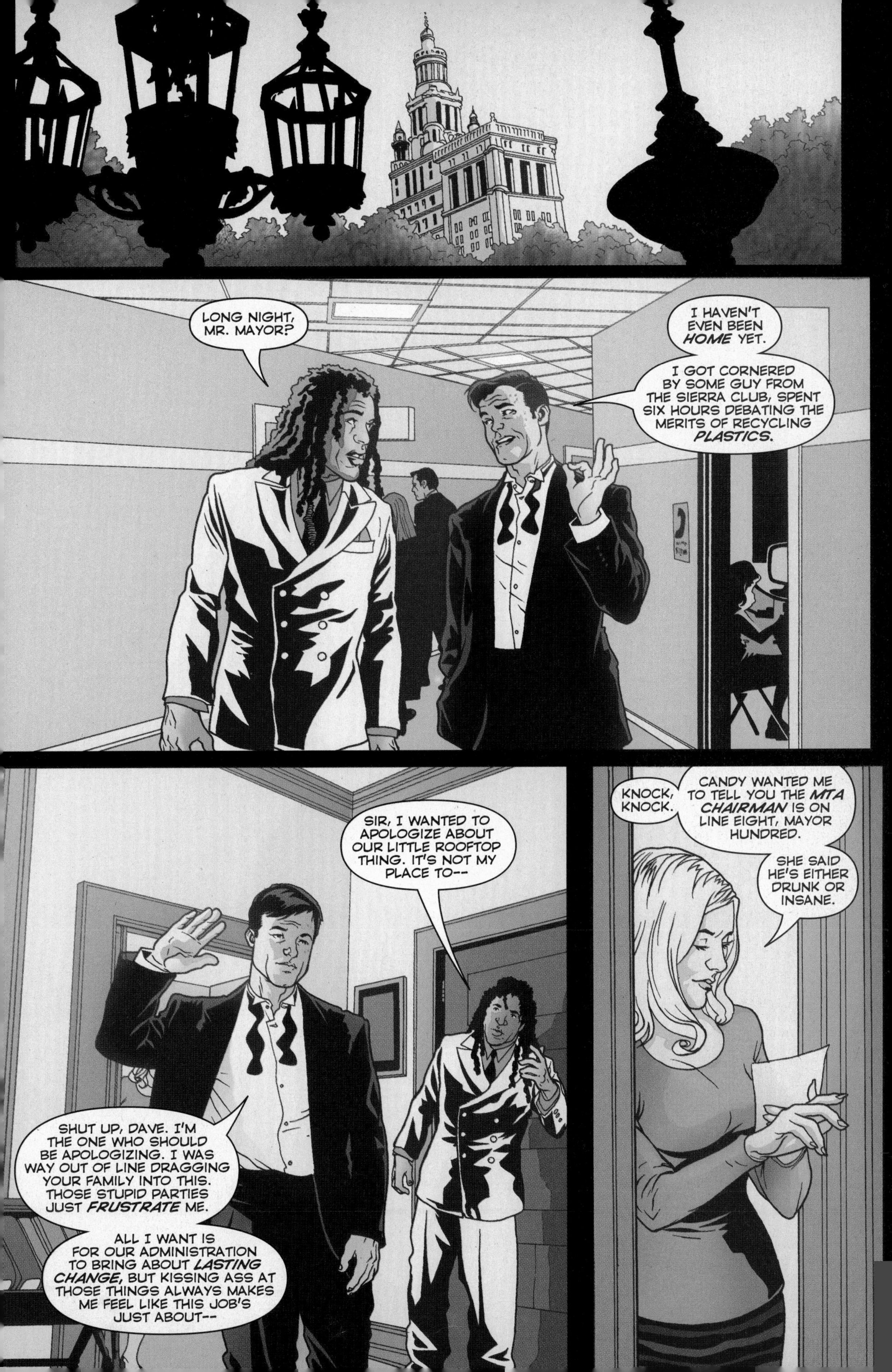
LONG NIGHT, MR. MAYOR?
I HAVEN'T EVEN BEEN HOME YET.
I GOT CORNERED BY SOME GUY FROM THE SIERRA CLUB, SPENT SIX HOURS DEBATING THE MERITS OF RECYCLING PLASTICS.
SIR, I WANTED TO APOLOGIZE ABOUT OUR LITTLE ROOFTOP THING. IT'S NOT MY PLACE TO--
SHUT UP, DAVE. I'M THE ONE WHO SHOULD BE APOLOGIZING. I WAS WAY OUT OF LINE DRAGGING YOUR FAMILY INTO THIS. THOSE STUPID PARTIES JUST FRUSTRATE ME.
ALL I WANT IS FOR OUR ADMINISTRATION TO BRING ABOUT LASTING CHANGE, BUT KISSING ASS AT THOSE THINGS ALWAYS MAKES ME FEEL LIKE THIS JOB'S JUST ABOUT--
KNOCK, KNOCK.
CANDY WANTED ME TO TELL YOU THE MTA CHAIRMAN IS ON LINE EIGHT, MAYOR HUNDRED.
SHE SAID HE'S EITHER DRUNK OR INSANE.

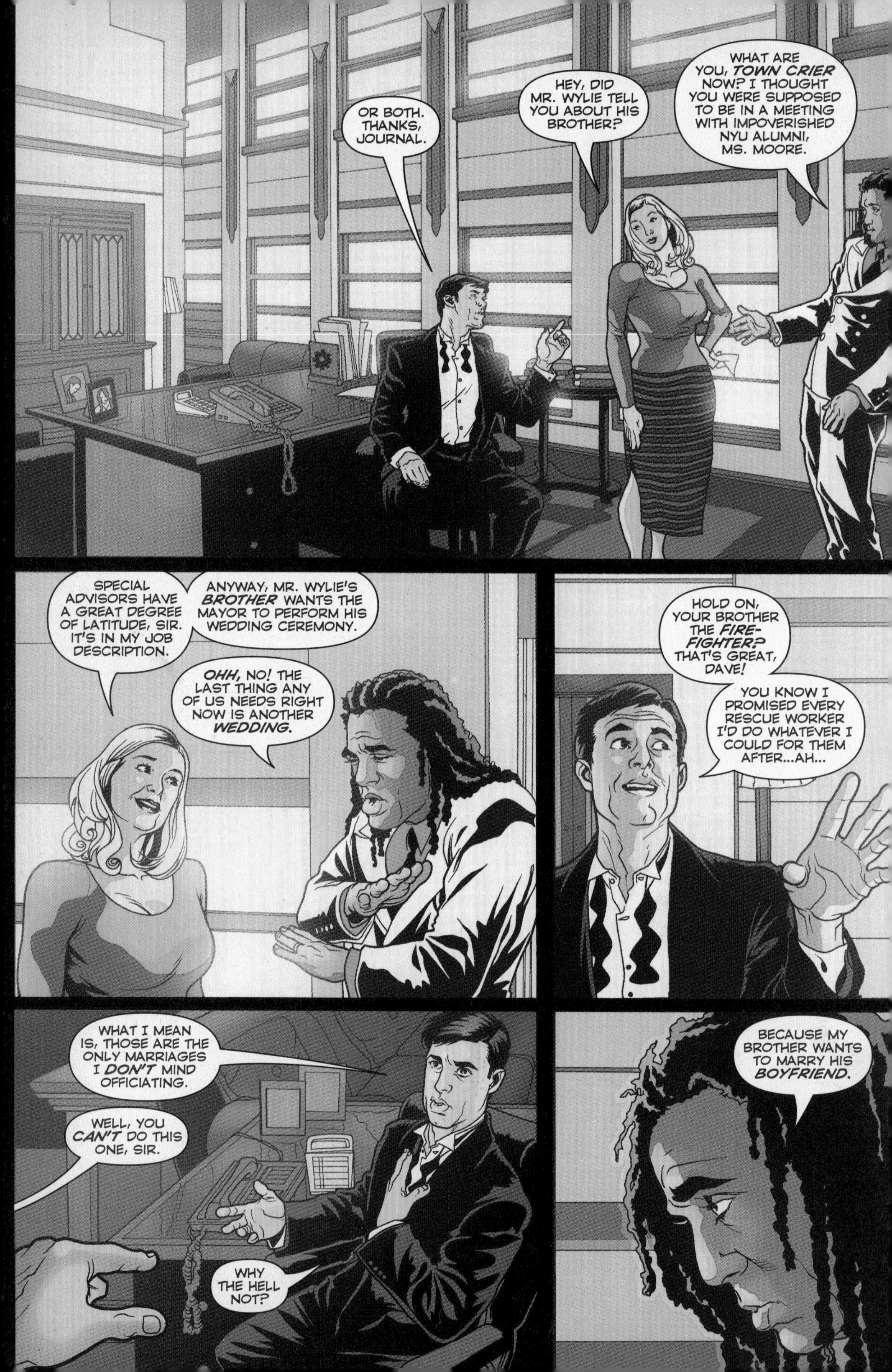
OR BOTH. THANKS, JOURNAL.
HEY, DID MR. WYLIE TELL YOU ABOUT HIS BROTHER?
WHAT ARE YOU, *TOWN CRIER* NOW? I THOUGHT YOU WERE SUPPOSED TO BE IN A MEETING WITH IMPOVERISHED NYU ALUMNI, MS. MOORE.
SPECIAL ADVISORS HAVE A GREAT DEGREE OF LATITUDE, SIR. IT'S IN MY JOB DESCRIPTION.
ANYWAY, MR. WYLIE'S *BROTHER* WANTS THE MAYOR TO PERFORM HIS WEDDING CEREMONY.
*OHH,* NO! THE LAST THING ANY OF US NEEDS RIGHT NOW IS ANOTHER *WEDDING*.
HOLD ON, YOUR BROTHER THE *FIRE-FIGHTER?* THAT'S GREAT, DAVE!
YOU KNOW I PROMISED EVERY RESCUE WORKER I'D DO WHATEVER I COULD FOR THEM AFTER...AH...
WHAT I MEAN IS, THOSE ARE THE ONLY MARRIAGES I *DON'T* MIND OFFICIATING.
WELL, YOU *CAN'T* DO THIS ONE, SIR.
WHY THE HELL NOT?
BECAUSE MY BROTHER WANTS TO MARRY HIS *BOYFRIEND*.

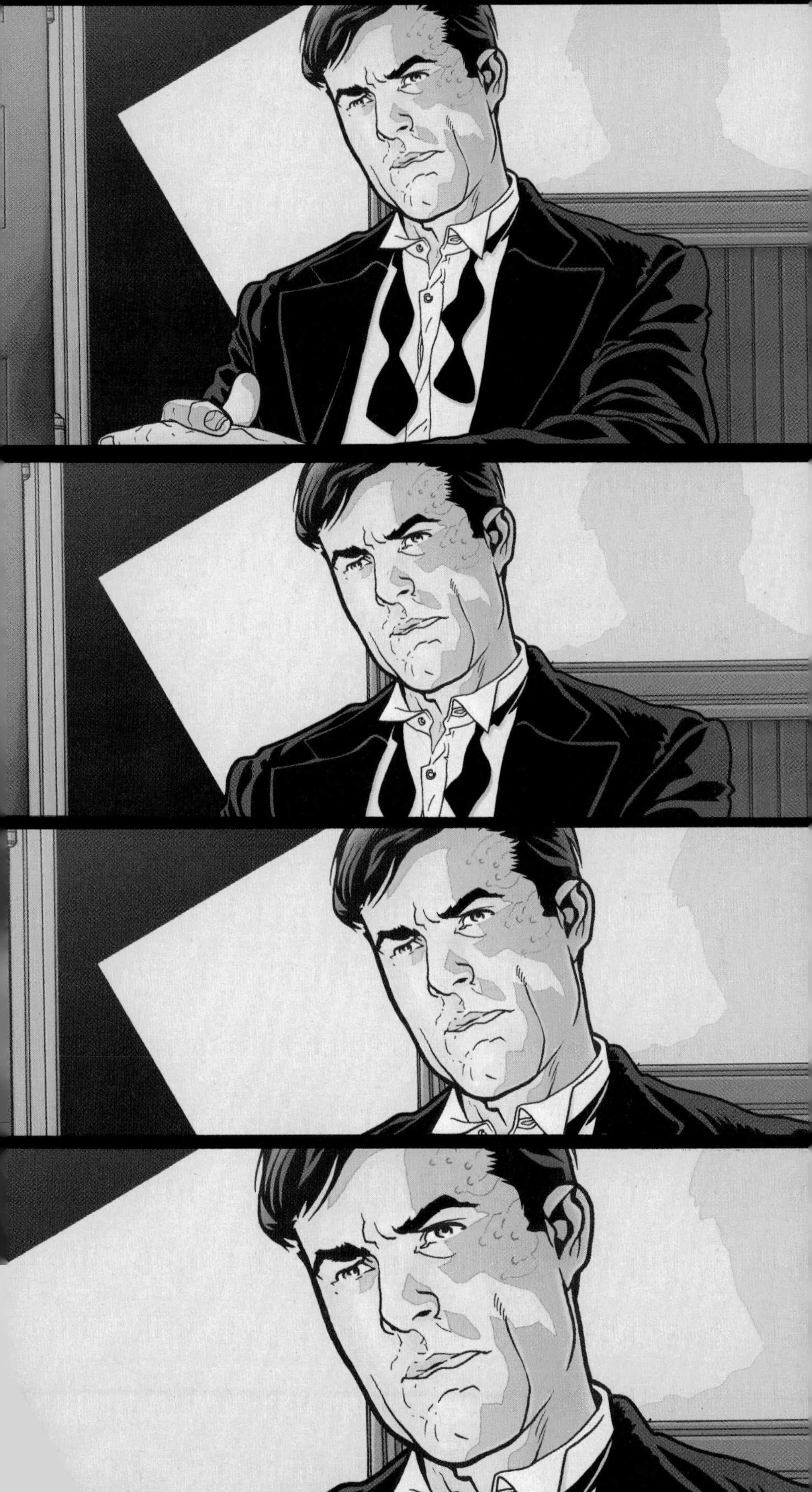

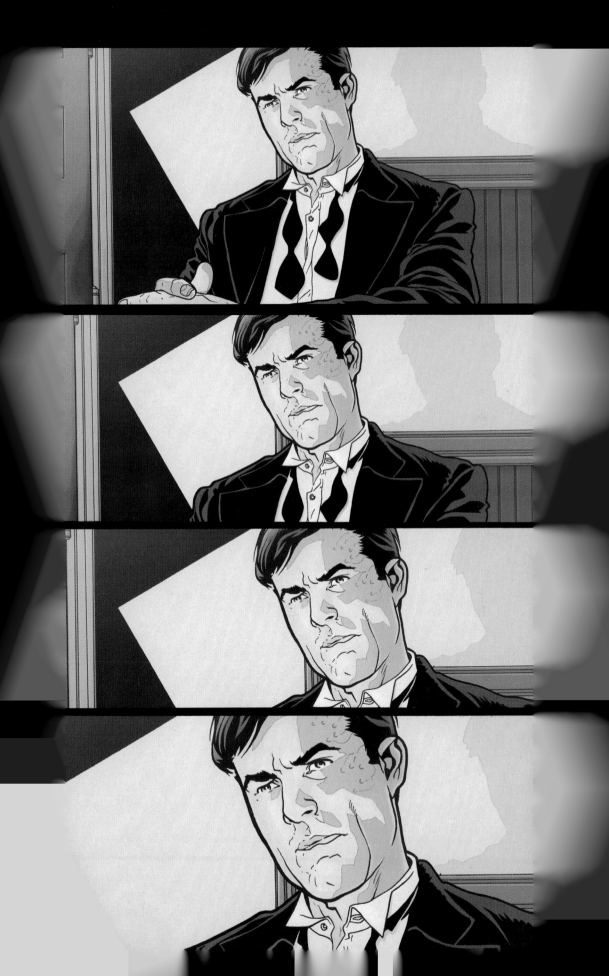

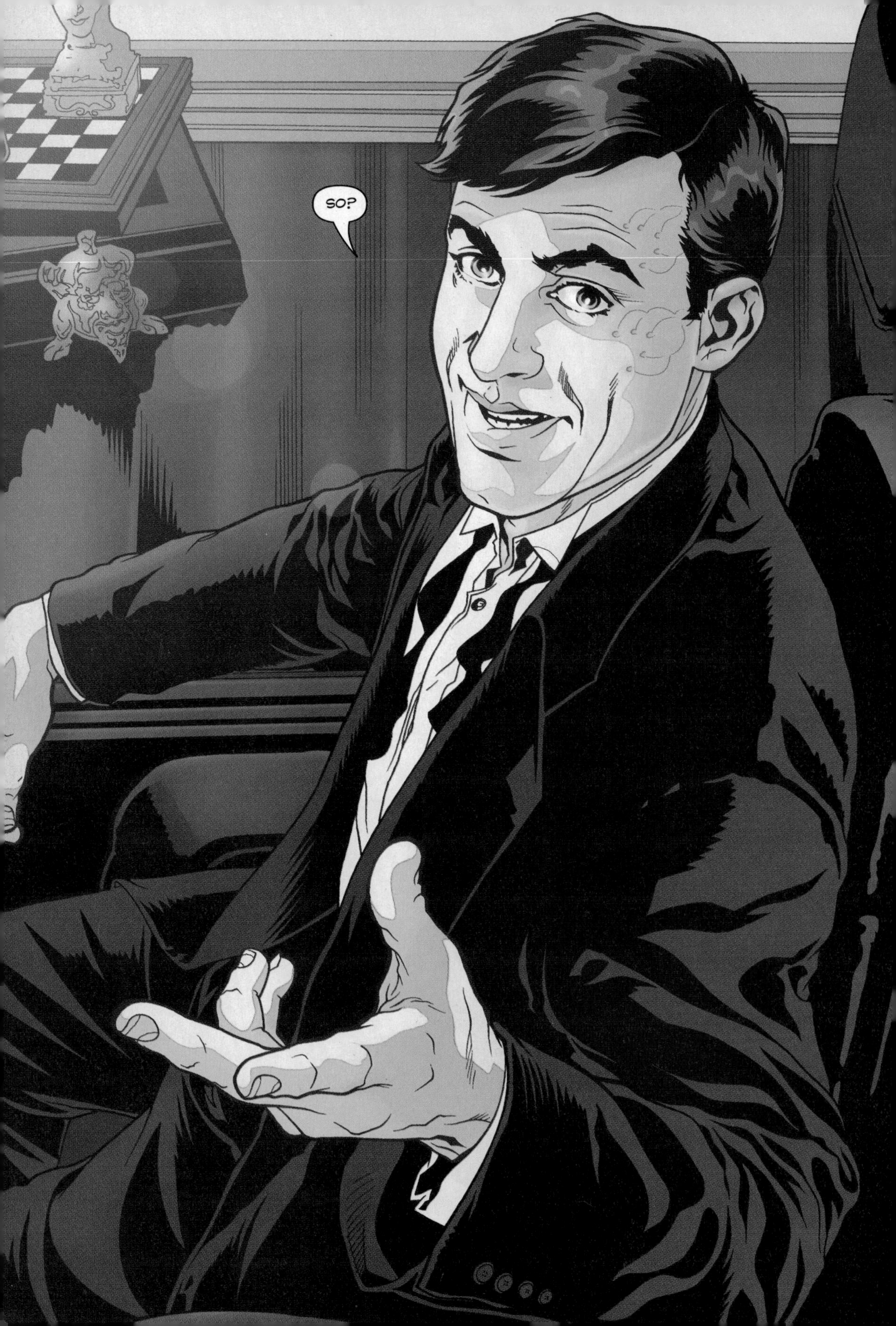
SO?

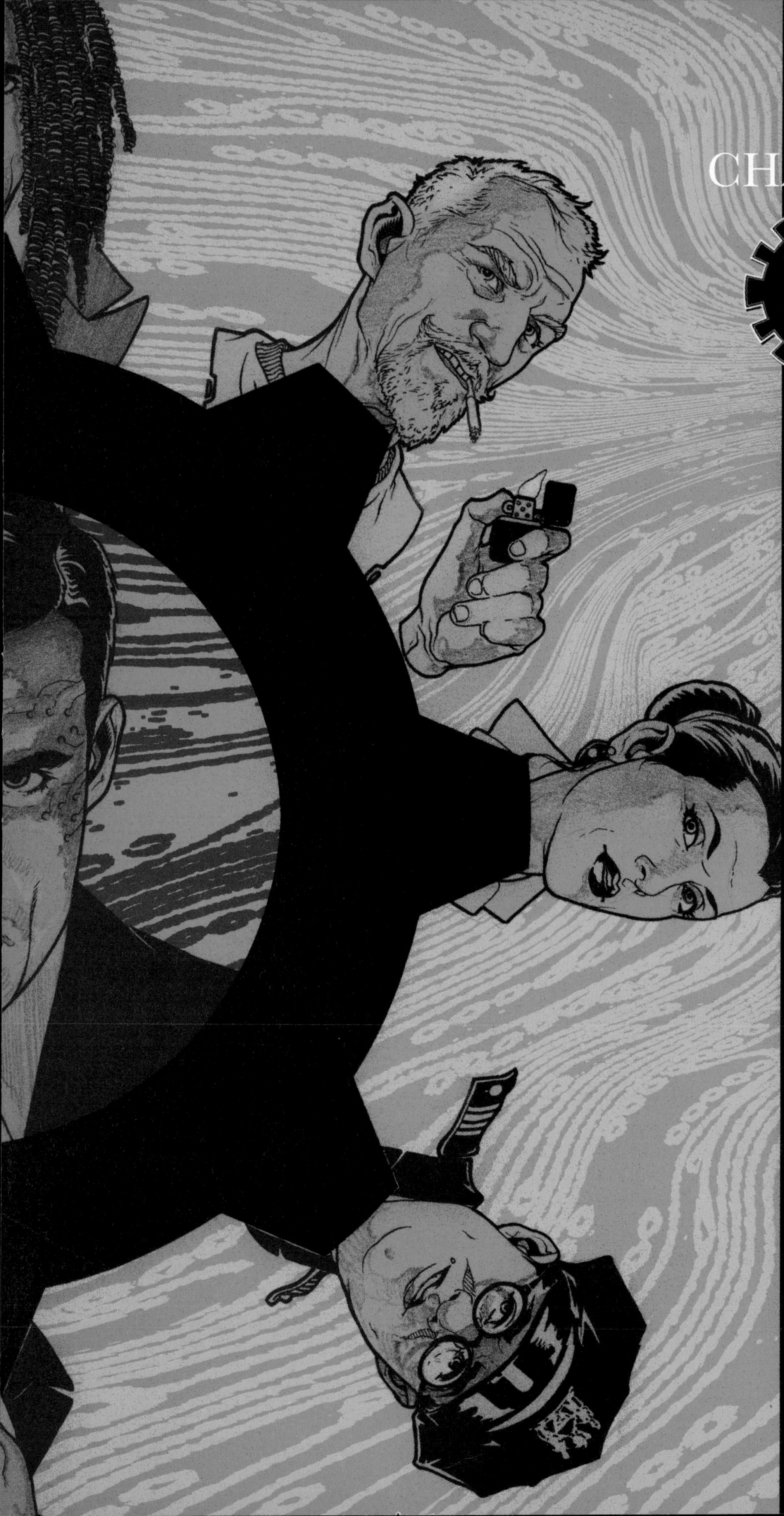

# CHAPTER 2

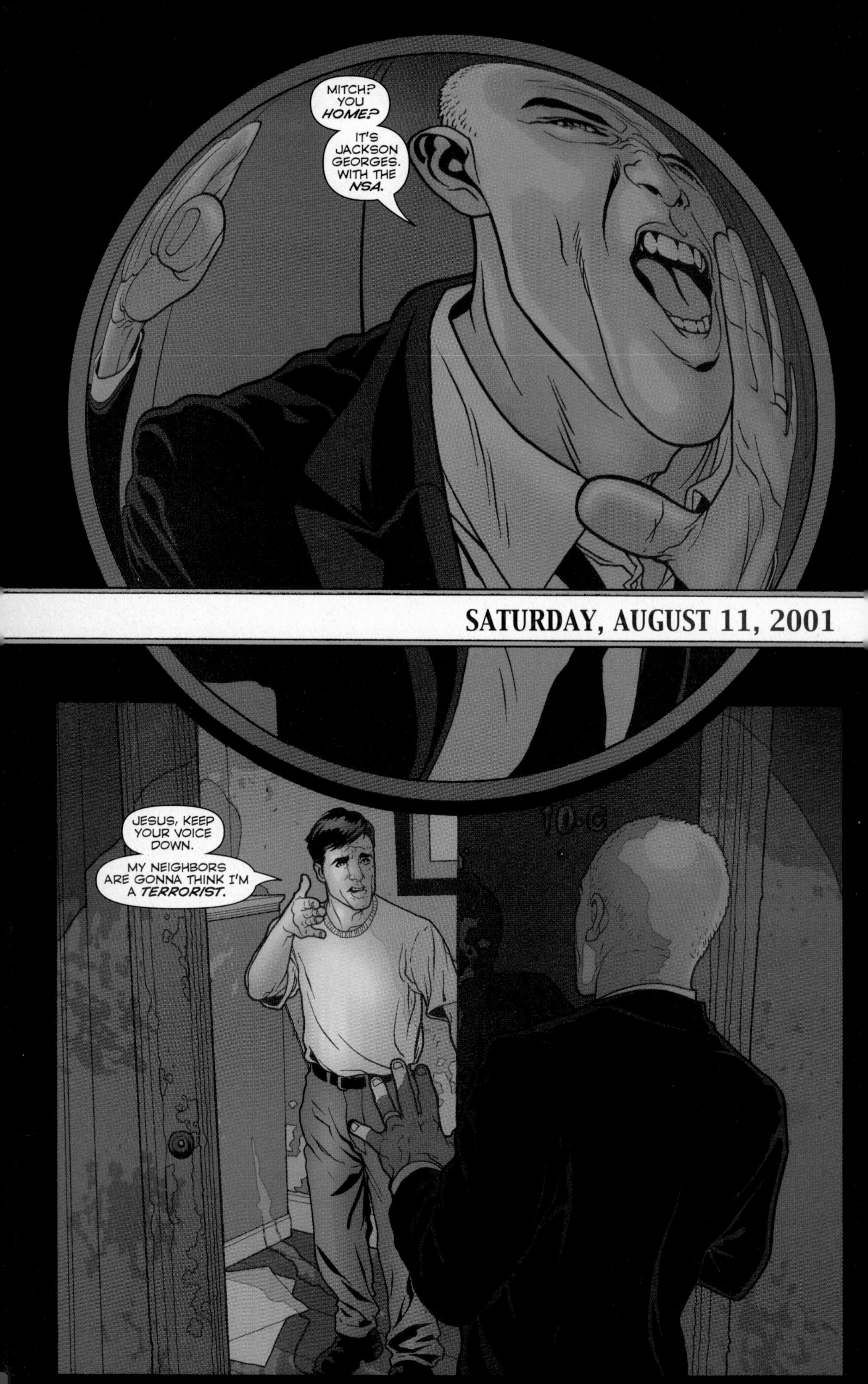
MITCH? YOU HOME?
IT'S JACKSON GEORGES. WITH THE NSA.
SATURDAY, AUGUST 11, 2001
10-G
JESUS, KEEP YOUR VOICE DOWN.
MY NEIGHBORS ARE GONNA THINK I'M A TERRORIST.

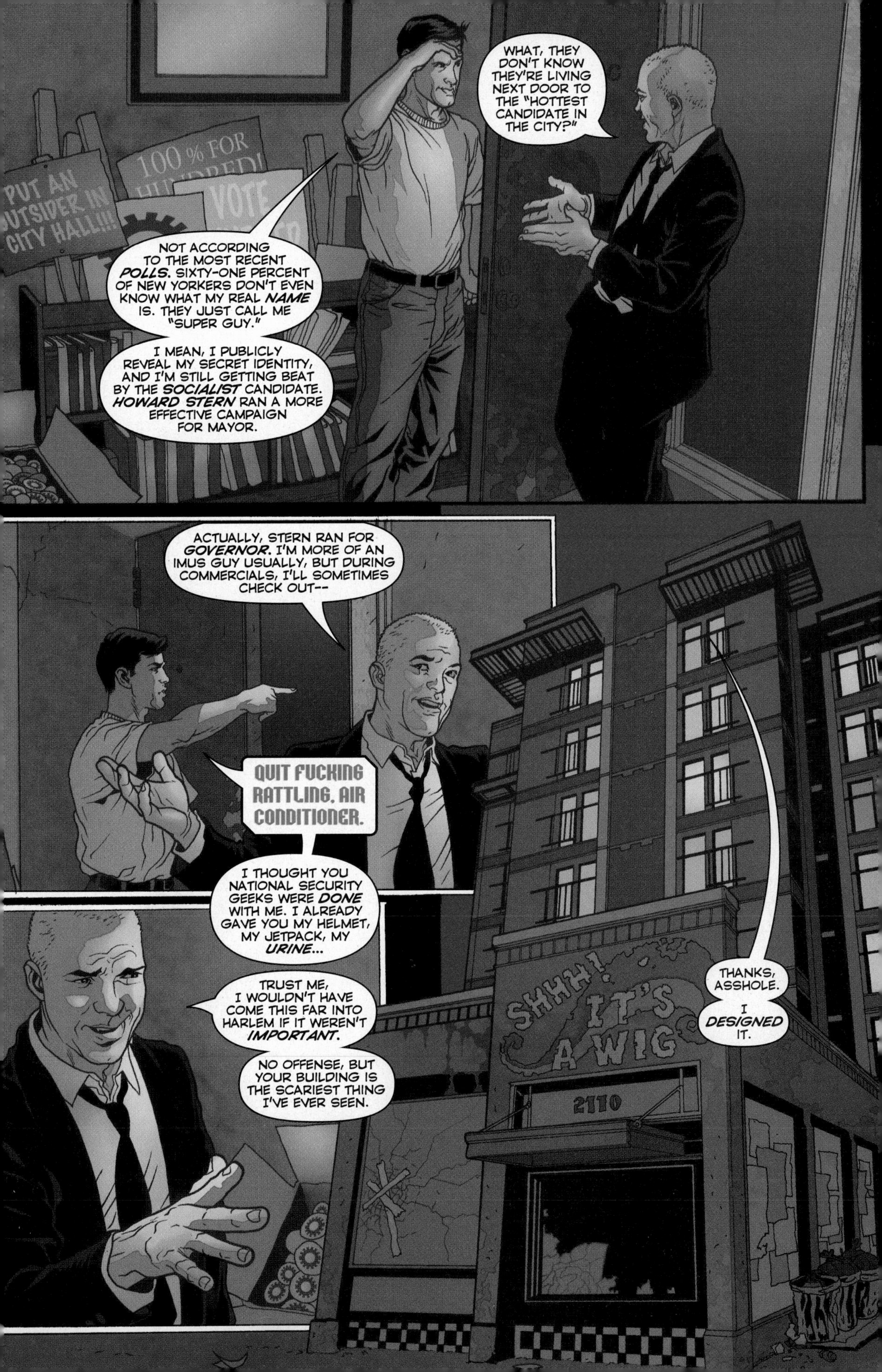

WHAT, THEY DON'T KNOW THEY'RE LIVING NEXT DOOR TO THE "HOTTEST CANDIDATE IN THE CITY?"
PUT AN OUTSIDER IN CITY HALL!!!
100 % FOR
VOTE
NOT ACCORDING TO THE MOST RECENT POLLS. SIXTY-ONE PERCENT OF NEW YORKERS DON'T EVEN KNOW WHAT MY REAL NAME IS. THEY JUST CALL ME "SUPER GUY."
I MEAN, I PUBLICLY REVEAL MY SECRET IDENTITY, AND I'M STILL GETTING BEAT BY THE SOCIALIST CANDIDATE. HOWARD STERN RAN A MORE EFFECTIVE CAMPAIGN FOR MAYOR.
ACTUALLY, STERN RAN FOR GOVERNOR. I'M MORE OF AN IMUS GUY USUALLY, BUT DURING COMMERCIALS, I'LL SOMETIMES CHECK OUT--
QUIT FUCKING RATTLING, AIR CONDITIONER.
I THOUGHT YOU NATIONAL SECURITY GEEKS WERE DONE WITH ME. I ALREADY GAVE YOU MY HELMET, MY JETPACK, MY URINE...
TRUST ME, I WOULDN'T HAVE COME THIS FAR INTO HARLEM IF IT WEREN'T IMPORTANT.
NO OFFENSE, BUT YOUR BUILDING IS THE SCARIEST THING I'VE EVER SEEN.
THANKS, ASSHOLE.
I DESIGNED IT.
SHHH! IT'S A WIG
2110

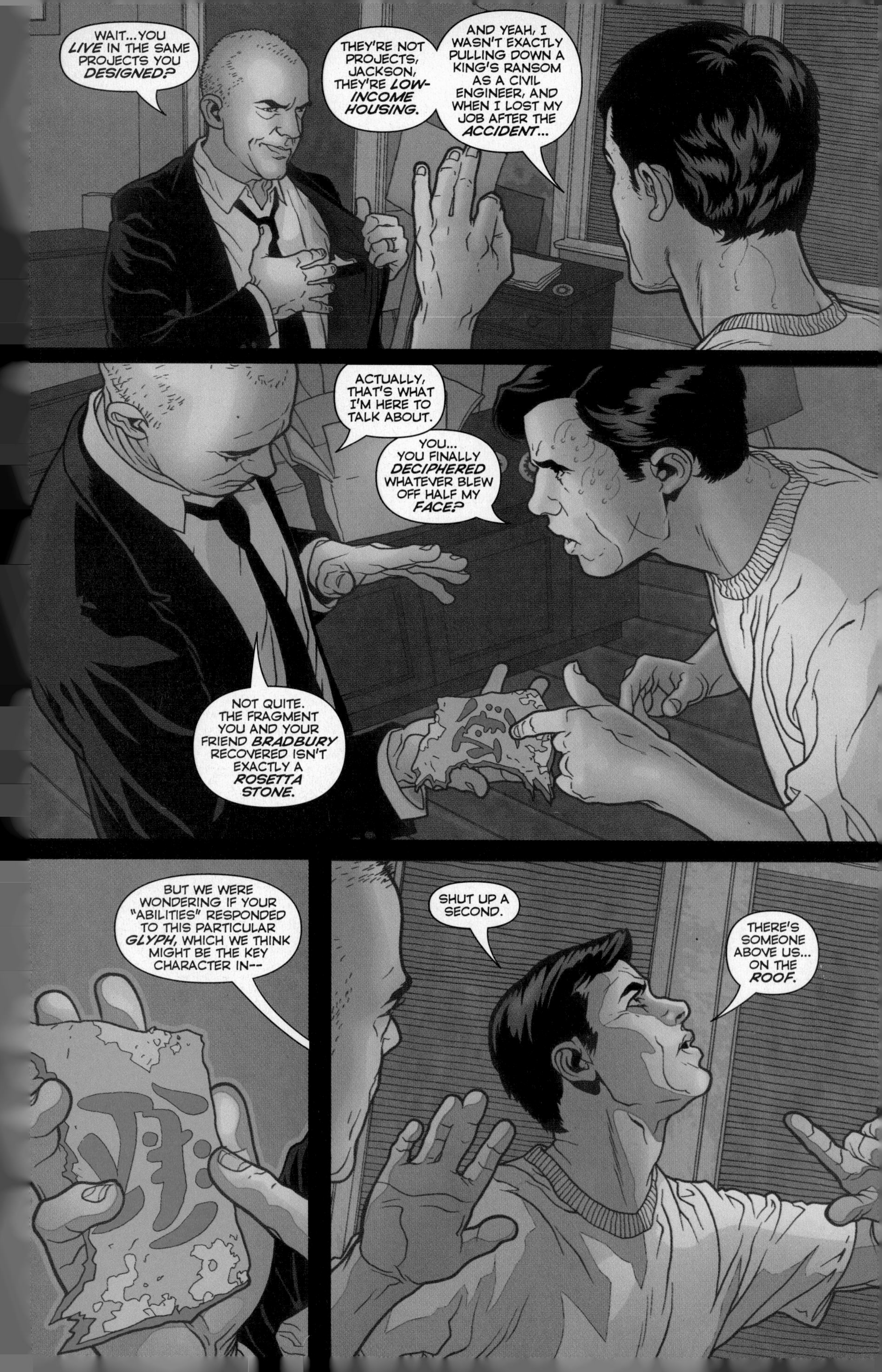
WAIT...YOU LIVE IN THE SAME PROJECTS YOU DESIGNED?
THEY'RE NOT PROJECTS, JACKSON, THEY'RE LOW-INCOME HOUSING.
AND YEAH, I WASN'T EXACTLY PULLING DOWN A KING'S RANSOM AS A CIVIL ENGINEER, AND WHEN I LOST MY JOB AFTER THE ACCIDENT...
ACTUALLY, THAT'S WHAT I'M HERE TO TALK ABOUT.
YOU... YOU FINALLY DECIPHERED WHATEVER BLEW OFF HALF MY FACE?
NOT QUITE. THE FRAGMENT YOU AND YOUR FRIEND BRADBURY RECOVERED ISN'T EXACTLY A ROSETTA STONE.
BUT WE WERE WONDERING IF YOUR "ABILITIES" RESPONDED TO THIS PARTICULAR GLYPH, WHICH WE THINK MIGHT BE THE KEY CHARACTER IN--
SHUT UP A SECOND.
THERE'S SOMEONE ABOVE US... ON THE ROOF.

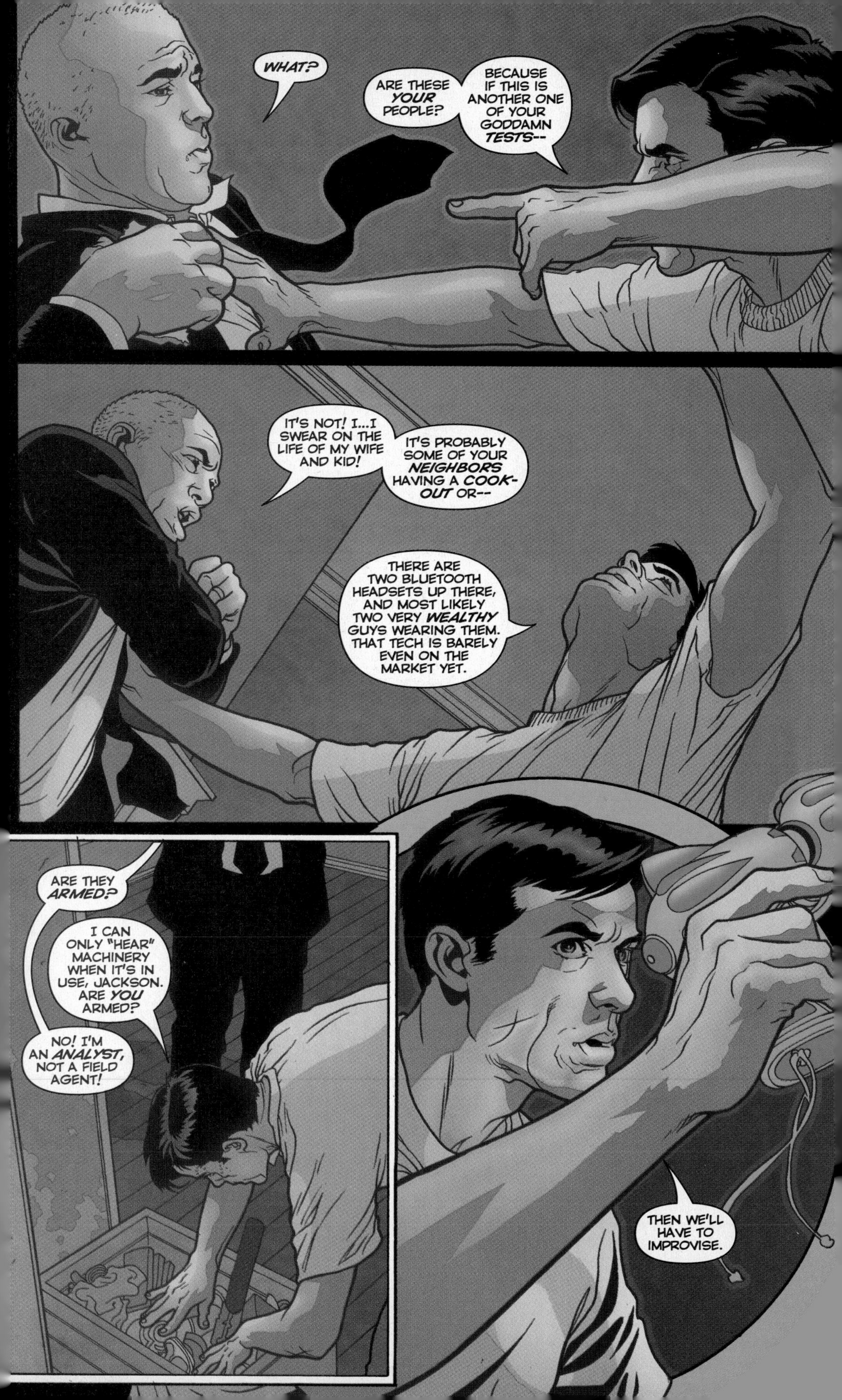
WHAT?
ARE THESE YOUR PEOPLE?
BECAUSE IF THIS IS ANOTHER ONE OF YOUR GODDAMN TESTS--
IT'S NOT! I...I SWEAR ON THE LIFE OF MY WIFE AND KID!
IT'S PROBABLY SOME OF YOUR NEIGHBORS HAVING A COOK-OUT OR--
THERE ARE TWO BLUETOOTH HEADSETS UP THERE, AND MOST LIKELY TWO VERY WEALTHY GUYS WEARING THEM. THAT TECH IS BARELY EVEN ON THE MARKET YET.
ARE THEY ARMED?
I CAN ONLY "HEAR" MACHINERY WHEN IT'S IN USE, JACKSON. ARE YOU ARMED?
NO! I'M AN ANALYST, NOT A FIELD AGENT!
THEN WE'LL HAVE TO IMPROVISE.

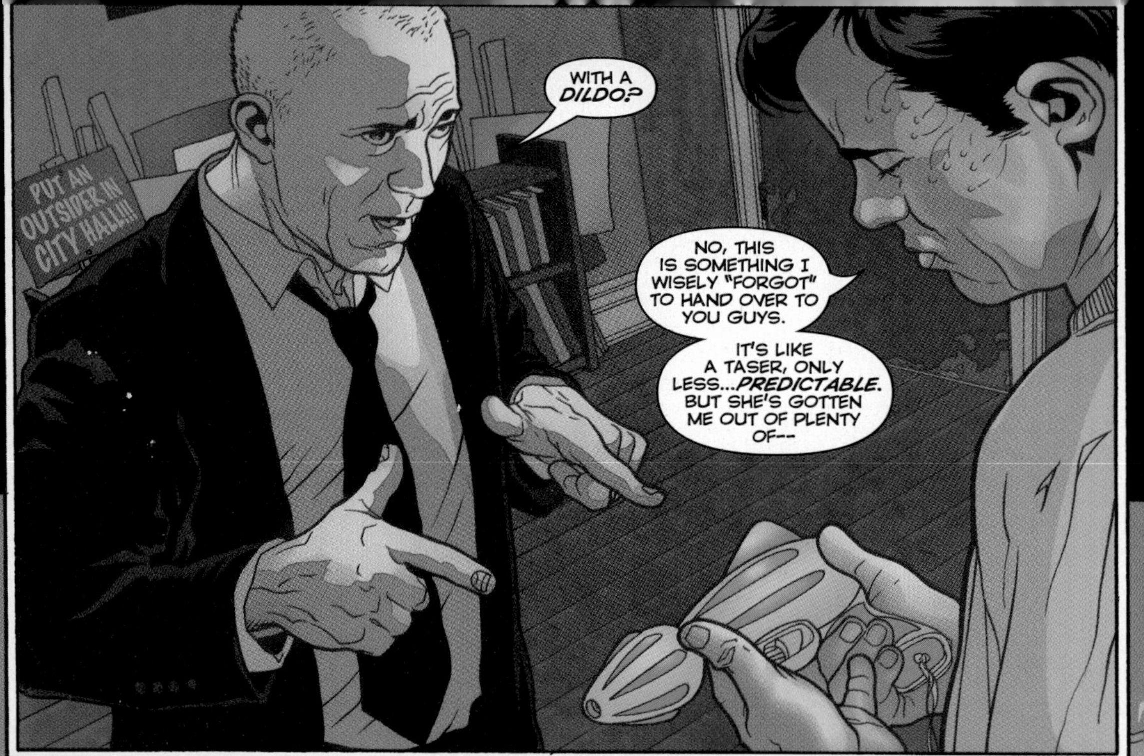
PUT AN OUTSIDER IN CITY HALL!!!
WITH A *DILDO?*
NO, THIS IS SOMETHING I WISELY "FORGOT" TO HAND OVER TO YOU GUYS.
IT'S LIKE A TASER, ONLY LESS...*PREDICTABLE.* BUT SHE'S GOTTEN ME OUT OF PLENTY OF--

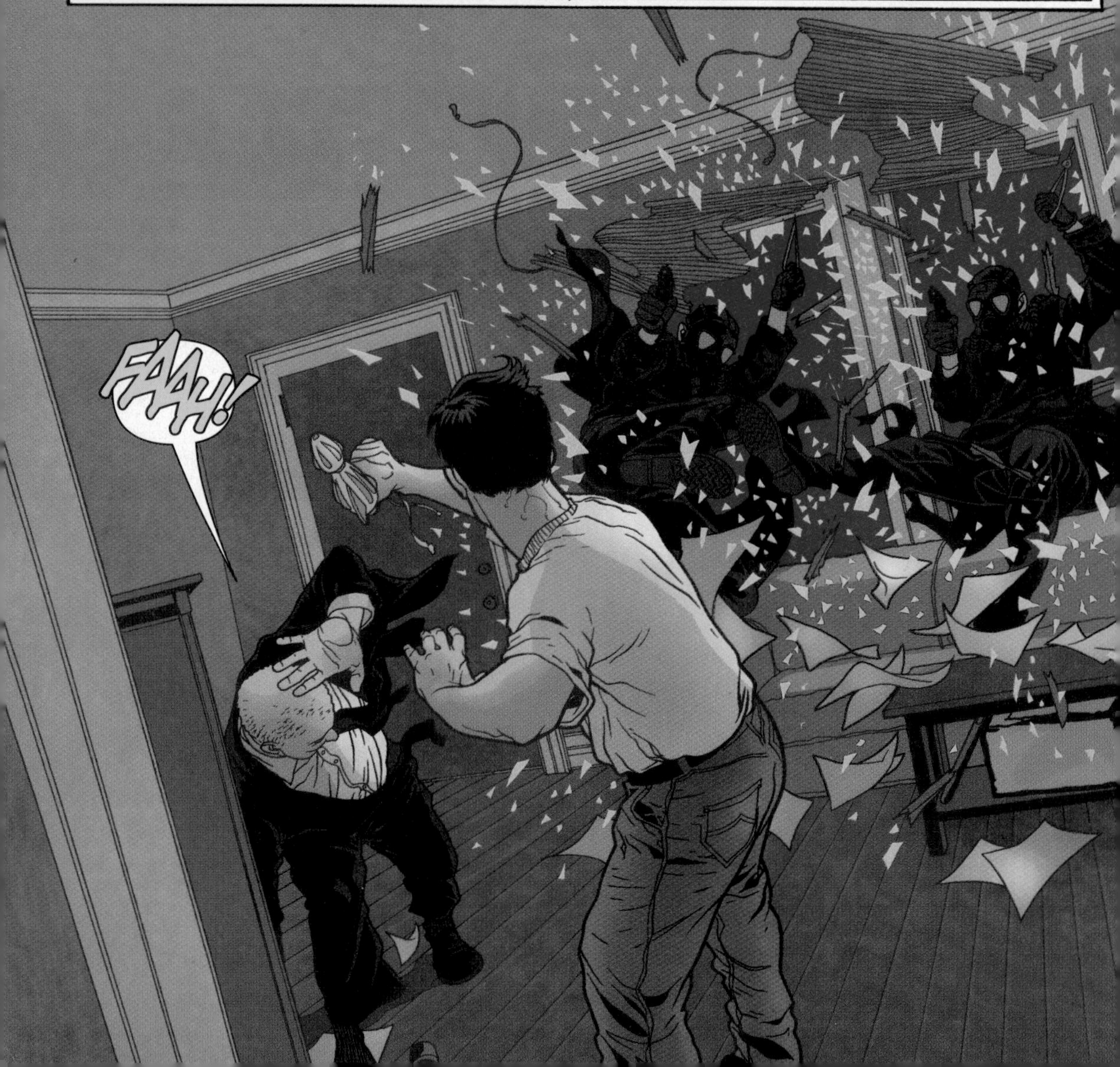
FAAAH!

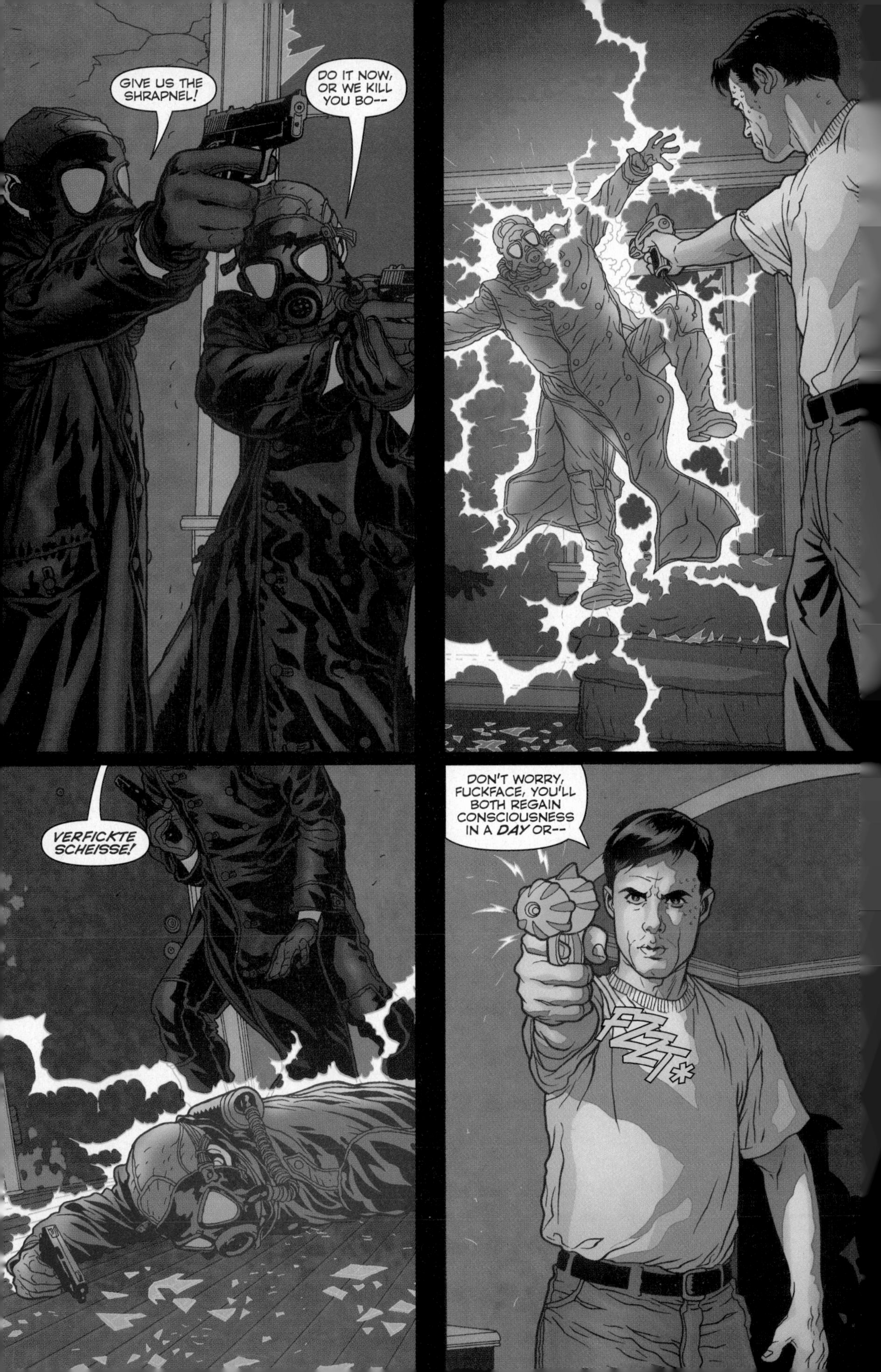
GIVE US THE SHRAPNEL!
DO IT NOW, OR WE KILL YOU BO--
VERFICKTE SCHEISSE!
DON'T WORRY, FUCKFACE, YOU'LL BOTH REGAIN CONSCIOUSNESS IN A DAY OR--
FZZZT*

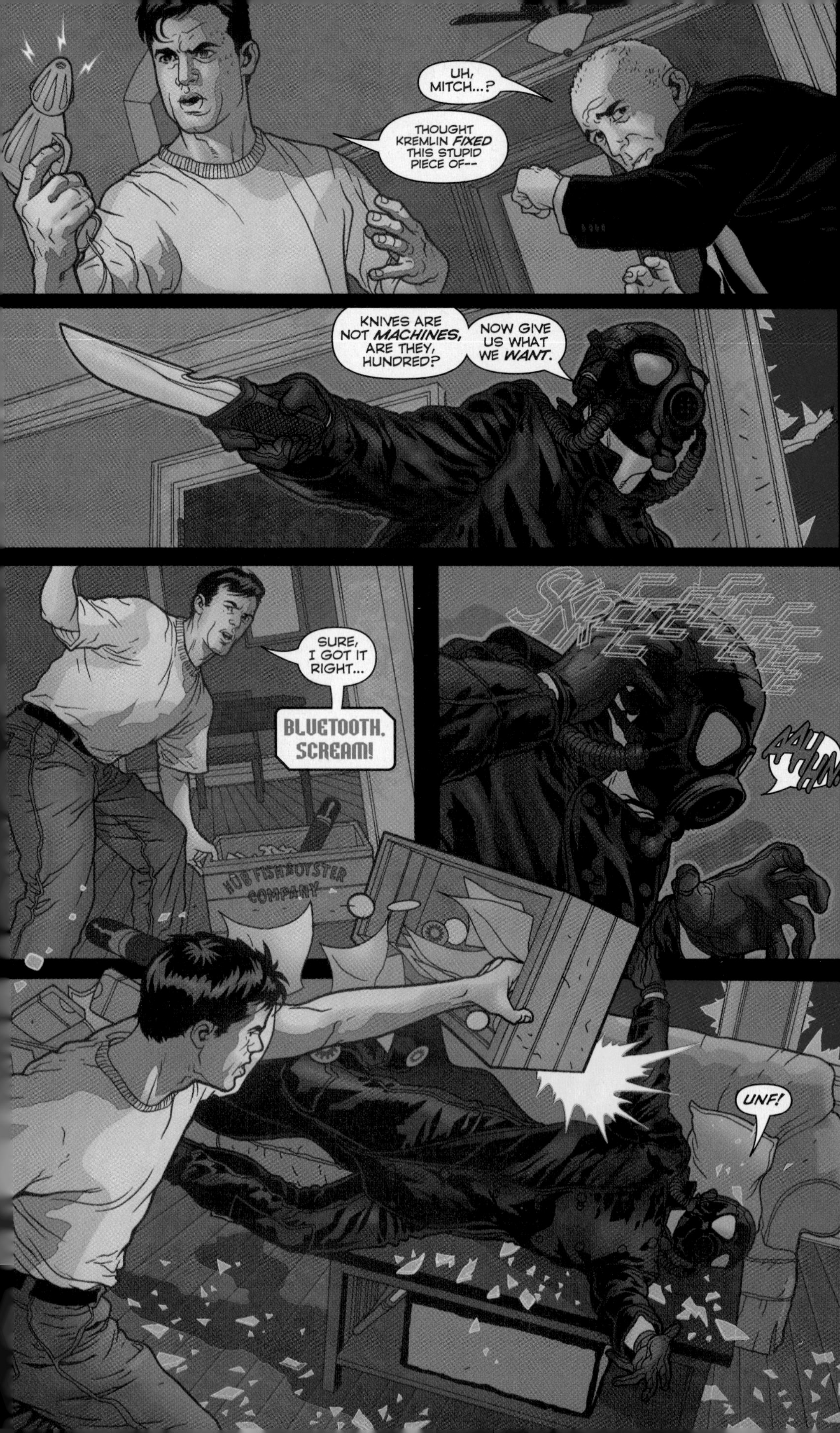

UH, MITCH...?
THOUGHT KREMLIN FIXED THIS STUPID PIECE OF--
KNIVES ARE NOT MACHINES, ARE THEY, HUNDRED?
NOW GIVE US WHAT WE WANT.
SURE, I GOT IT RIGHT...
BLUETOOTH, SCREAM!
HUB FISH & OYSTER COMPANY
UNF!

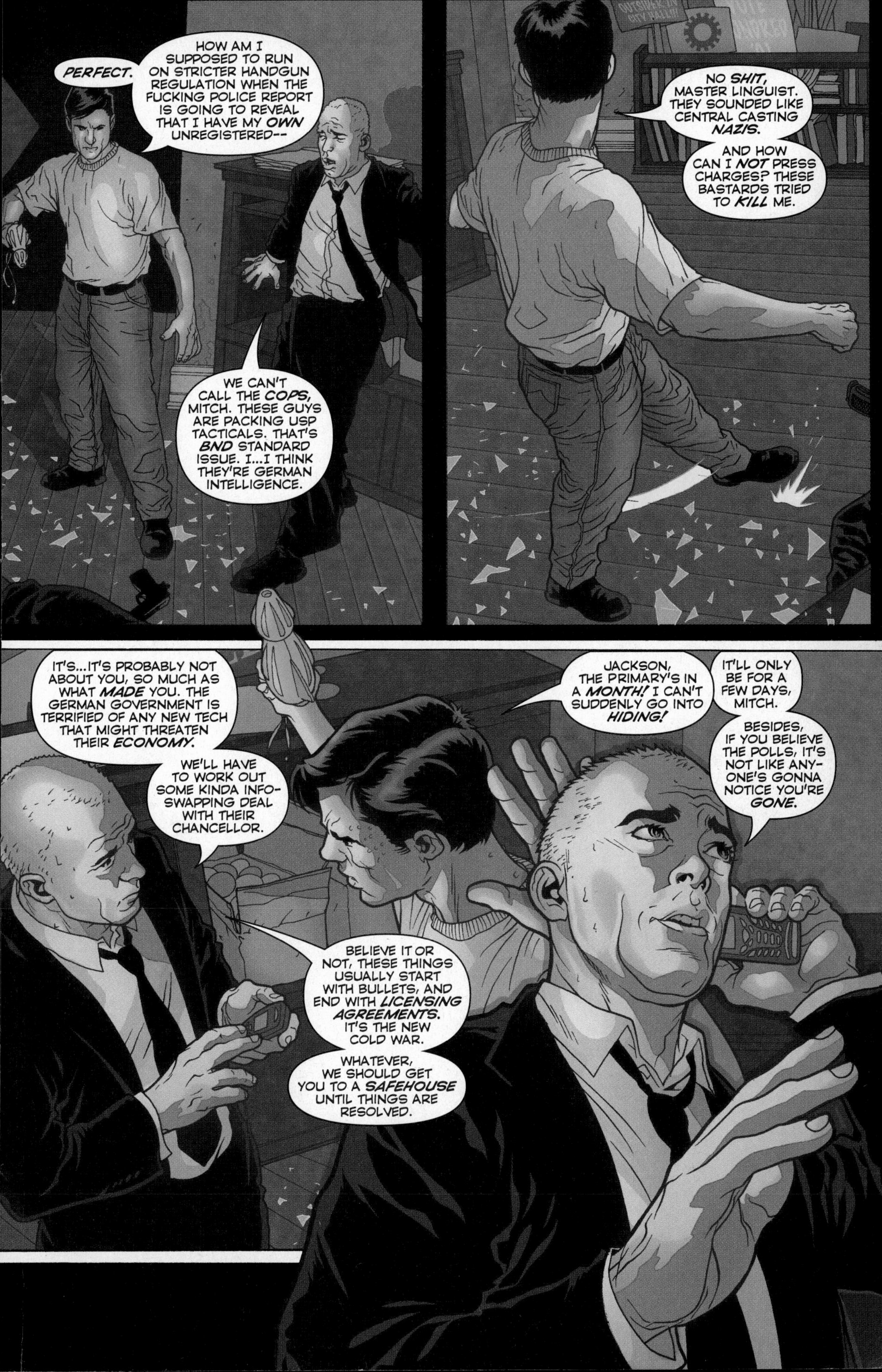
PERFECT.
HOW AM I SUPPOSED TO RUN ON STRICTER HANDGUN REGULATION WHEN THE FUCKING POLICE REPORT IS GOING TO REVEAL THAT I HAVE MY OWN UNREGISTERED--
WE CAN'T CALL THE COPS, MITCH. THESE GUYS ARE PACKING USP TACTICALS. THAT'S BND STANDARD ISSUE. I...I THINK THEY'RE GERMAN INTELLIGENCE.
NO SHIT, MASTER LINGUIST. THEY SOUNDED LIKE CENTRAL CASTING NAZIS.
AND HOW CAN I NOT PRESS CHARGES? THESE BASTARDS TRIED TO KILL ME.
IT'S...IT'S PROBABLY NOT ABOUT YOU, SO MUCH AS WHAT MADE YOU. THE GERMAN GOVERNMENT IS TERRIFIED OF ANY NEW TECH THAT MIGHT THREATEN THEIR ECONOMY.
WE'LL HAVE TO WORK OUT SOME KINDA INFO-SWAPPING DEAL WITH THEIR CHANCELLOR.
BELIEVE IT OR NOT, THESE THINGS USUALLY START WITH BULLETS, AND END WITH LICENSING AGREEMENTS. IT'S THE NEW COLD WAR.
WHATEVER, WE SHOULD GET YOU TO A SAFEHOUSE UNTIL THINGS ARE RESOLVED.
JACKSON, THE PRIMARY'S IN A MONTH! I CAN'T SUDDENLY GO INTO HIDING!
IT'LL ONLY BE FOR A FEW DAYS, MITCH.
BESIDES, IF YOU BELIEVE THE POLLS, IT'S NOT LIKE ANY-ONE'S GONNA NOTICE YOU'RE GONE.

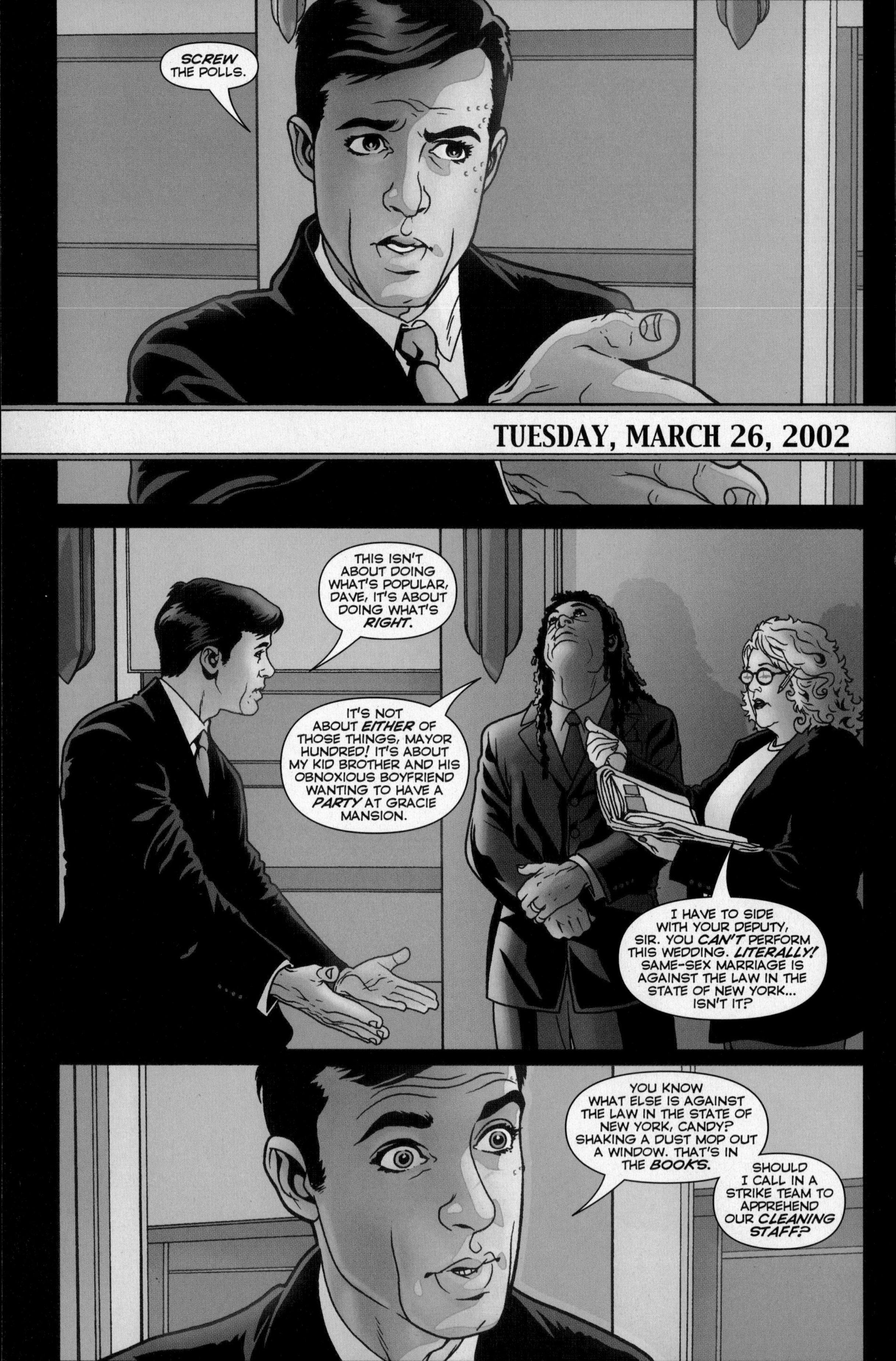
SCREW THE POLLS.
TUESDAY, MARCH 26, 2002
THIS ISN'T ABOUT DOING WHAT'S POPULAR, DAVE, IT'S ABOUT DOING WHAT'S RIGHT.
IT'S NOT ABOUT EITHER OF THOSE THINGS, MAYOR HUNDRED! IT'S ABOUT MY KID BROTHER AND HIS OBNOXIOUS BOYFRIEND WANTING TO HAVE A PARTY AT GRACIE MANSION.
I HAVE TO SIDE WITH YOUR DEPUTY, SIR. YOU CAN'T PERFORM THIS WEDDING. LITERALLY! SAME-SEX MARRIAGE IS AGAINST THE LAW IN THE STATE OF NEW YORK... ISN'T IT?
YOU KNOW WHAT ELSE IS AGAINST THE LAW IN THE STATE OF NEW YORK, CANDY? SHAKING A DUST MOP OUT A WINDOW. THAT'S IN THE BOOKS.
SHOULD I CALL IN A STRIKE TEAM TO APPREHEND OUR CLEANING STAFF?

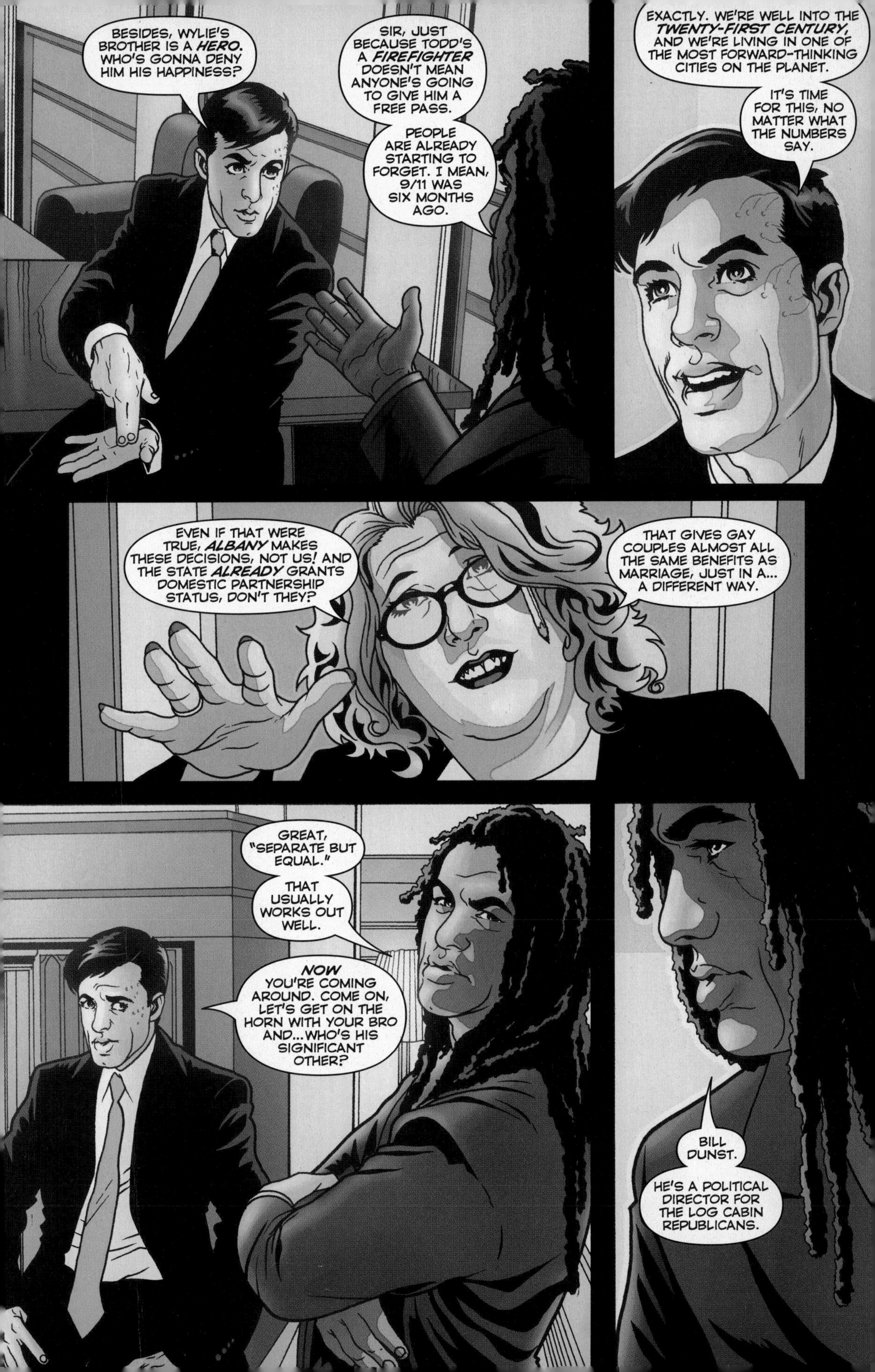
BESIDES, WYLIE'S BROTHER IS A HERO. WHO'S GONNA DENY HIM HIS HAPPINESS?
SIR, JUST BECAUSE TODD'S A FIREFIGHTER DOESN'T MEAN ANYONE'S GOING TO GIVE HIM A FREE PASS.
PEOPLE ARE ALREADY STARTING TO FORGET. I MEAN, 9/11 WAS SIX MONTHS AGO.
EXACTLY. WE'RE WELL INTO THE TWENTY-FIRST CENTURY, AND WE'RE LIVING IN ONE OF THE MOST FORWARD-THINKING CITIES ON THE PLANET.
IT'S TIME FOR THIS, NO MATTER WHAT THE NUMBERS SAY.
EVEN IF THAT WERE TRUE, ALBANY MAKES THESE DECISIONS, NOT US! AND THE STATE ALREADY GRANTS DOMESTIC PARTNERSHIP STATUS, DON'T THEY?
THAT GIVES GAY COUPLES ALMOST ALL THE SAME BENEFITS AS MARRIAGE, JUST IN A... A DIFFERENT WAY.
GREAT, "SEPARATE BUT EQUAL."
THAT USUALLY WORKS OUT WELL.
NOW YOU'RE COMING AROUND. COME ON, LET'S GET ON THE HORN WITH YOUR BRO AND...WHO'S HIS SIGNIFICANT OTHER?
BILL DUNST.
HE'S A POLITICAL DIRECTOR FOR THE LOG CABIN REPUBLICANS.

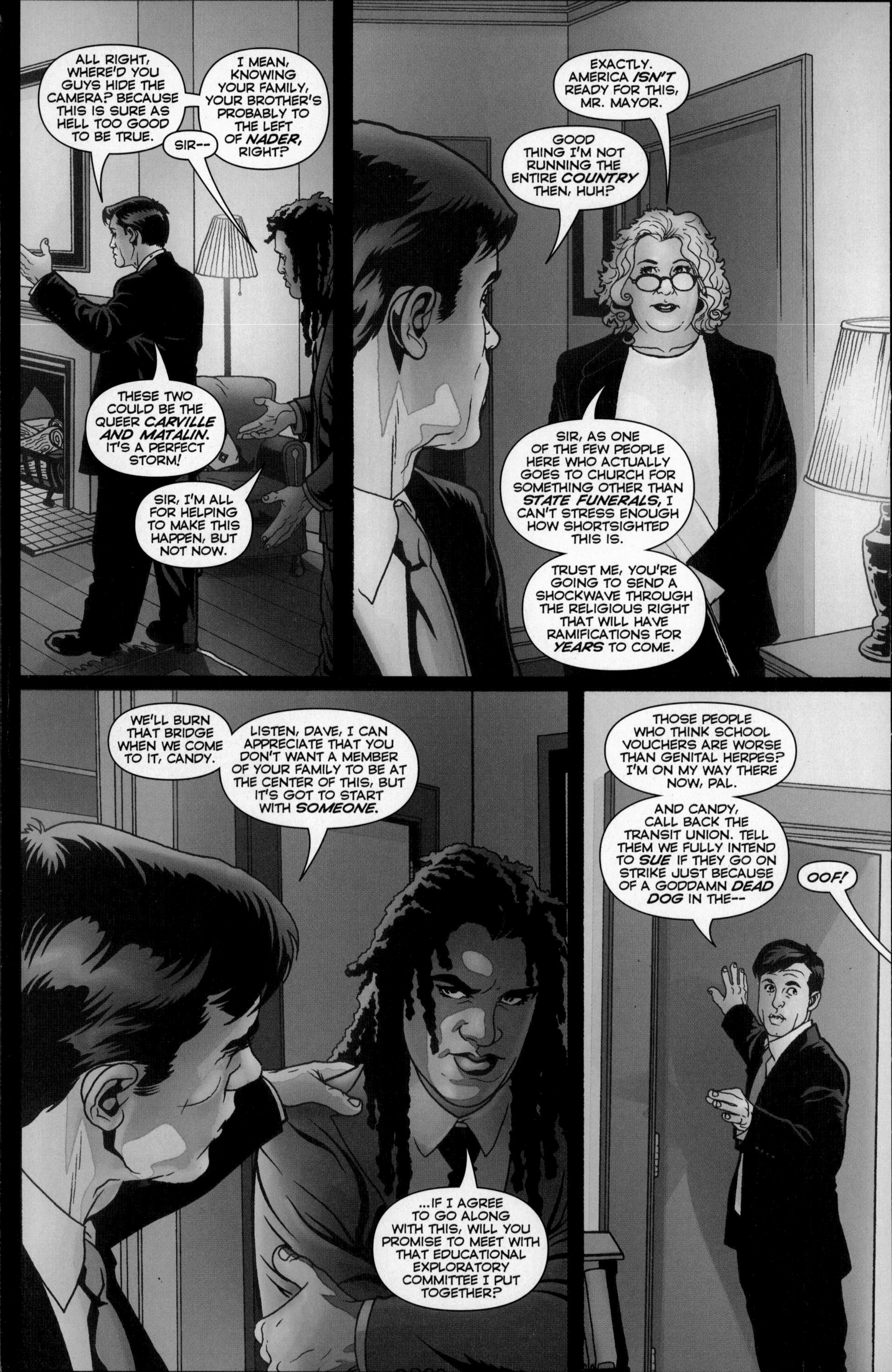
ALL RIGHT, WHERE'D YOU GUYS HIDE THE CAMERA? BECAUSE THIS IS SURE AS HELL TOO GOOD TO BE TRUE.
SIR--
I MEAN, KNOWING YOUR FAMILY, YOUR BROTHER'S PROBABLY TO THE LEFT OF NADER, RIGHT?
THESE TWO COULD BE THE QUEER CARVILLE AND MATALIN. IT'S A PERFECT STORM!
SIR, I'M ALL FOR HELPING TO MAKE THIS HAPPEN, BUT NOT NOW.
EXACTLY. AMERICA ISN'T READY FOR THIS, MR. MAYOR.
GOOD THING I'M NOT RUNNING THE ENTIRE COUNTRY THEN, HUH?
SIR, AS ONE OF THE FEW PEOPLE HERE WHO ACTUALLY GOES TO CHURCH FOR SOMETHING OTHER THAN STATE FUNERALS, I CAN'T STRESS ENOUGH HOW SHORTSIGHTED THIS IS.
TRUST ME, YOU'RE GOING TO SEND A SHOCKWAVE THROUGH THE RELIGIOUS RIGHT THAT WILL HAVE RAMIFICATIONS FOR YEARS TO COME.
WE'LL BURN THAT BRIDGE WHEN WE COME TO IT, CANDY.
LISTEN, DAVE, I CAN APPRECIATE THAT YOU DON'T WANT A MEMBER OF YOUR FAMILY TO BE AT THE CENTER OF THIS, BUT IT'S GOT TO START WITH SOMEONE.
...IF I AGREE TO GO ALONG WITH THIS, WILL YOU PROMISE TO MEET WITH THAT EDUCATIONAL EXPLORATORY COMMITTEE I PUT TOGETHER?
THOSE PEOPLE WHO THINK SCHOOL VOUCHERS ARE WORSE THAN GENITAL HERPES? I'M ON MY WAY THERE NOW, PAL.
AND CANDY, CALL BACK THE TRANSIT UNION. TELL THEM WE FULLY INTEND TO SUE IF THEY GO ON STRIKE JUST BECAUSE OF A GODDAMN DEAD DOG IN THE--
OOF!

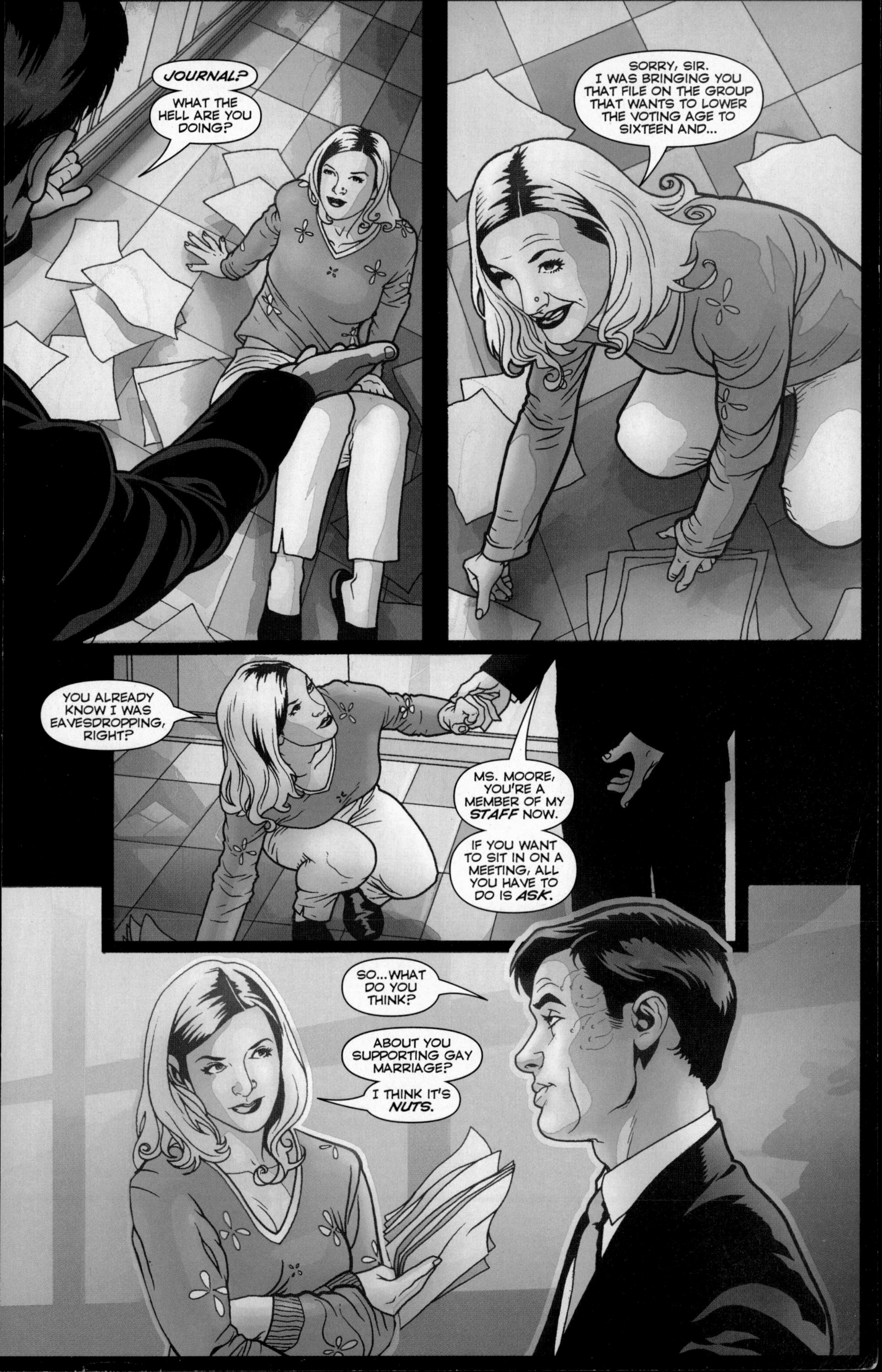
JOURNAL?
WHAT THE HELL ARE YOU DOING?
SORRY, SIR. I WAS BRINGING YOU THAT FILE ON THE GROUP THAT WANTS TO LOWER THE VOTING AGE TO SIXTEEN AND...
YOU ALREADY KNOW I WAS EAVESDROPPING, RIGHT?
MS. MOORE, YOU'RE A MEMBER OF MY STAFF NOW.
IF YOU WANT TO SIT IN ON A MEETING, ALL YOU HAVE TO DO IS ASK.
SO...WHAT DO YOU THINK?
ABOUT YOU SUPPORTING GAY MARRIAGE?
I THINK IT'S NUTS.

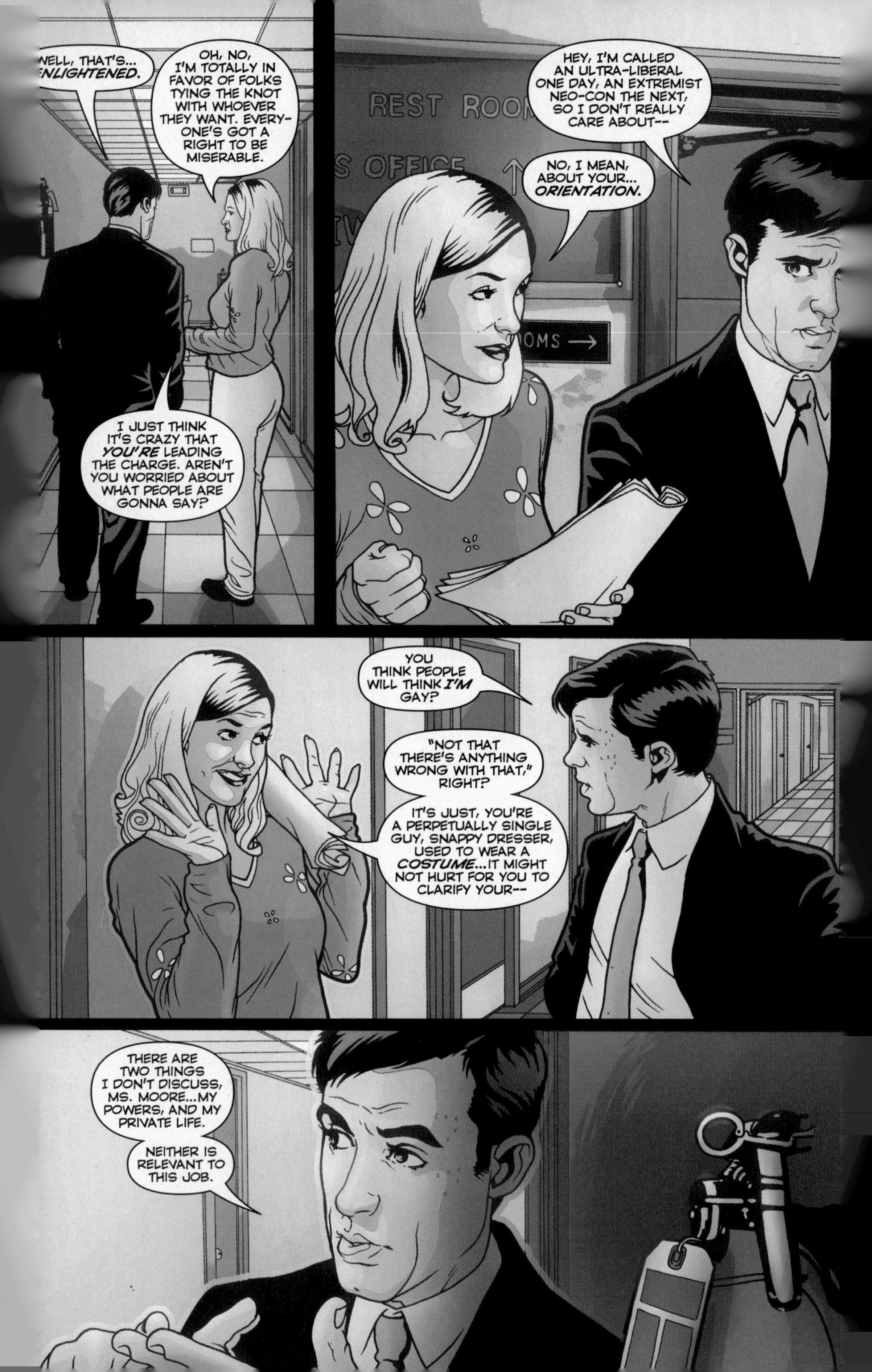
WELL, THAT'S... ENLIGHTENED.
OH, NO, I'M TOTALLY IN FAVOR OF FOLKS TYING THE KNOT WITH WHOEVER THEY WANT. EVERYONE'S GOT A RIGHT TO BE MISERABLE.
I JUST THINK IT'S CRAZY THAT *YOU'RE* LEADING THE CHARGE. AREN'T YOU WORRIED ABOUT WHAT PEOPLE ARE GONNA SAY?
REST ROOM
S OFFICE
HEY, I'M CALLED AN ULTRA-LIBERAL ONE DAY, AN EXTREMIST NEO-CON THE NEXT, SO I DON'T REALLY CARE ABOUT--
NO, I MEAN, ABOUT YOUR... *ORIENTATION.*
OMS →
YOU THINK PEOPLE WILL THINK *I'M* GAY?
"NOT THAT THERE'S ANYTHING WRONG WITH THAT," RIGHT?
IT'S JUST, YOU'RE A PERPETUALLY SINGLE GUY, SNAPPY DRESSER, USED TO WEAR A *COSTUME*...IT MIGHT NOT HURT FOR YOU TO CLARIFY YOUR--
THERE ARE TWO THINGS I DON'T DISCUSS, MS. MOORE...MY POWERS, AND MY PRIVATE LIFE.
NEITHER IS RELEVANT TO THIS JOB.

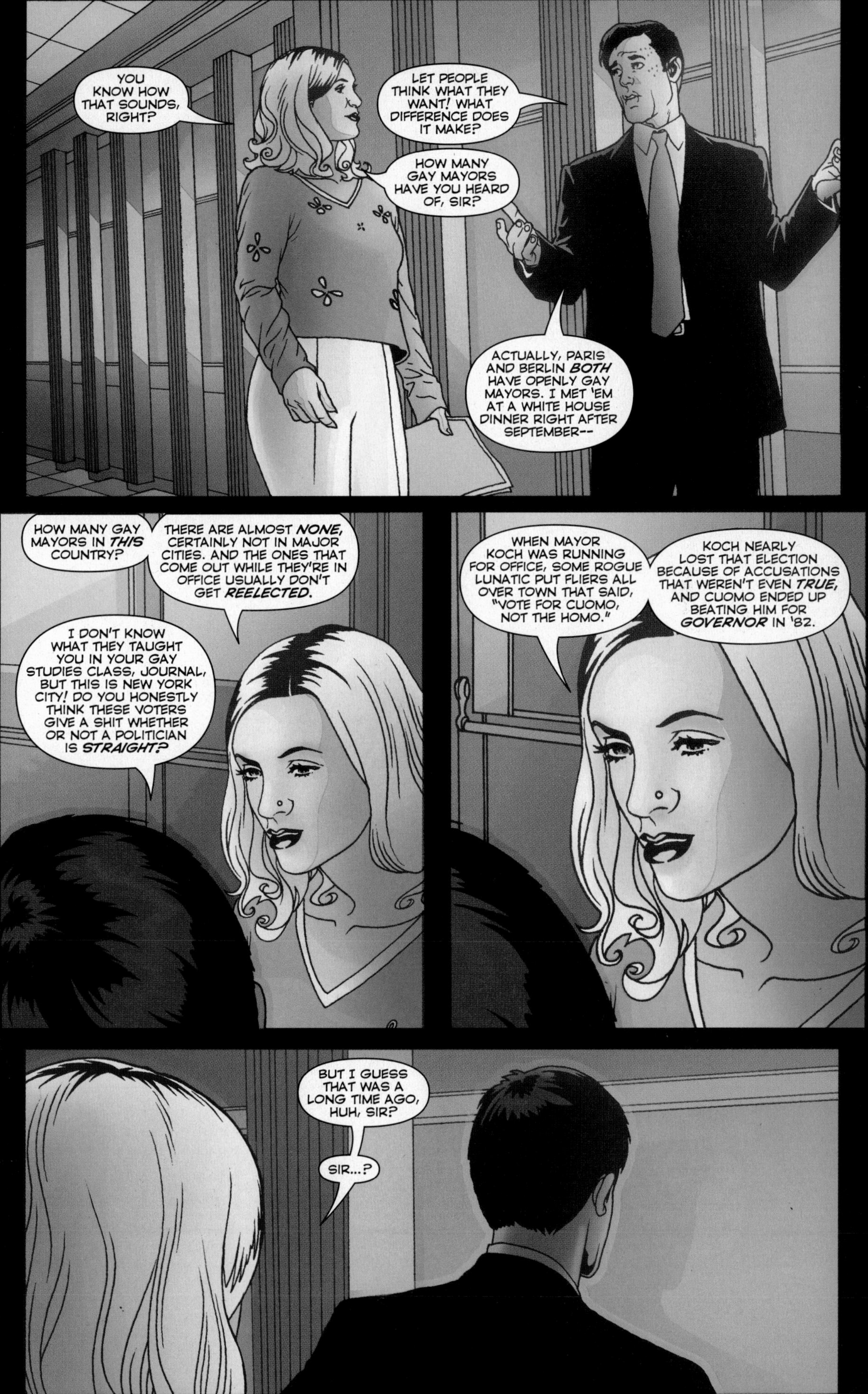
YOU KNOW HOW THAT SOUNDS, RIGHT?
LET PEOPLE THINK WHAT THEY WANT! WHAT DIFFERENCE DOES IT MAKE?
HOW MANY GAY MAYORS HAVE YOU HEARD OF, SIR?
ACTUALLY, PARIS AND BERLIN BOTH HAVE OPENLY GAY MAYORS. I MET 'EM AT A WHITE HOUSE DINNER RIGHT AFTER SEPTEMBER--
HOW MANY GAY MAYORS IN THIS COUNTRY?
THERE ARE ALMOST NONE, CERTAINLY NOT IN MAJOR CITIES. AND THE ONES THAT COME OUT WHILE THEY'RE IN OFFICE USUALLY DON'T GET REELECTED.
I DON'T KNOW WHAT THEY TAUGHT YOU IN YOUR GAY STUDIES CLASS, JOURNAL, BUT THIS IS NEW YORK CITY! DO YOU HONESTLY THINK THESE VOTERS GIVE A SHIT WHETHER OR NOT A POLITICIAN IS STRAIGHT?
WHEN MAYOR KOCH WAS RUNNING FOR OFFICE, SOME ROGUE LUNATIC PUT FLIERS ALL OVER TOWN THAT SAID, "VOTE FOR CUOMO, NOT THE HOMO."
KOCH NEARLY LOST THAT ELECTION BECAUSE OF ACCUSATIONS THAT WEREN'T EVEN TRUE, AND CUOMO ENDED UP BEATING HIM FOR GOVERNOR IN '82.
BUT I GUESS THAT WAS A LONG TIME AGO, HUH, SIR?
SIR...?

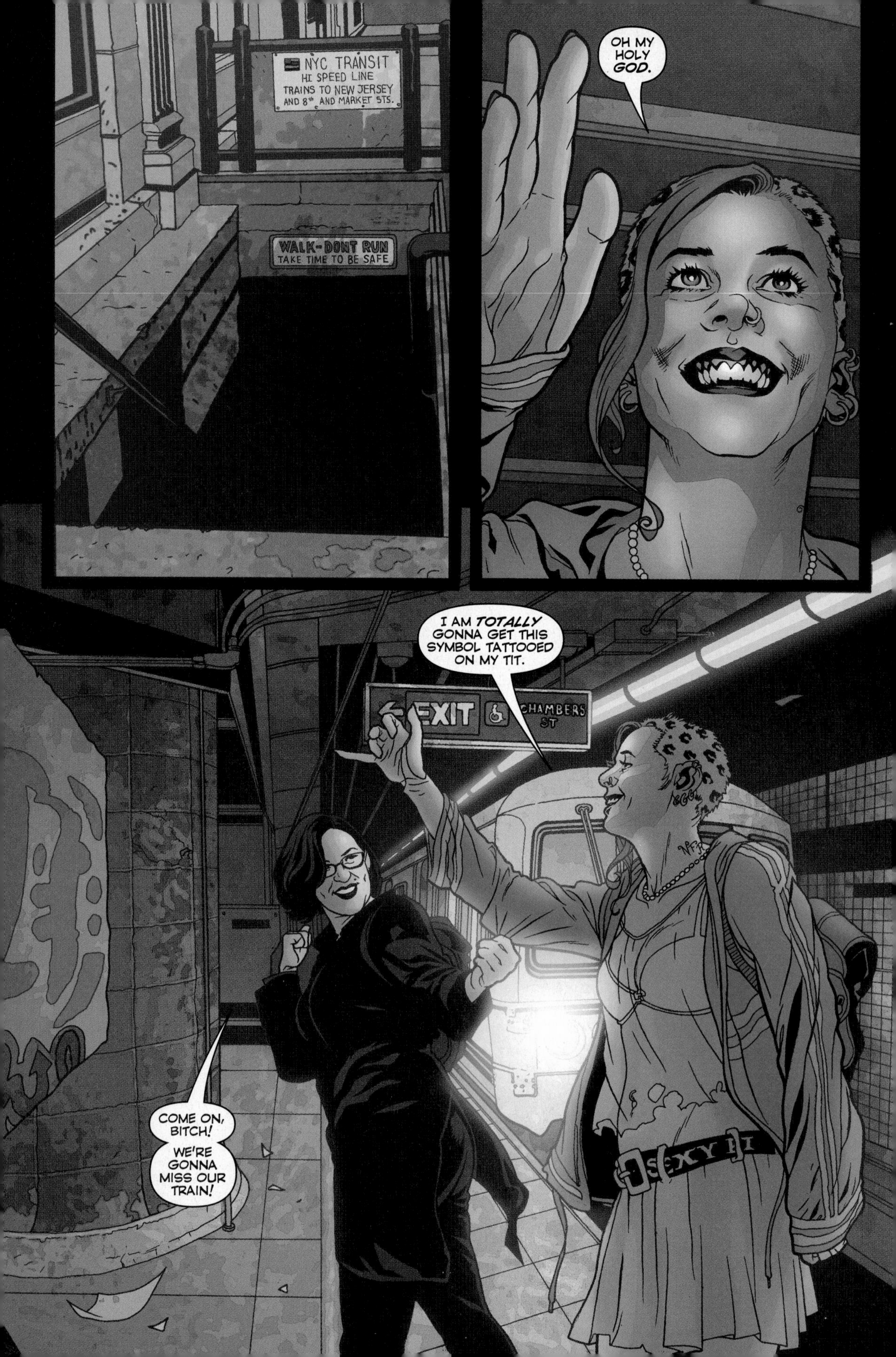
NYC TRANSIT
HI SPEED LINE
TRAINS TO NEW JERSEY
AND 8th AND MARKET STS.
WALK-DONT RUN
TAKE TIME TO BE SAFE
OH MY HOLY *GOD.*
I AM *TOTALLY* GONNA GET THIS SYMBOL TATTOOED ON MY TIT.
EXIT
CHAMBERS ST
COME ON, BITCH!
WE'RE GONNA MISS OUR TRAIN!

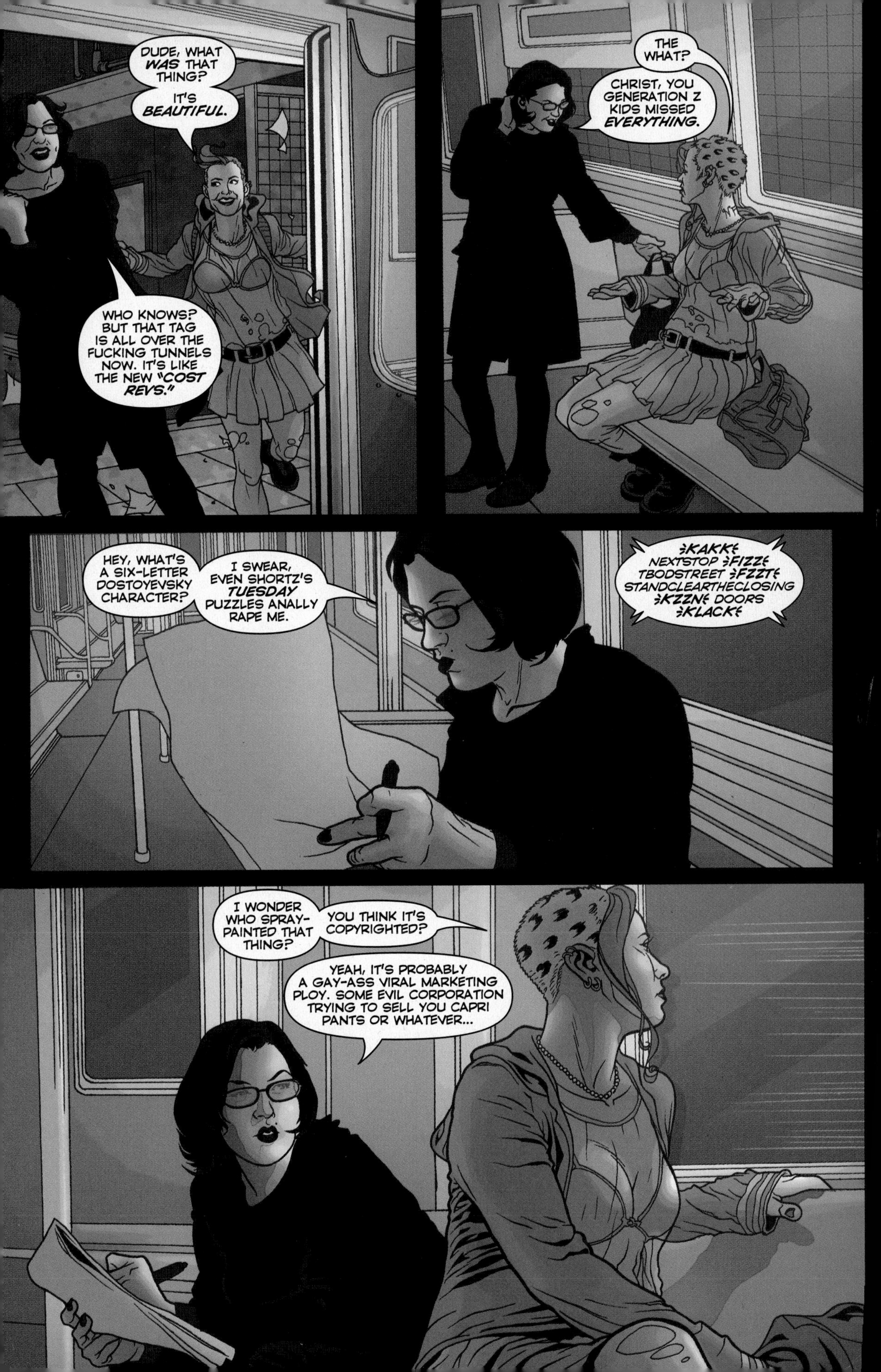
DUDE, WHAT WAS THAT THING?
IT'S BEAUTIFUL.
WHO KNOWS? BUT THAT TAG IS ALL OVER THE FUCKING TUNNELS NOW. IT'S LIKE THE NEW "COST REVS."
THE WHAT?
CHRIST, YOU GENERATION Z KIDS MISSED EVERYTHING.
HEY, WHAT'S A SIX-LETTER DOSTOYEVSKY CHARACTER?
I SWEAR, EVEN SHORTZ'S TUESDAY PUZZLES ANALLY RAPE ME.
KAKK NEXTSTOP FIZZ TBODSTREET FZZT STANDCLEARTHECLOSING KZZN DOORS KLACK
I WONDER WHO SPRAY-PAINTED THAT THING?
YOU THINK IT'S COPYRIGHTED?
YEAH, IT'S PROBABLY A GAY-ASS VIRAL MARKETING PLOY. SOME EVIL CORPORATION TRYING TO SELL YOU CAPRI PANTS OR WHATEVER...

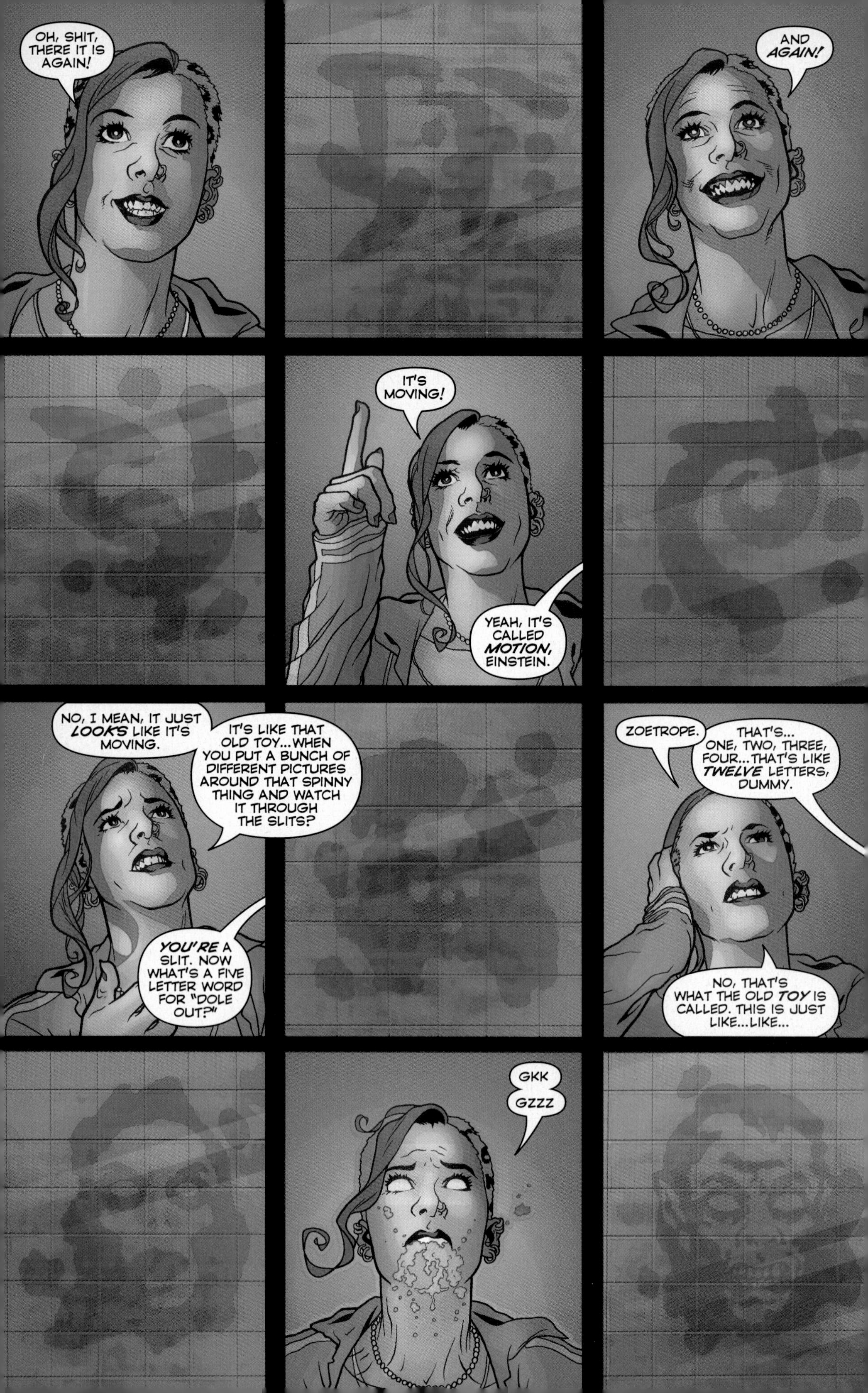
OH, SHIT, THERE IT IS AGAIN!
AND AGAIN!
IT'S MOVING!
YEAH, IT'S CALLED MOTION, EINSTEIN.
NO, I MEAN, IT JUST LOOKS LIKE IT'S MOVING.
IT'S LIKE THAT OLD TOY...WHEN YOU PUT A BUNCH OF DIFFERENT PICTURES AROUND THAT SPINNY THING AND WATCH IT THROUGH THE SLITS?
YOU'RE A SLIT. NOW WHAT'S A FIVE LETTER WORD FOR "DOLE OUT?"
ZOETROPE.
THAT'S... ONE, TWO, THREE, FOUR...THAT'S LIKE TWELVE LETTERS, DUMMY.
NO, THAT'S WHAT THE OLD TOY IS CALLED. THIS IS JUST LIKE...LIKE...
GKK
GZZZ

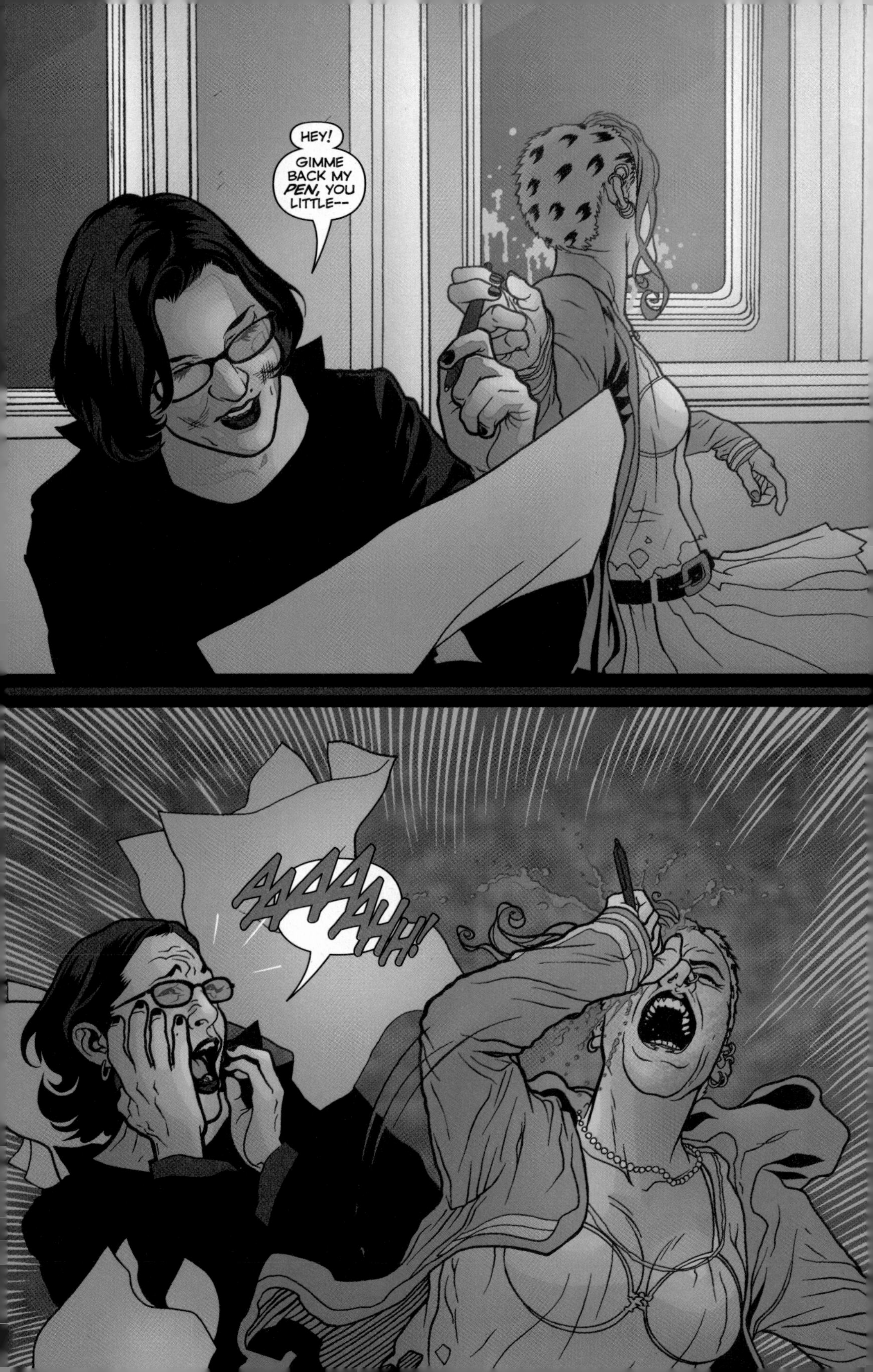
HEY!
GIMME BACK MY PEN, YOU LITTLE--
AAAAAHH!

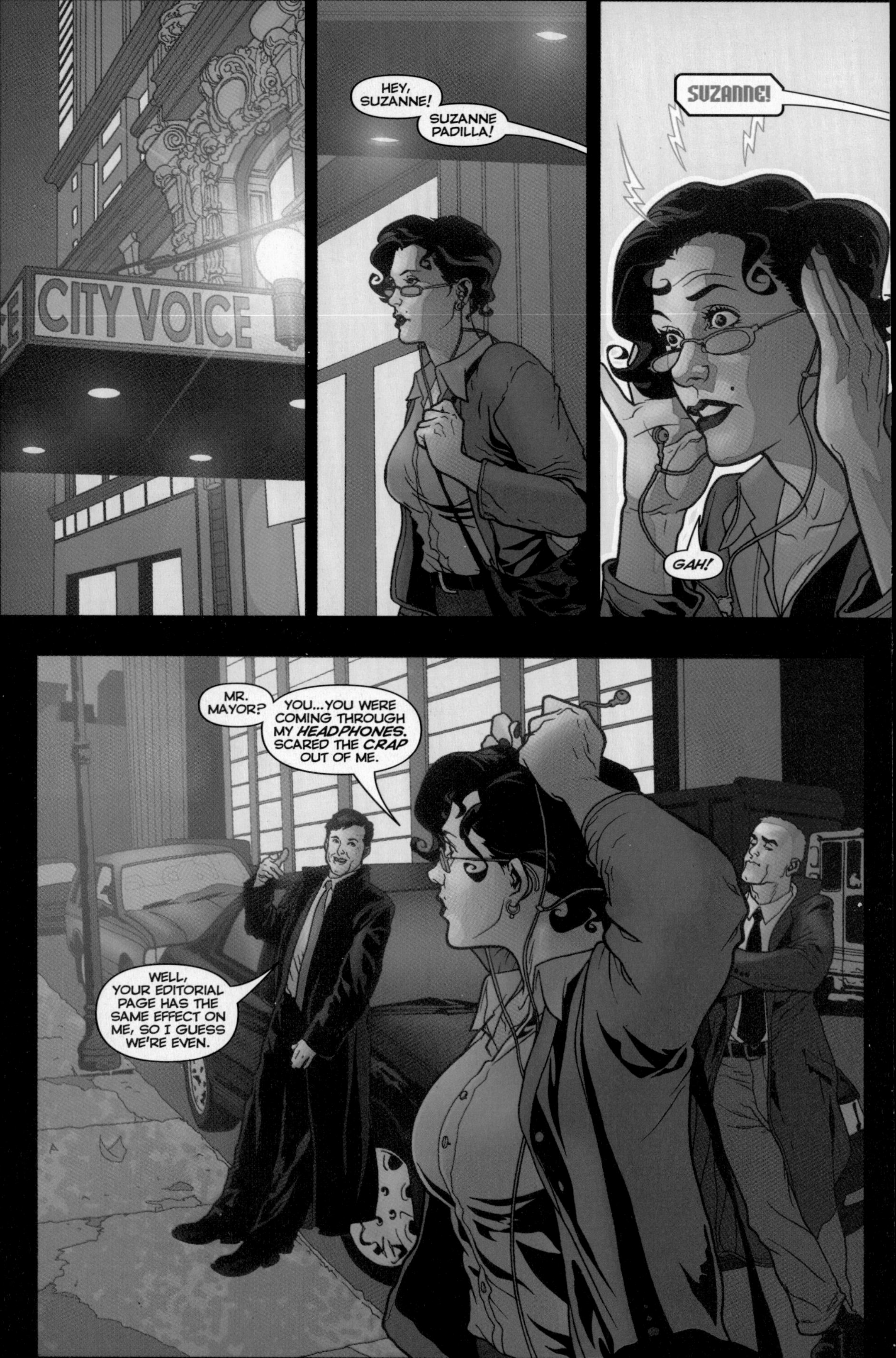
CITY VOICE
HEY, SUZANNE!
SUZANNE PADILLA!
SUZANNE!
GAH!
MR. MAYOR?
YOU...YOU WERE COMING THROUGH MY HEADPHONES. SCARED THE CRAP OUT OF ME.
WELL, YOUR EDITORIAL PAGE HAS THE SAME EFFECT ON ME, SO I GUESS WE'RE EVEN.

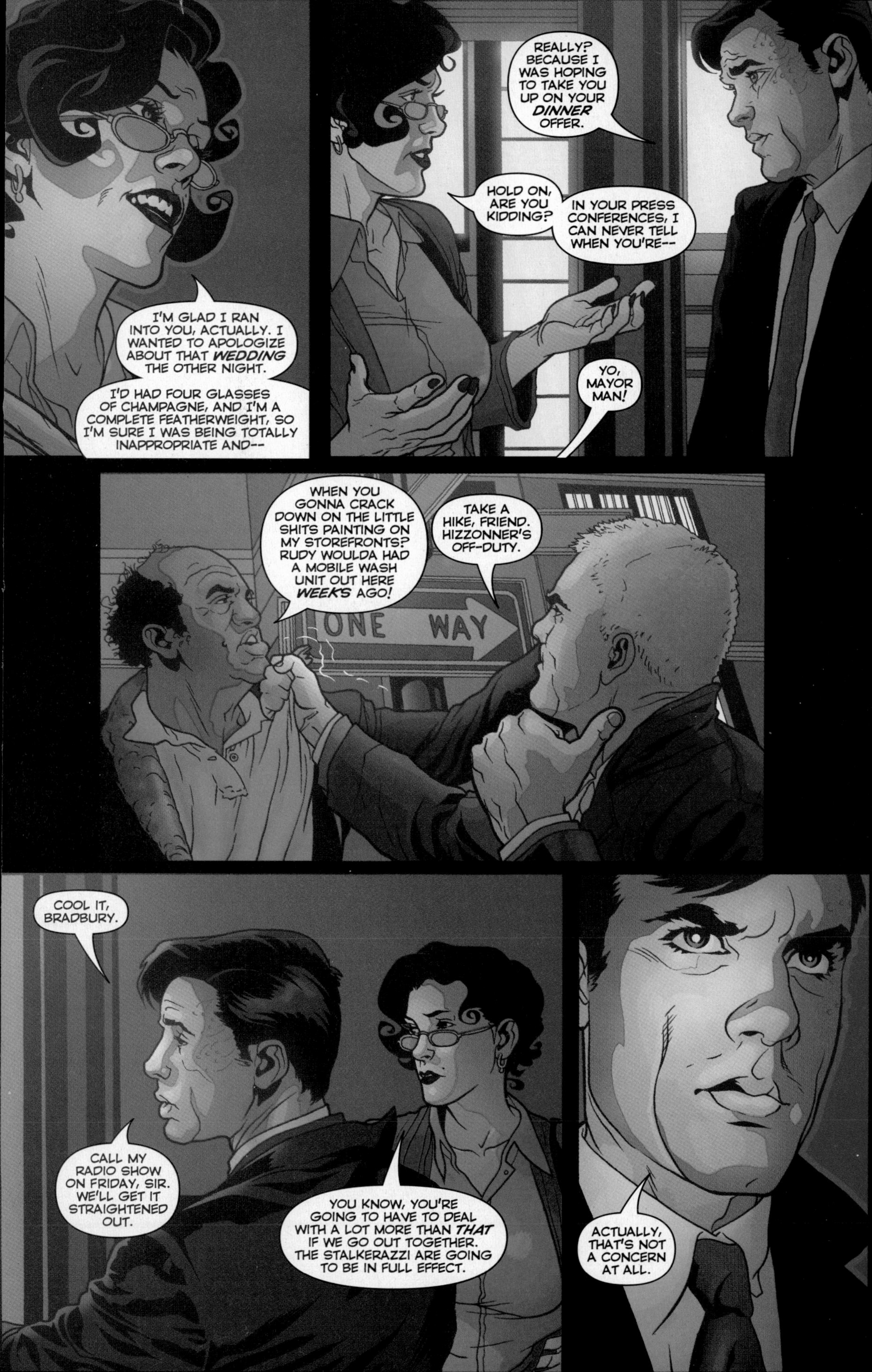
I'M GLAD I RAN INTO YOU, ACTUALLY. I WANTED TO APOLOGIZE ABOUT THAT *WEDDING* THE OTHER NIGHT.
I'D HAD FOUR GLASSES OF CHAMPAGNE, AND I'M A COMPLETE FEATHERWEIGHT, SO I'M SURE I WAS BEING TOTALLY INAPPROPRIATE AND--
REALLY? BECAUSE I WAS HOPING TO TAKE YOU UP ON YOUR *DINNER* OFFER.
HOLD ON, ARE YOU KIDDING?
IN YOUR PRESS CONFERENCES, I CAN NEVER TELL WHEN YOU'RE--
YO, MAYOR MAN!
WHEN YOU GONNA CRACK DOWN ON THE LITTLE SHITS PAINTING ON MY STOREFRONTS? RUDY WOULDA HAD A MOBILE WASH UNIT OUT HERE *WEEKS* AGO!
TAKE A HIKE, FRIEND. HIZZONNER'S OFF-DUTY.
ONE WAY
COOL IT, BRADBURY.
CALL MY RADIO SHOW ON FRIDAY, SIR. WE'LL GET IT STRAIGHTENED OUT.
YOU KNOW, YOU'RE GOING TO HAVE TO DEAL WITH A LOT MORE THAN *THAT* IF WE GO OUT TOGETHER. THE STALKERAZZI ARE GOING TO BE IN FULL EFFECT.
ACTUALLY, THAT'S NOT A CONCERN AT ALL.

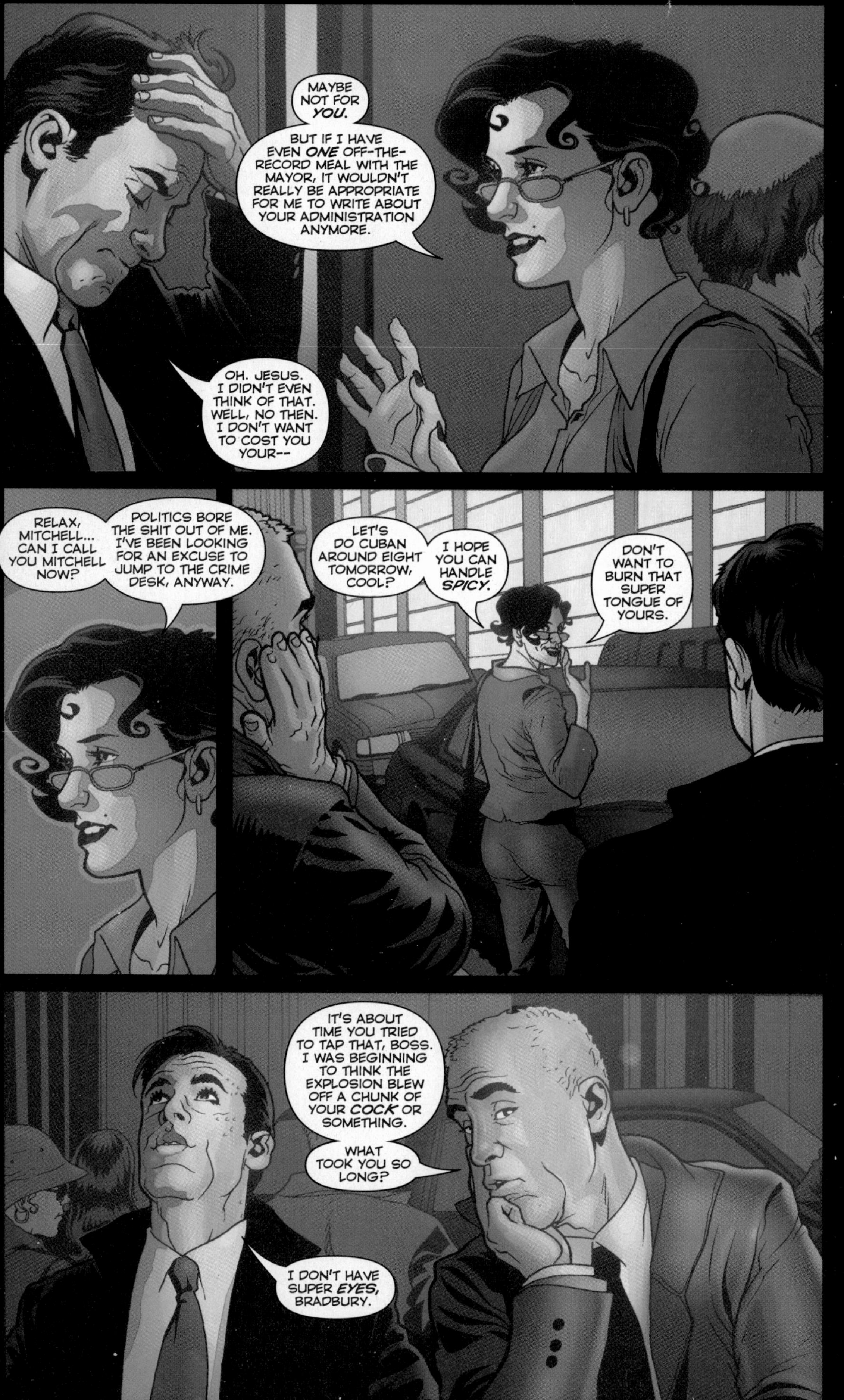
MAYBE NOT FOR *YOU.*
BUT IF I HAVE EVEN *ONE* OFF-THE-RECORD MEAL WITH THE MAYOR, IT WOULDN'T REALLY BE APPROPRIATE FOR ME TO WRITE ABOUT YOUR ADMINISTRATION ANYMORE.
OH. JESUS. I DIDN'T EVEN THINK OF THAT. WELL, NO THEN. I DON'T WANT TO COST YOU YOUR--
RELAX, MITCHELL... CAN I CALL YOU MITCHELL NOW?
POLITICS BORE THE SHIT OUT OF ME. I'VE BEEN LOOKING FOR AN EXCUSE TO JUMP TO THE CRIME DESK, ANYWAY.
LET'S DO CUBAN AROUND EIGHT TOMORROW, COOL?
I HOPE YOU CAN HANDLE *SPICY.*
DON'T WANT TO BURN THAT SUPER TONGUE OF YOURS.
IT'S ABOUT TIME YOU TRIED TO TAP THAT, BOSS. I WAS BEGINNING TO THINK THE EXPLOSION BLEW OFF A CHUNK OF YOUR *COCK* OR SOMETHING.
WHAT TOOK YOU SO LONG?
I DON'T HAVE SUPER *EYES,* BRADBURY.

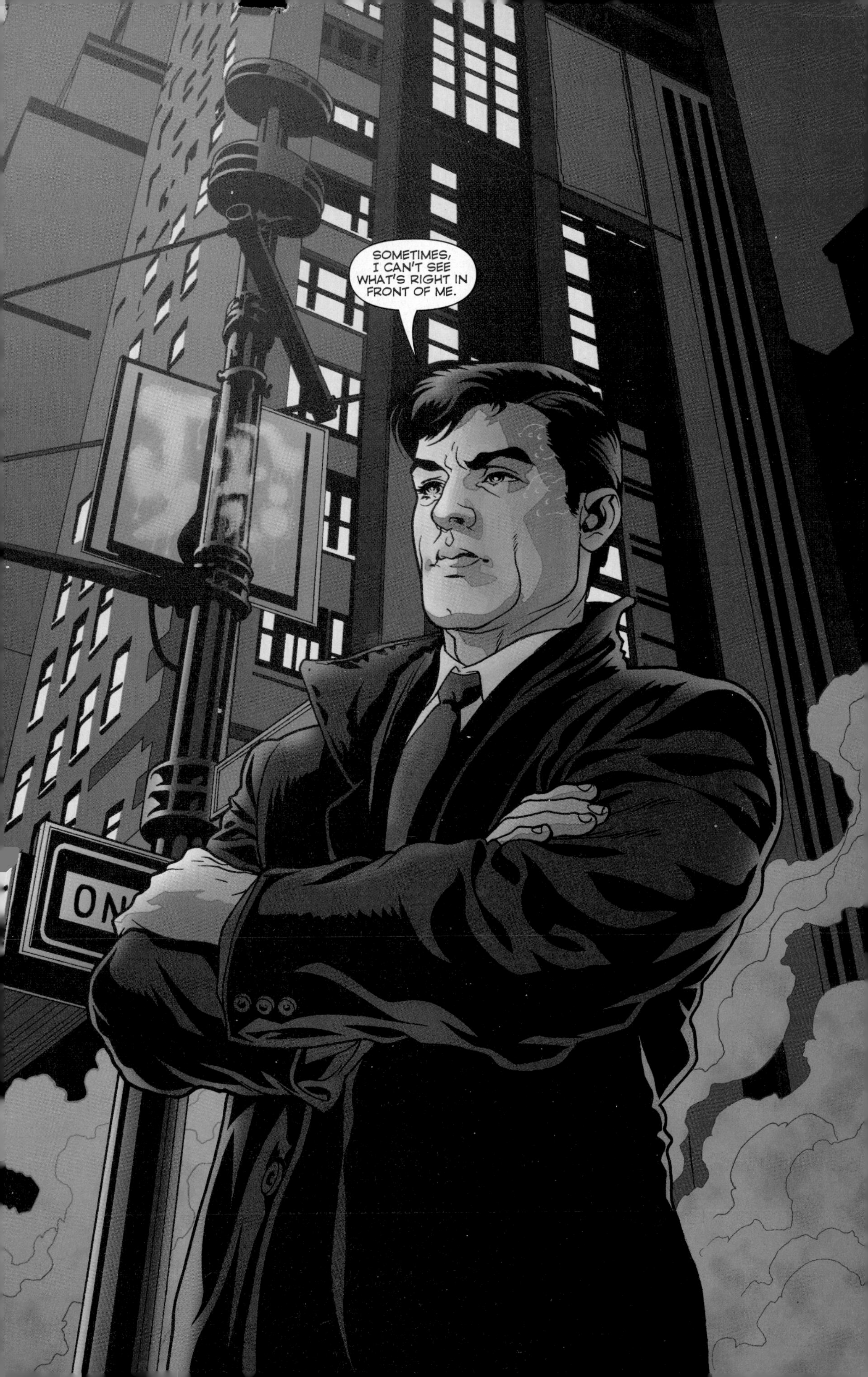
SOMETIMES, I CAN'T SEE WHAT'S RIGHT IN FRONT OF ME.
ON

# CHAPTER 3

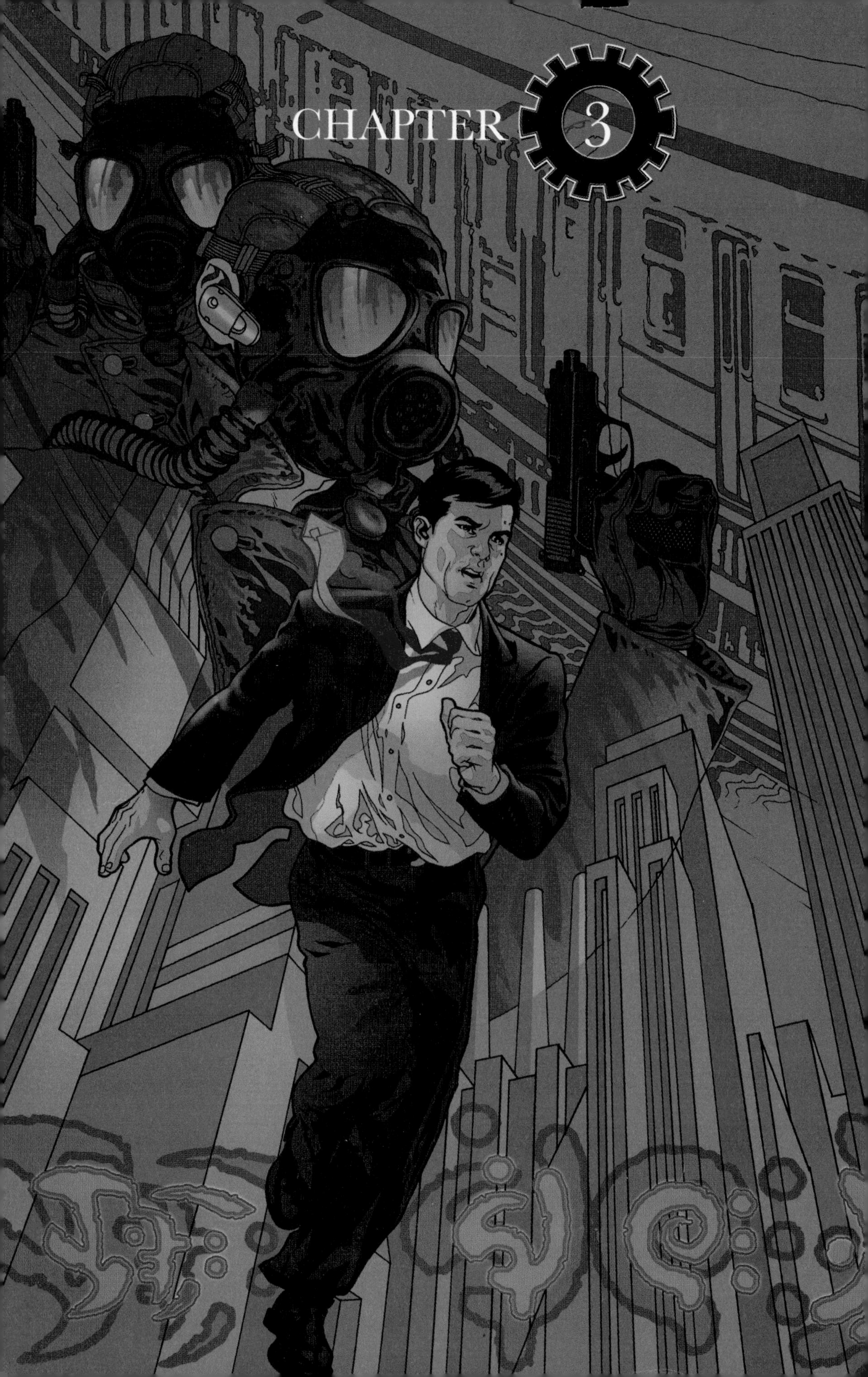

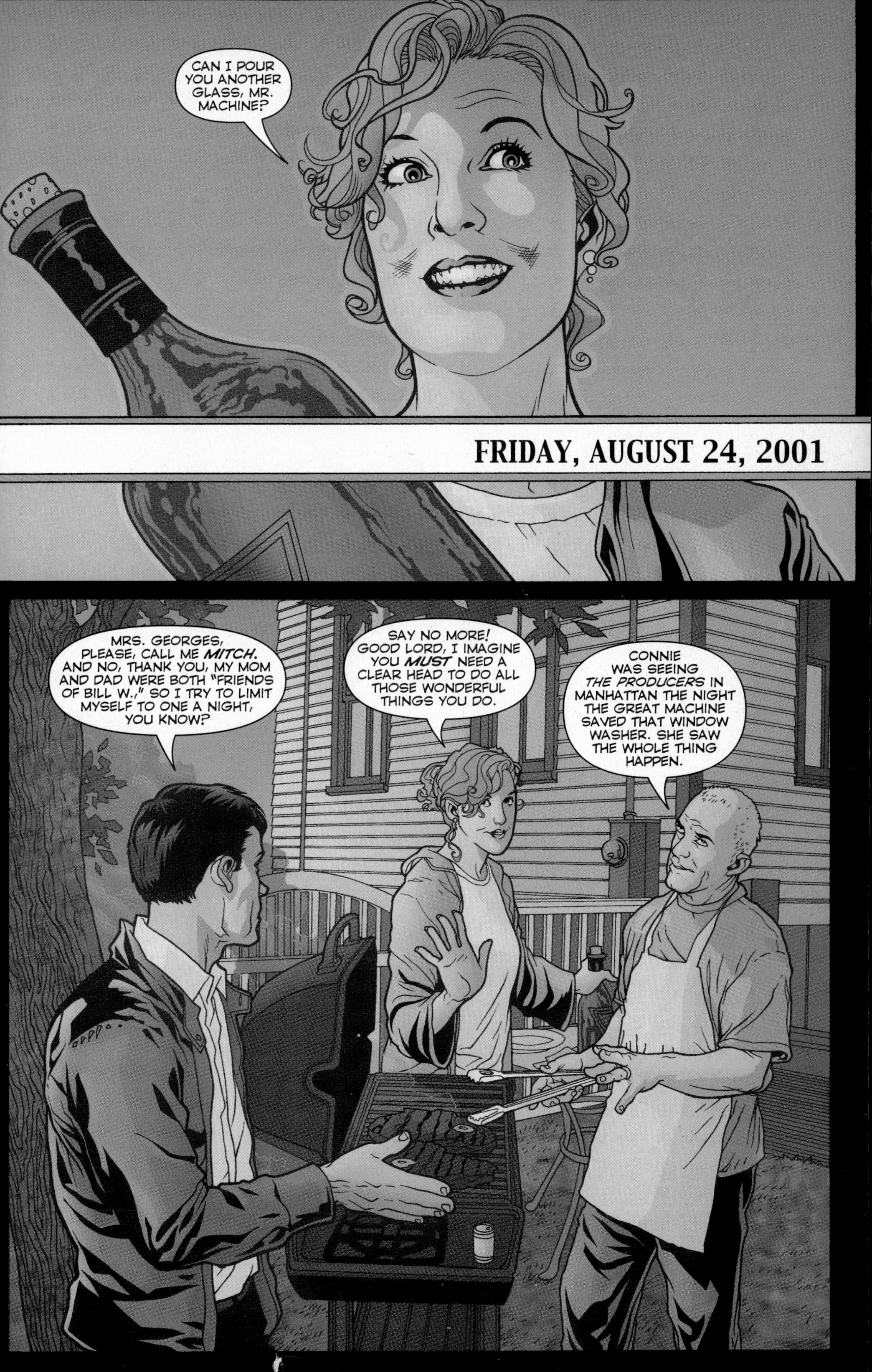
CAN I POUR YOU ANOTHER GLASS, MR. MACHINE?
FRIDAY, AUGUST 24, 2001
MRS. GEORGES, PLEASE, CALL ME MITCH. AND NO, THANK YOU, MY MOM AND DAD WERE BOTH "FRIENDS OF BILL W.;" SO I TRY TO LIMIT MYSELF TO ONE A NIGHT, YOU KNOW?
SAY NO MORE! GOOD LORD, I IMAGINE YOU MUST NEED A CLEAR HEAD TO DO ALL THOSE WONDERFUL THINGS YOU DO.
CONNIE WAS SEEING THE PRODUCERS IN MANHATTAN THE NIGHT THE GREAT MACHINE SAVED THAT WINDOW WASHER. SHE SAW THE WHOLE THING HAPPEN.

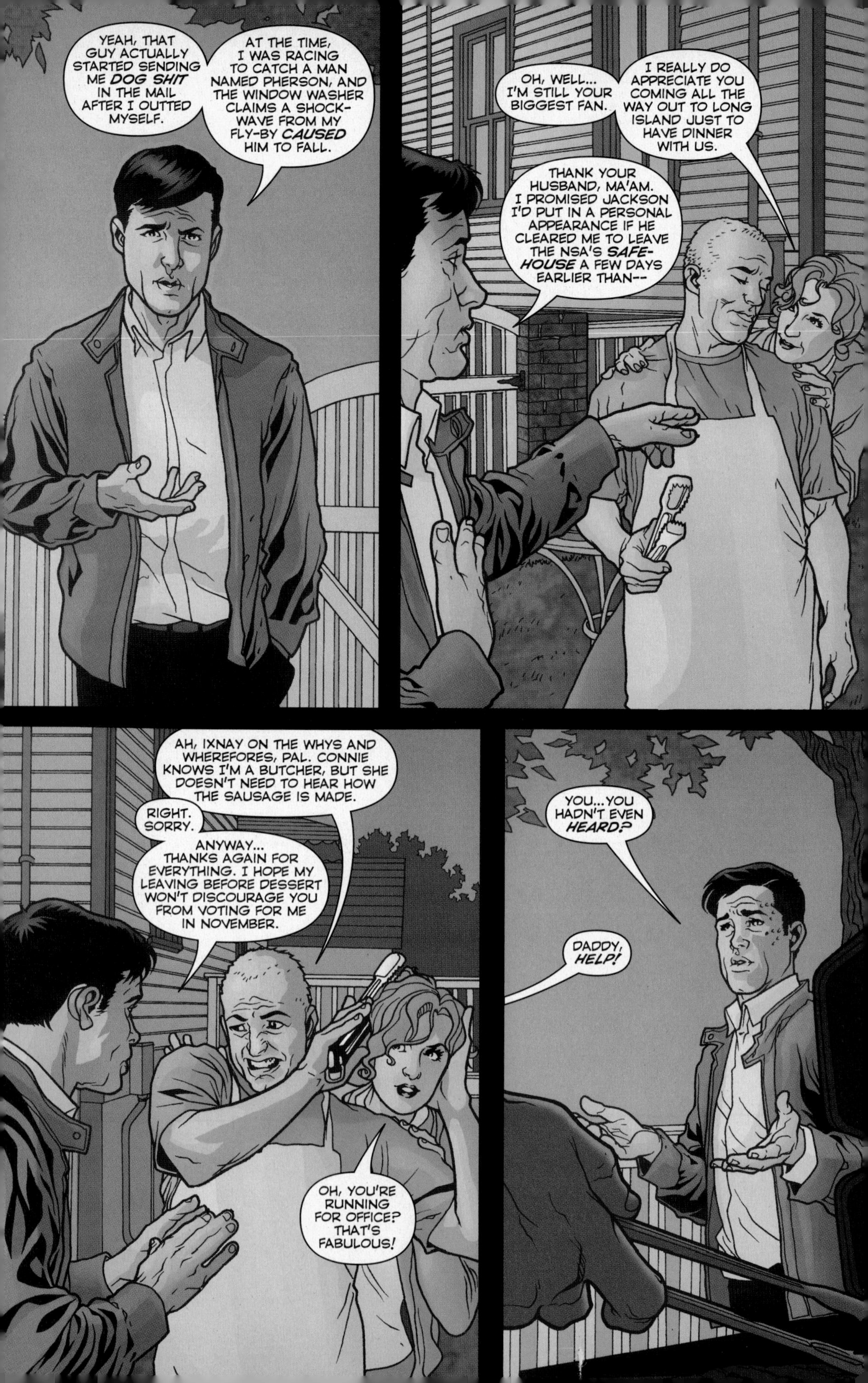
YEAH, THAT GUY ACTUALLY STARTED SENDING ME DOG SHIT IN THE MAIL AFTER I OUTTED MYSELF.
AT THE TIME, I WAS RACING TO CATCH A MAN NAMED PHERSON, AND THE WINDOW WASHER CLAIMS A SHOCK-WAVE FROM MY FLY-BY CAUSED HIM TO FALL.
OH, WELL... I'M STILL YOUR BIGGEST FAN.
I REALLY DO APPRECIATE YOU COMING ALL THE WAY OUT TO LONG ISLAND JUST TO HAVE DINNER WITH US.
THANK YOUR HUSBAND, MA'AM. I PROMISED JACKSON I'D PUT IN A PERSONAL APPEARANCE IF HE CLEARED ME TO LEAVE THE NSA'S SAFE-HOUSE A FEW DAYS EARLIER THAN--
AH, IXNAY ON THE WHYS AND WHEREFORES, PAL. CONNIE KNOWS I'M A BUTCHER, BUT SHE DOESN'T NEED TO HEAR HOW THE SAUSAGE IS MADE.
RIGHT. SORRY.
ANYWAY... THANKS AGAIN FOR EVERYTHING. I HOPE MY LEAVING BEFORE DESSERT WON'T DISCOURAGE YOU FROM VOTING FOR ME IN NOVEMBER.
OH, YOU'RE RUNNING FOR OFFICE? THAT'S FABULOUS!
YOU...YOU HADN'T EVEN HEARD?
DADDY, HELP!

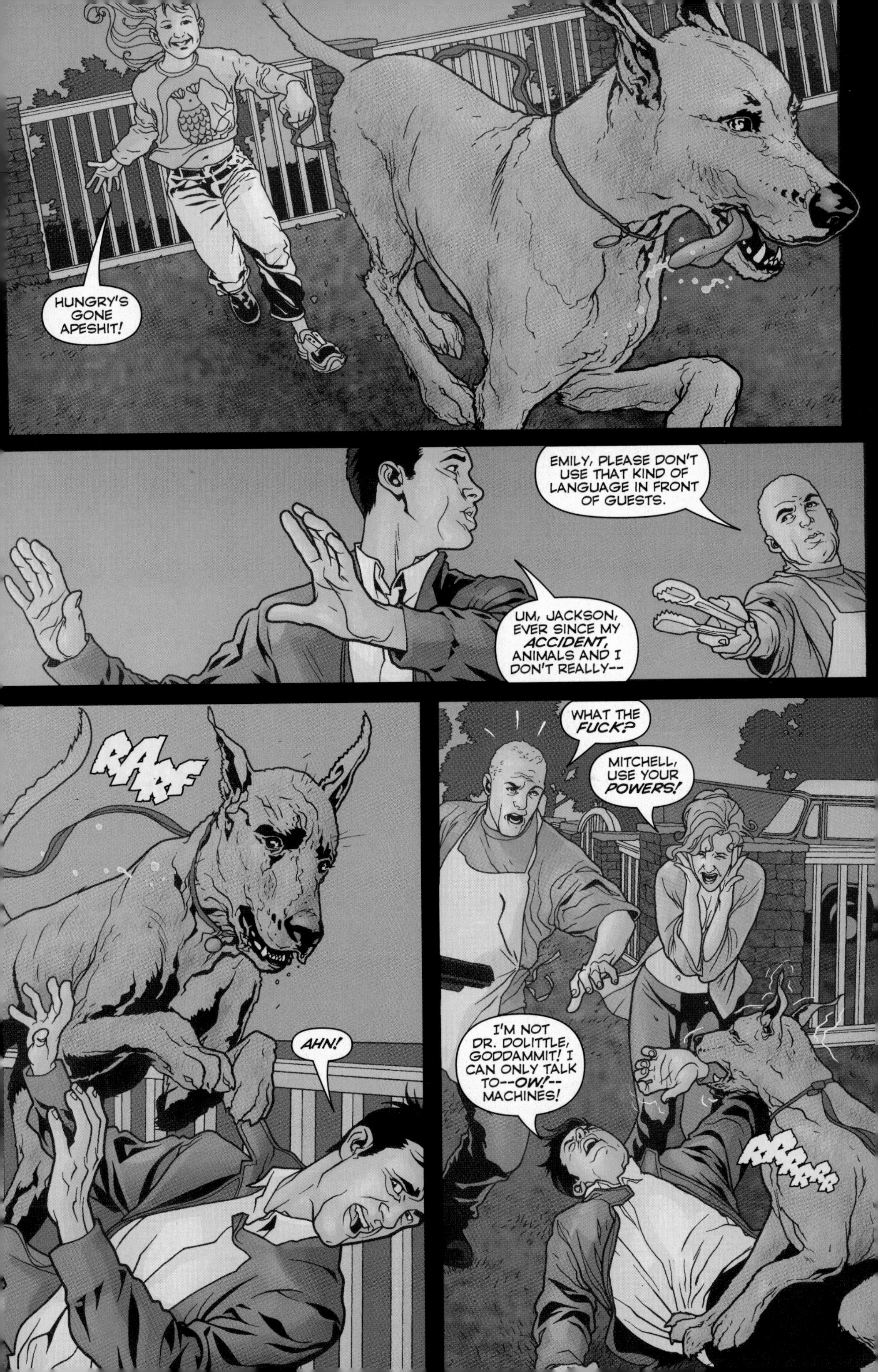
HUNGRY'S GONE APESHIT!
EMILY, PLEASE DON'T USE THAT KIND OF LANGUAGE IN FRONT OF GUESTS.
UM, JACKSON, EVER SINCE MY ACCIDENT, ANIMALS AND I DON'T REALLY--
RARF
AHN!
WHAT THE FUCK?
MITCHELL, USE YOUR POWERS!
I'M NOT DR. DOLITTLE, GODDAMMIT! I CAN ONLY TALK TO--OW!--MACHINES!
RRRRR

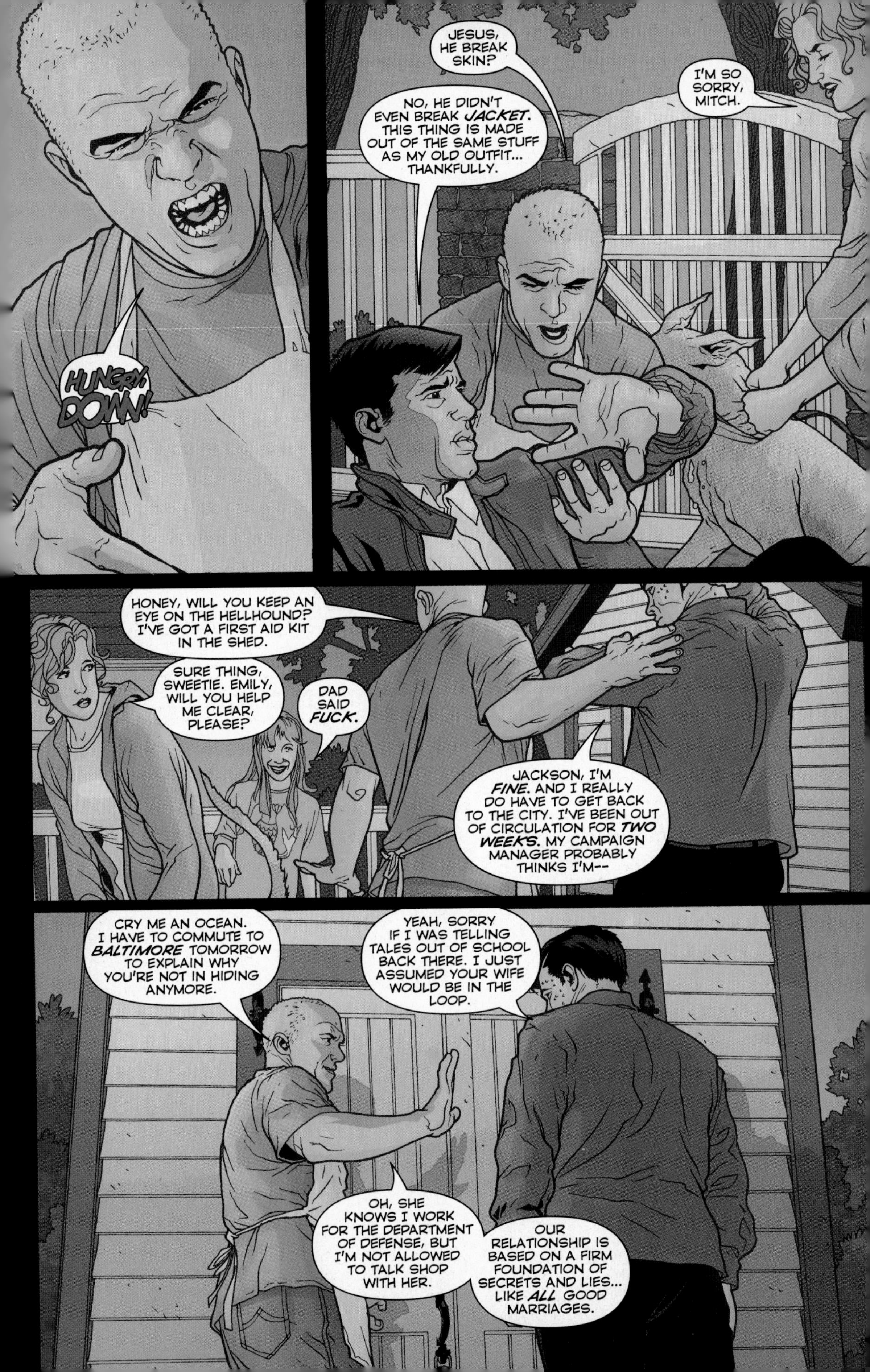
HUNGRY, DOWN!
JESUS, HE BREAK SKIN?
NO, HE DIDN'T EVEN BREAK JACKET. THIS THING IS MADE OUT OF THE SAME STUFF AS MY OLD OUTFIT... THANKFULLY.
I'M SO SORRY, MITCH.
HONEY, WILL YOU KEEP AN EYE ON THE HELLHOUND? I'VE GOT A FIRST AID KIT IN THE SHED.
SURE THING, SWEETIE. EMILY, WILL YOU HELP ME CLEAR, PLEASE?
DAD SAID FUCK.
JACKSON, I'M FINE. AND I REALLY DO HAVE TO GET BACK TO THE CITY. I'VE BEEN OUT OF CIRCULATION FOR TWO WEEKS. MY CAMPAIGN MANAGER PROBABLY THINKS I'M--
CRY ME AN OCEAN. I HAVE TO COMMUTE TO BALTIMORE TOMORROW TO EXPLAIN WHY YOU'RE NOT IN HIDING ANYMORE.
YEAH, SORRY IF I WAS TELLING TALES OUT OF SCHOOL BACK THERE. I JUST ASSUMED YOUR WIFE WOULD BE IN THE LOOP.
OH, SHE KNOWS I WORK FOR THE DEPARTMENT OF DEFENSE, BUT I'M NOT ALLOWED TO TALK SHOP WITH HER.
OUR RELATIONSHIP IS BASED ON A FIRM FOUNDATION OF SECRETS AND LIES... LIKE ALL GOOD MARRIAGES.

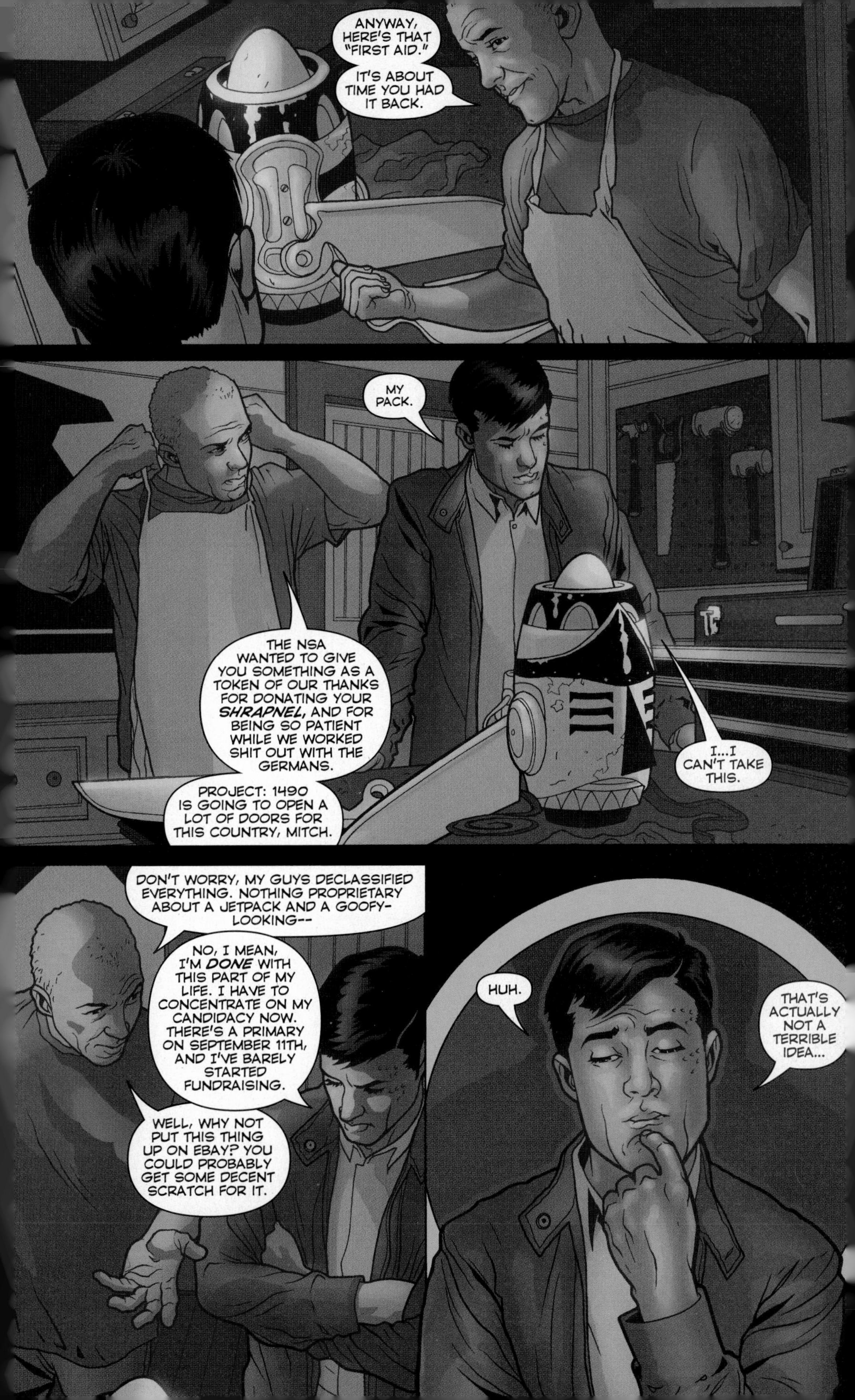
ANYWAY, HERE'S THAT "FIRST AID."
IT'S ABOUT TIME YOU HAD IT BACK.
MY PACK.
THE NSA WANTED TO GIVE YOU SOMETHING AS A TOKEN OF OUR THANKS FOR DONATING YOUR *SHRAPNEL,* AND FOR BEING SO PATIENT WHILE WE WORKED SHIT OUT WITH THE GERMANS.
PROJECT: 1490 IS GOING TO OPEN A LOT OF DOORS FOR THIS COUNTRY, MITCH.
I...I CAN'T TAKE THIS.
DON'T WORRY, MY GUYS DECLASSIFIED EVERYTHING. NOTHING PROPRIETARY ABOUT A JETPACK AND A GOOFY-LOOKING--
NO, I MEAN, I'M *DONE* WITH THIS PART OF MY LIFE. I HAVE TO CONCENTRATE ON MY CANDIDACY NOW. THERE'S A PRIMARY ON SEPTEMBER 11TH, AND I'VE BARELY STARTED FUNDRAISING.
WELL, WHY NOT PUT THIS THING UP ON EBAY? YOU COULD PROBABLY GET SOME DECENT SCRATCH FOR IT.
HUH.
THAT'S ACTUALLY NOT A TERRIBLE IDEA...

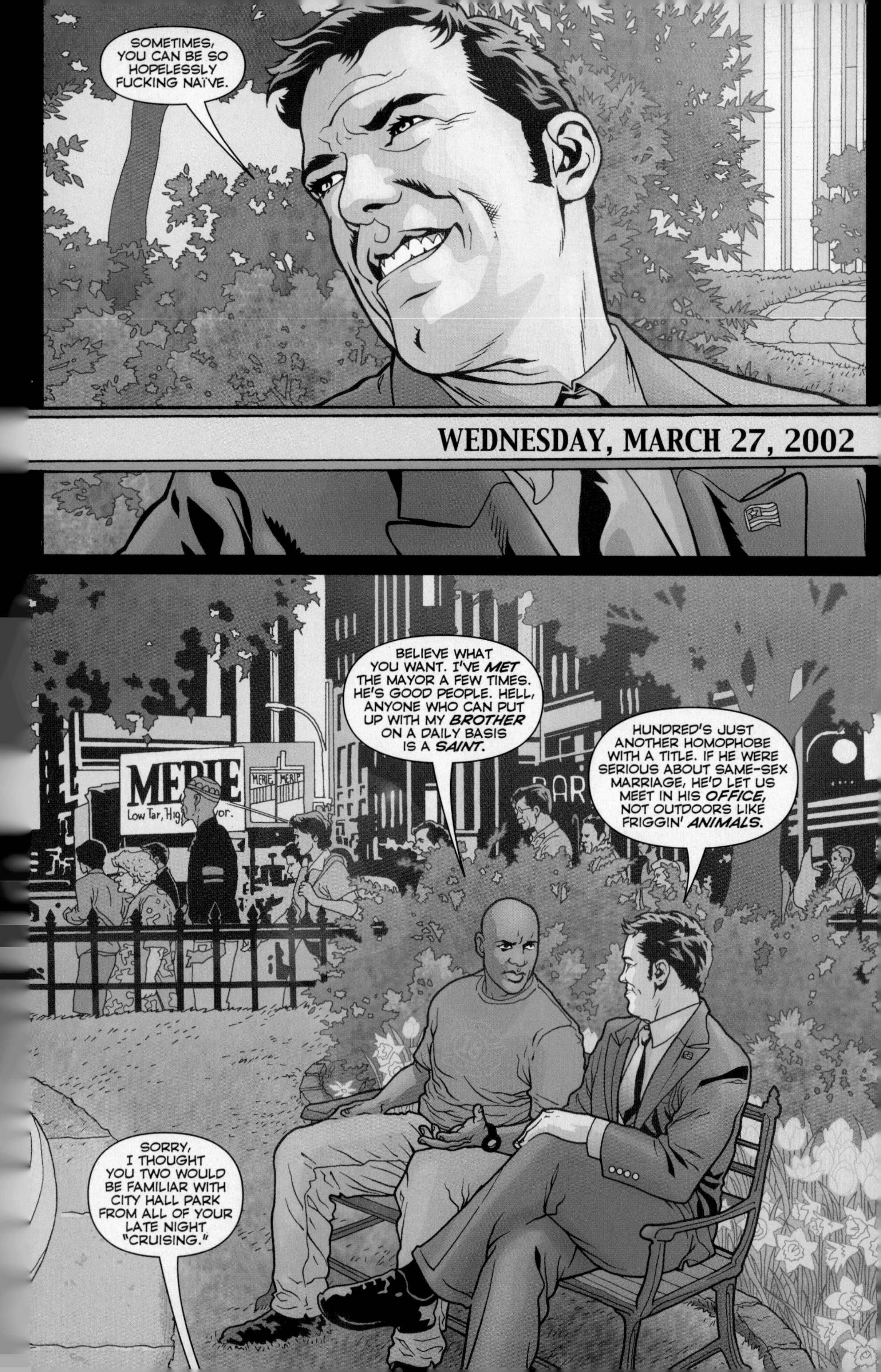
SOMETIMES, YOU CAN BE SO HOPELESSLY FUCKING NAÏVE.
WEDNESDAY, MARCH 27, 2002
MERIE
Low Tar, Hig... ...vor.
MERIE MERIE
BELIEVE WHAT YOU WANT. I'VE MET THE MAYOR A FEW TIMES. HE'S GOOD PEOPLE. HELL, ANYONE WHO CAN PUT UP WITH MY BROTHER ON A DAILY BASIS IS A SAINT.
HUNDRED'S JUST ANOTHER HOMOPHOBE WITH A TITLE. IF HE WERE SERIOUS ABOUT SAME-SEX MARRIAGE, HE'D LET US MEET IN HIS OFFICE, NOT OUTDOORS LIKE FRIGGIN' ANIMALS.
SORRY, I THOUGHT YOU TWO WOULD BE FAMILIAR WITH CITY HALL PARK FROM ALL OF YOUR LATE NIGHT "CRUISING."

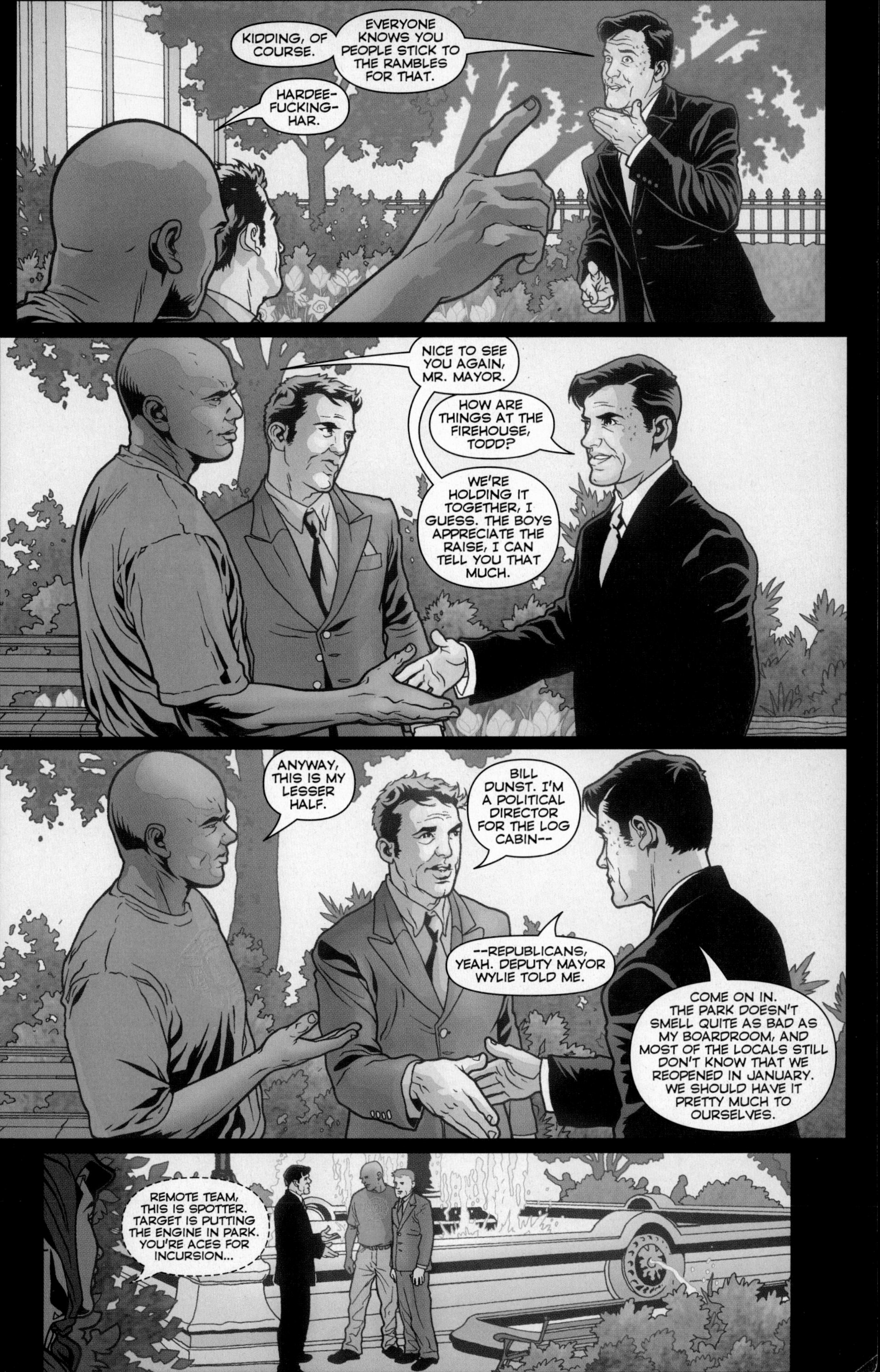
KIDDING, OF COURSE.
EVERYONE KNOWS YOU PEOPLE STICK TO THE RAMBLES FOR THAT.
HARDEE-FUCKING-HAR.
NICE TO SEE YOU AGAIN, MR. MAYOR.
HOW ARE THINGS AT THE FIREHOUSE, TODD?
WE'RE HOLDING IT TOGETHER, I GUESS. THE BOYS APPRECIATE THE RAISE, I CAN TELL YOU THAT MUCH.
ANYWAY, THIS IS MY LESSER HALF.
BILL DUNST. I'M A POLITICAL DIRECTOR FOR THE LOG CABIN--
--REPUBLICANS, YEAH. DEPUTY MAYOR WYLIE TOLD ME.
COME ON IN. THE PARK DOESN'T SMELL QUITE AS BAD AS MY BOARDROOM, AND MOST OF THE LOCALS STILL DON'T KNOW THAT WE REOPENED IN JANUARY. WE SHOULD HAVE IT PRETTY MUCH TO OURSELVES.
REMOTE TEAM, THIS IS SPOTTER. TARGET IS PUTTING THE ENGINE IN PARK. YOU'RE ACES FOR INCURSION...

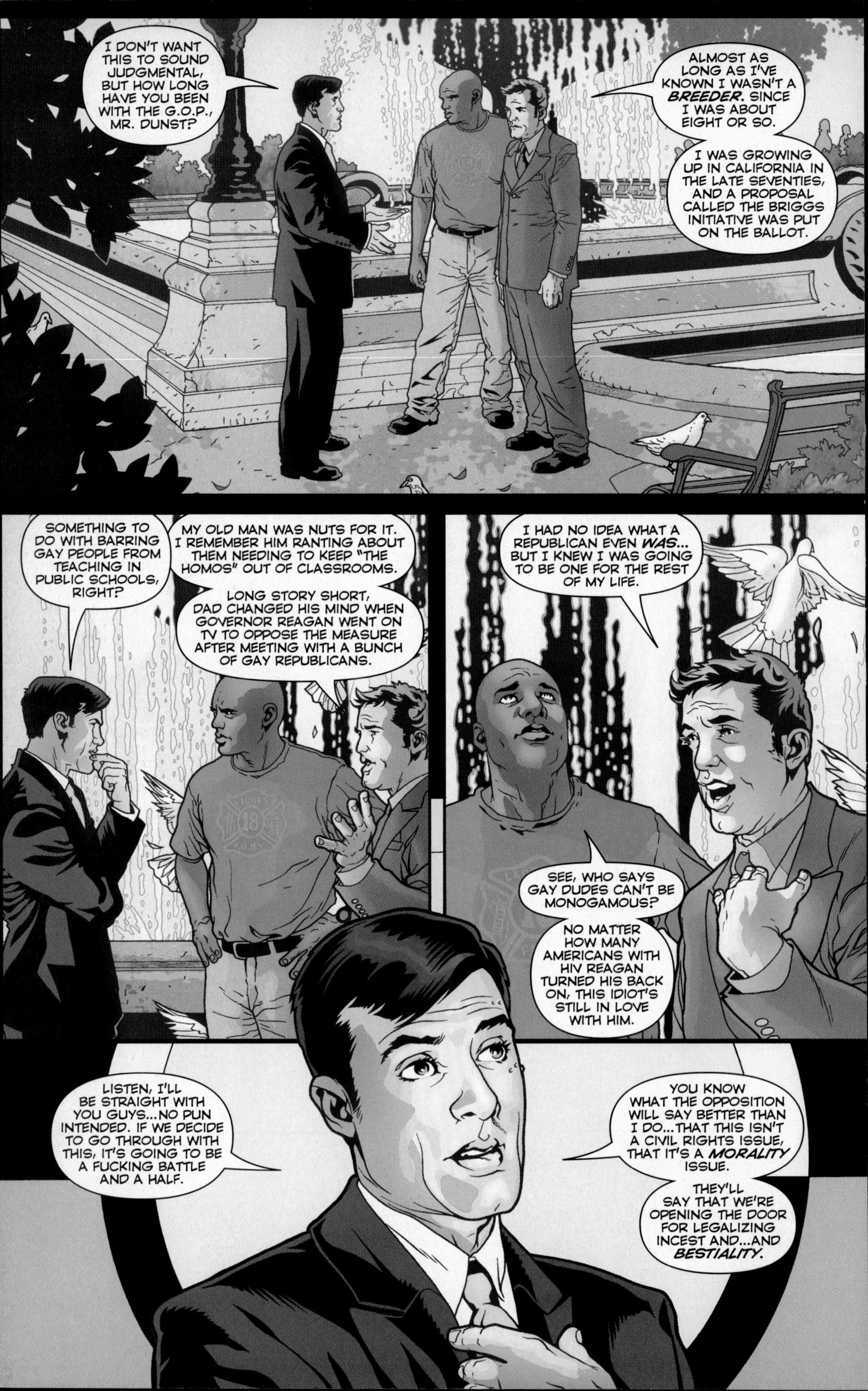
I DON'T WANT THIS TO SOUND JUDGMENTAL, BUT HOW LONG HAVE YOU BEEN WITH THE G.O.P., MR. DUNST?
ALMOST AS LONG AS I'VE KNOWN I WASN'T A BREEDER. SINCE I WAS ABOUT EIGHT OR SO.
I WAS GROWING UP IN CALIFORNIA IN THE LATE SEVENTIES, AND A PROPOSAL CALLED THE BRIGGS INITIATIVE WAS PUT ON THE BALLOT.
SOMETHING TO DO WITH BARRING GAY PEOPLE FROM TEACHING IN PUBLIC SCHOOLS, RIGHT?
MY OLD MAN WAS NUTS FOR IT. I REMEMBER HIM RANTING ABOUT THEM NEEDING TO KEEP "THE HOMOS" OUT OF CLASSROOMS.
LONG STORY SHORT, DAD CHANGED HIS MIND WHEN GOVERNOR REAGAN WENT ON TV TO OPPOSE THE MEASURE AFTER MEETING WITH A BUNCH OF GAY REPUBLICANS.
I HAD NO IDEA WHAT A REPUBLICAN EVEN WAS... BUT I KNEW I WAS GOING TO BE ONE FOR THE REST OF MY LIFE.
SEE, WHO SAYS GAY DUDES CAN'T BE MONOGAMOUS?
NO MATTER HOW MANY AMERICANS WITH HIV REAGAN TURNED HIS BACK ON, THIS IDIOT'S STILL IN LOVE WITH HIM.
LISTEN, I'LL BE STRAIGHT WITH YOU GUYS...NO PUN INTENDED. IF WE DECIDE TO GO THROUGH WITH THIS, IT'S GOING TO BE A FUCKING BATTLE AND A HALF.
YOU KNOW WHAT THE OPPOSITION WILL SAY BETTER THAN I DO...THAT THIS ISN'T A CIVIL RIGHTS ISSUE, THAT IT'S A MORALITY ISSUE.
THEY'LL SAY THAT WE'RE OPENING THE DOOR FOR LEGALIZING INCEST AND...AND BESTIALITY.

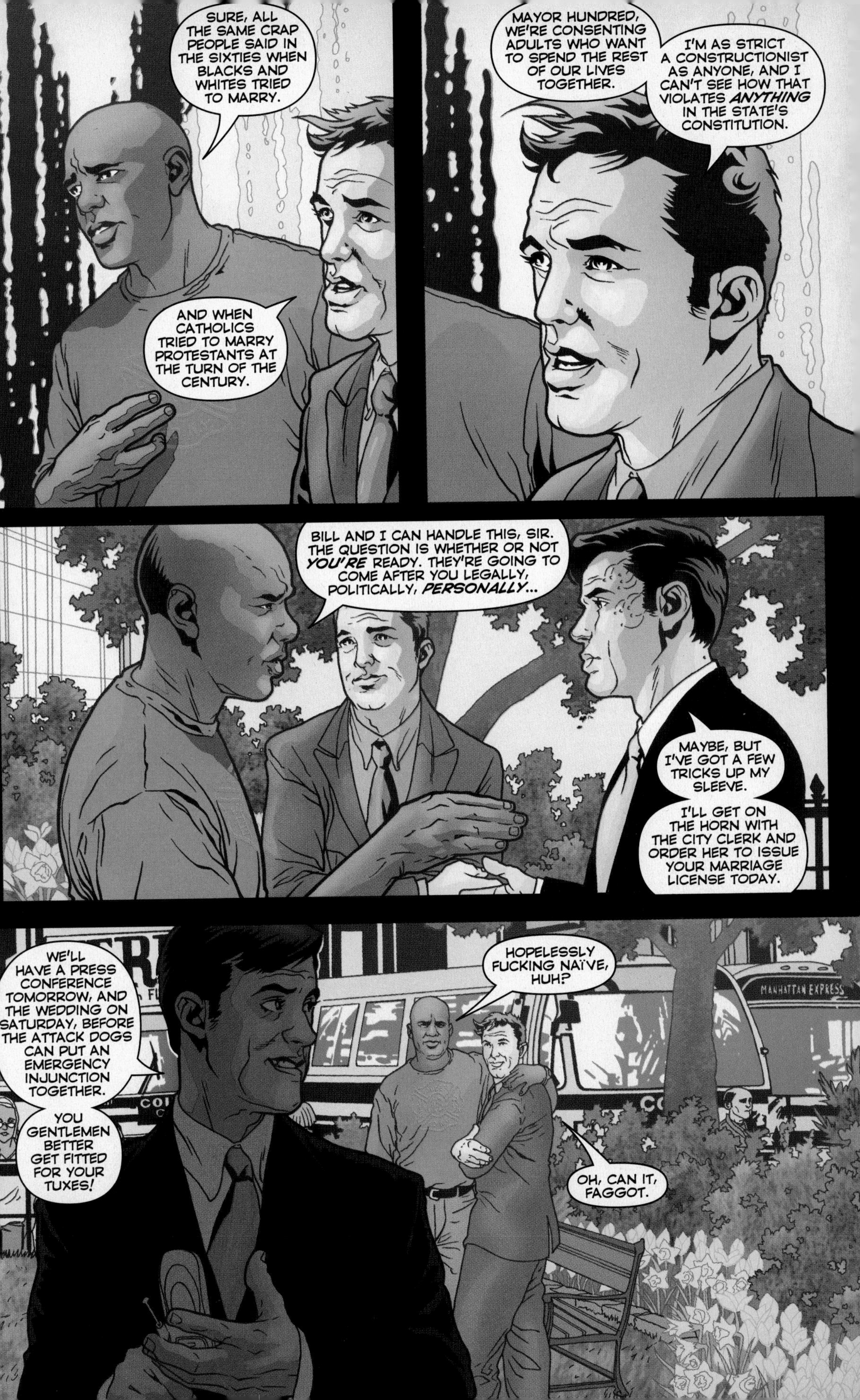
SURE, ALL THE SAME CRAP PEOPLE SAID IN THE SIXTIES WHEN BLACKS AND WHITES TRIED TO MARRY.
AND WHEN CATHOLICS TRIED TO MARRY PROTESTANTS AT THE TURN OF THE CENTURY.
MAYOR HUNDRED, WE'RE CONSENTING ADULTS WHO WANT TO SPEND THE REST OF OUR LIVES TOGETHER.
I'M AS STRICT A CONSTRUCTIONIST AS ANYONE, AND I CAN'T SEE HOW THAT VIOLATES *ANYTHING* IN THE STATE'S CONSTITUTION.
BILL AND I CAN HANDLE THIS, SIR. THE QUESTION IS WHETHER OR NOT *YOU'RE* READY. THEY'RE GOING TO COME AFTER YOU LEGALLY, POLITICALLY, *PERSONALLY*...
MAYBE, BUT I'VE GOT A FEW TRICKS UP MY SLEEVE.
I'LL GET ON THE HORN WITH THE CITY CLERK AND ORDER HER TO ISSUE YOUR MARRIAGE LICENSE TODAY.
WE'LL HAVE A PRESS CONFERENCE TOMORROW, AND THE WEDDING ON SATURDAY, BEFORE THE ATTACK DOGS CAN PUT AN EMERGENCY INJUNCTION TOGETHER.
YOU GENTLEMEN BETTER GET FITTED FOR YOUR TUXES!
HOPELESSLY FUCKING NAÏVE, HUH?
OH, CAN IT, FAGGOT.
MANHATTAN EXPRESS

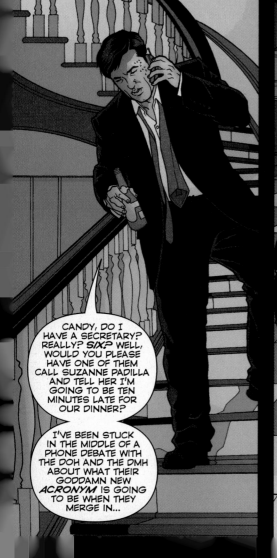

CANDY, DO I HAVE A SECRETARY? REALLY? *SIX?* WELL, WOULD YOU PLEASE HAVE ONE OF THEM CALL SUZANNE PADILLA AND TELL HER I'M GOING TO BE TEN MINUTES LATE FOR OUR DINNER?

I'VE BEEN STUCK IN THE MIDDLE OF A PHONE DEBATE WITH THE DOH AND THE DMH ABOUT WHAT THEIR GODDAMN NEW *ACRONYM* IS GOING TO BE WHEN THEY MERGE IN...

ACTUALLY, IT'S PROBABLY GOING TO BE MORE LIKE *FIFTEEN* MINUTES.

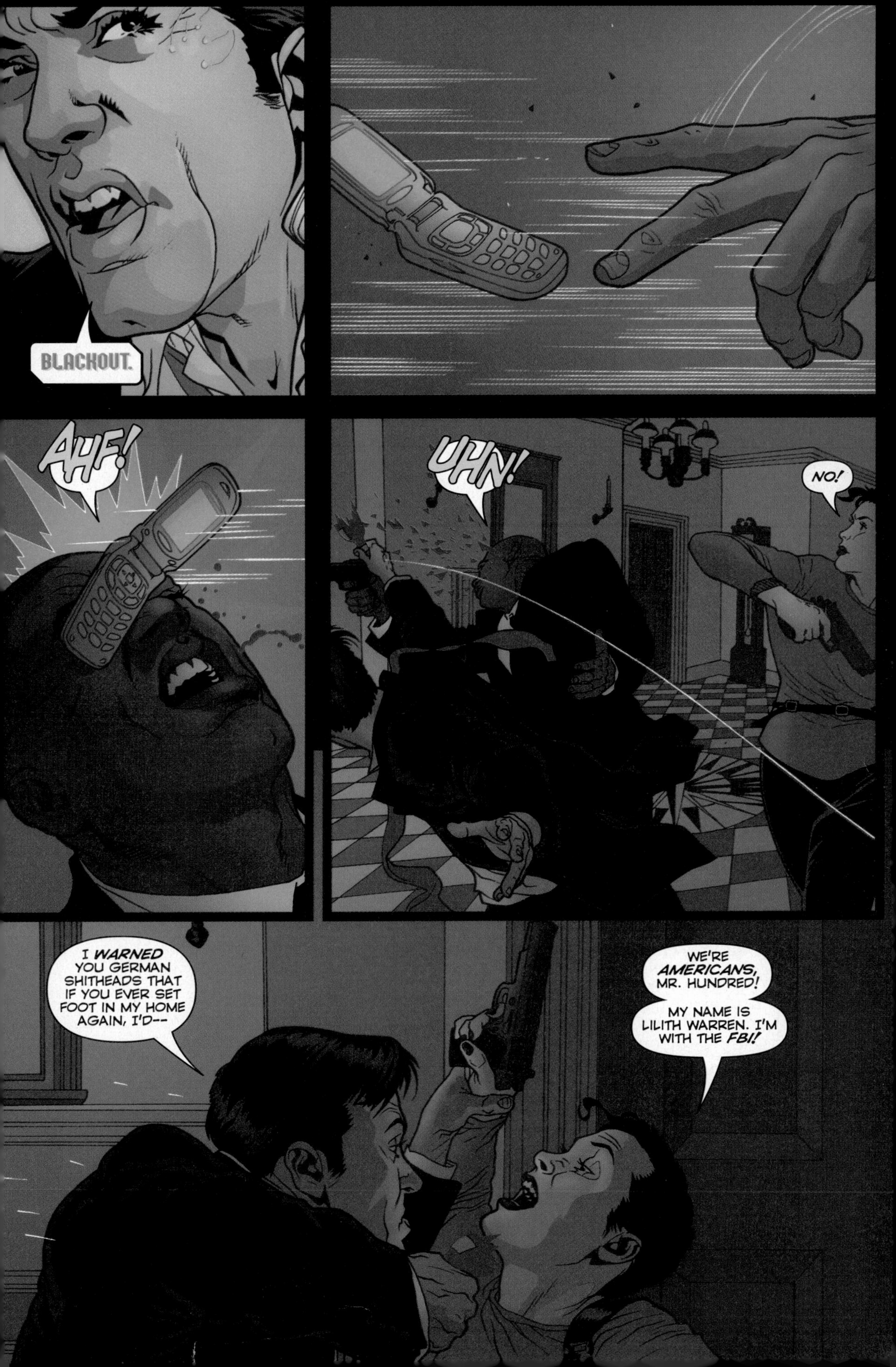
BLACKOUT.
AHF!
UHN!
NO!
I WARNED YOU GERMAN SHITHEADS THAT IF YOU EVER SET FOOT IN MY HOME AGAIN, I'D--
WE'RE AMERICANS, MR. HUNDRED!
MY NAME IS LILITH WARREN. I'M WITH THE FBI!

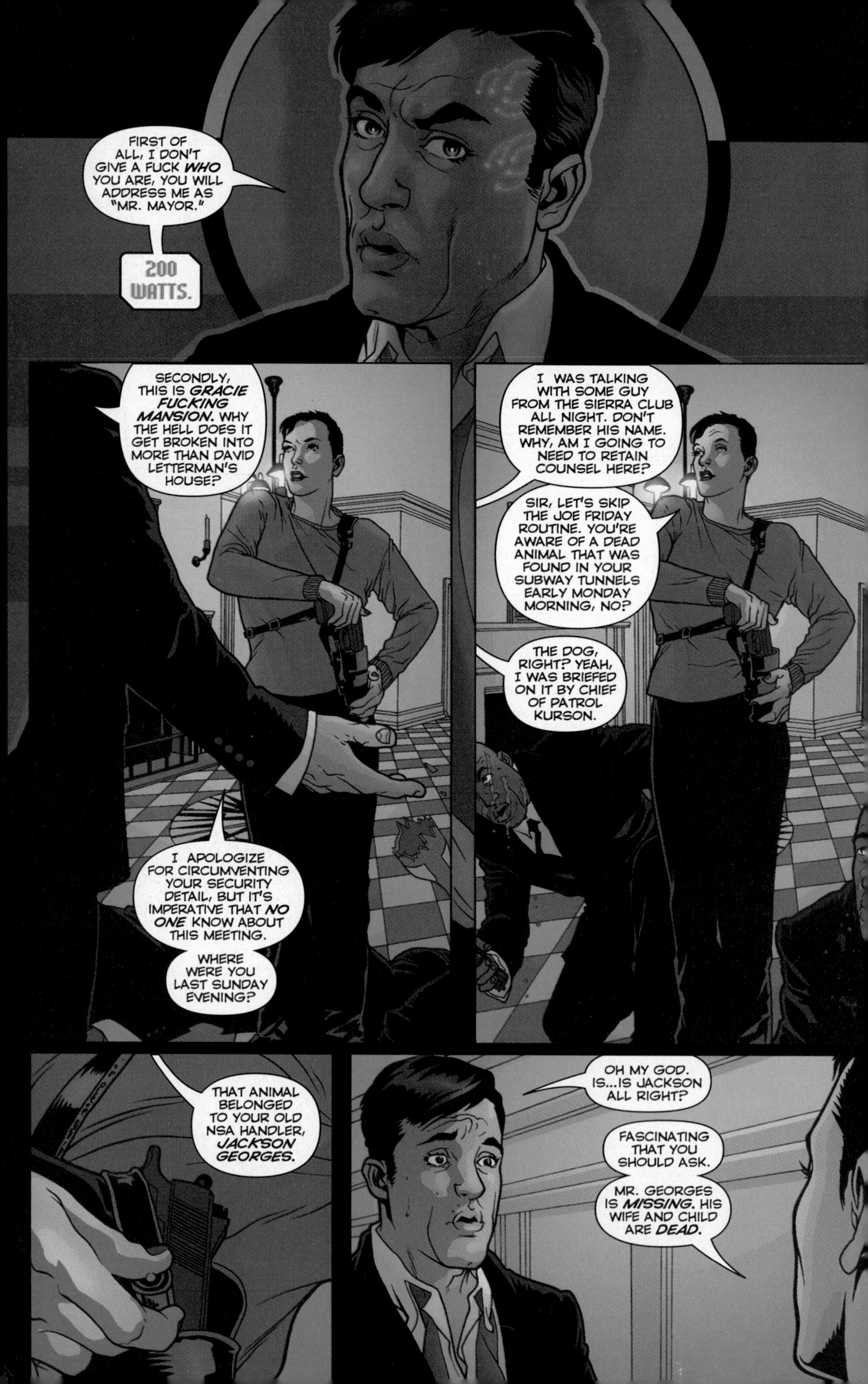
FIRST OF ALL, I DON'T GIVE A FUCK *WHO* YOU ARE, YOU WILL ADDRESS ME AS "MR. MAYOR."
200 WATTS.
SECONDLY, THIS IS *GRACIE FUCKING MANSION*. WHY THE HELL DOES IT GET BROKEN INTO MORE THAN DAVID LETTERMAN'S HOUSE?
I APOLOGIZE FOR CIRCUMVENTING YOUR SECURITY DETAIL, BUT IT'S IMPERATIVE THAT *NO ONE* KNOW ABOUT THIS MEETING.
WHERE WERE YOU LAST SUNDAY EVENING?
I WAS TALKING WITH SOME GUY FROM THE SIERRA CLUB ALL NIGHT. DON'T REMEMBER HIS NAME. WHY, AM I GOING TO NEED TO RETAIN COUNSEL HERE?
SIR, LET'S SKIP THE JOE FRIDAY ROUTINE. YOU'RE AWARE OF A DEAD ANIMAL THAT WAS FOUND IN YOUR SUBWAY TUNNELS EARLY MONDAY MORNING, NO?
THE DOG, RIGHT? YEAH, I WAS BRIEFED ON IT BY CHIEF OF PATROL KURSON.
THAT ANIMAL BELONGED TO YOUR OLD NSA HANDLER, *JACKSON GEORGES*.
OH MY GOD. IS...IS JACKSON ALL RIGHT?
FASCINATING THAT YOU SHOULD ASK.
MR. GEORGES IS *MISSING*. HIS WIFE AND CHILD ARE *DEAD*.

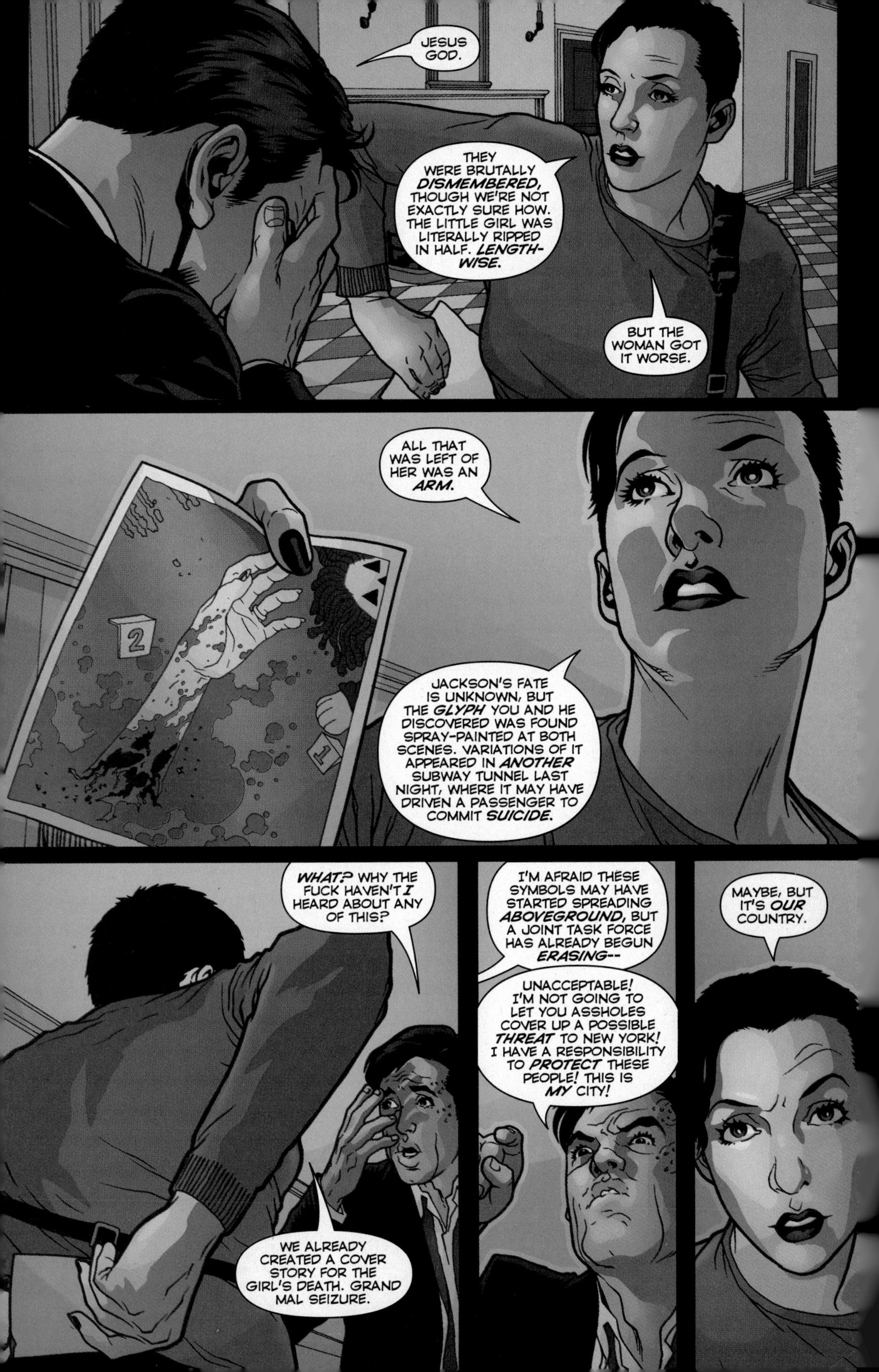
JESUS GOD.
THEY WERE BRUTALLY *DISMEMBERED*, THOUGH WE'RE NOT EXACTLY SURE HOW. THE LITTLE GIRL WAS LITERALLY RIPPED IN HALF. *LENGTH-WISE*.
BUT THE WOMAN GOT IT WORSE.
ALL THAT WAS LEFT OF HER WAS AN *ARM*.
JACKSON'S FATE IS UNKNOWN, BUT THE *GLYPH* YOU AND HE DISCOVERED WAS FOUND SPRAY-PAINTED AT BOTH SCENES. VARIATIONS OF IT APPEARED IN *ANOTHER* SUBWAY TUNNEL LAST NIGHT, WHERE IT MAY HAVE DRIVEN A PASSENGER TO COMMIT *SUICIDE*.
*WHAT?* WHY THE FUCK HAVEN'T *I* HEARD ABOUT ANY OF THIS?
WE ALREADY CREATED A COVER STORY FOR THE GIRL'S DEATH. GRAND MAL SEIZURE.
I'M AFRAID THESE SYMBOLS MAY HAVE STARTED SPREADING *ABOVEGROUND*, BUT A JOINT TASK FORCE HAS ALREADY BEGUN *ERASING*--
UNACCEPTABLE! I'M NOT GOING TO LET YOU ASSHOLES COVER UP A POSSIBLE *THREAT* TO NEW YORK! I HAVE A RESPONSIBILITY TO *PROTECT* THESE PEOPLE! THIS IS *MY* CITY!
MAYBE, BUT IT'S *OUR* COUNTRY.

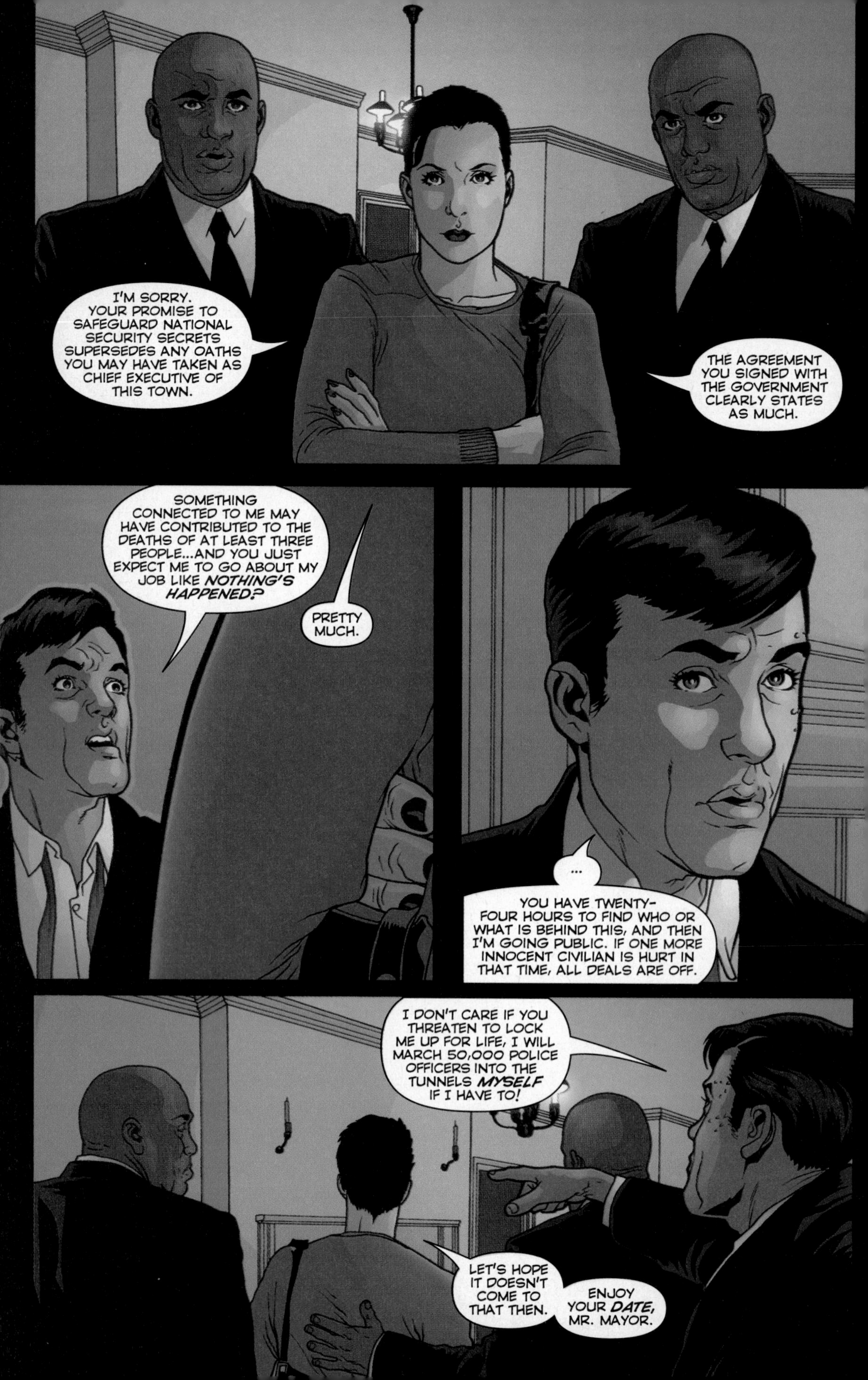
I'M SORRY. YOUR PROMISE TO SAFEGUARD NATIONAL SECURITY SECRETS SUPERSEDES ANY OATHS YOU MAY HAVE TAKEN AS CHIEF EXECUTIVE OF THIS TOWN.
THE AGREEMENT YOU SIGNED WITH THE GOVERNMENT CLEARLY STATES AS MUCH.
SOMETHING CONNECTED TO ME MAY HAVE CONTRIBUTED TO THE DEATHS OF AT LEAST THREE PEOPLE...AND YOU JUST EXPECT ME TO GO ABOUT MY JOB LIKE *NOTHING'S HAPPENED?*
PRETTY MUCH.
...
YOU HAVE TWENTY-FOUR HOURS TO FIND WHO OR WHAT IS BEHIND THIS, AND THEN I'M GOING PUBLIC. IF ONE MORE INNOCENT CIVILIAN IS HURT IN THAT TIME, ALL DEALS ARE OFF.
I DON'T CARE IF YOU THREATEN TO LOCK ME UP FOR LIFE, I WILL MARCH 50,000 POLICE OFFICERS INTO THE TUNNELS *MYSELF* IF I HAVE TO!
LET'S HOPE IT DOESN'T COME TO THAT THEN.
ENJOY YOUR *DATE,* MR. MAYOR.

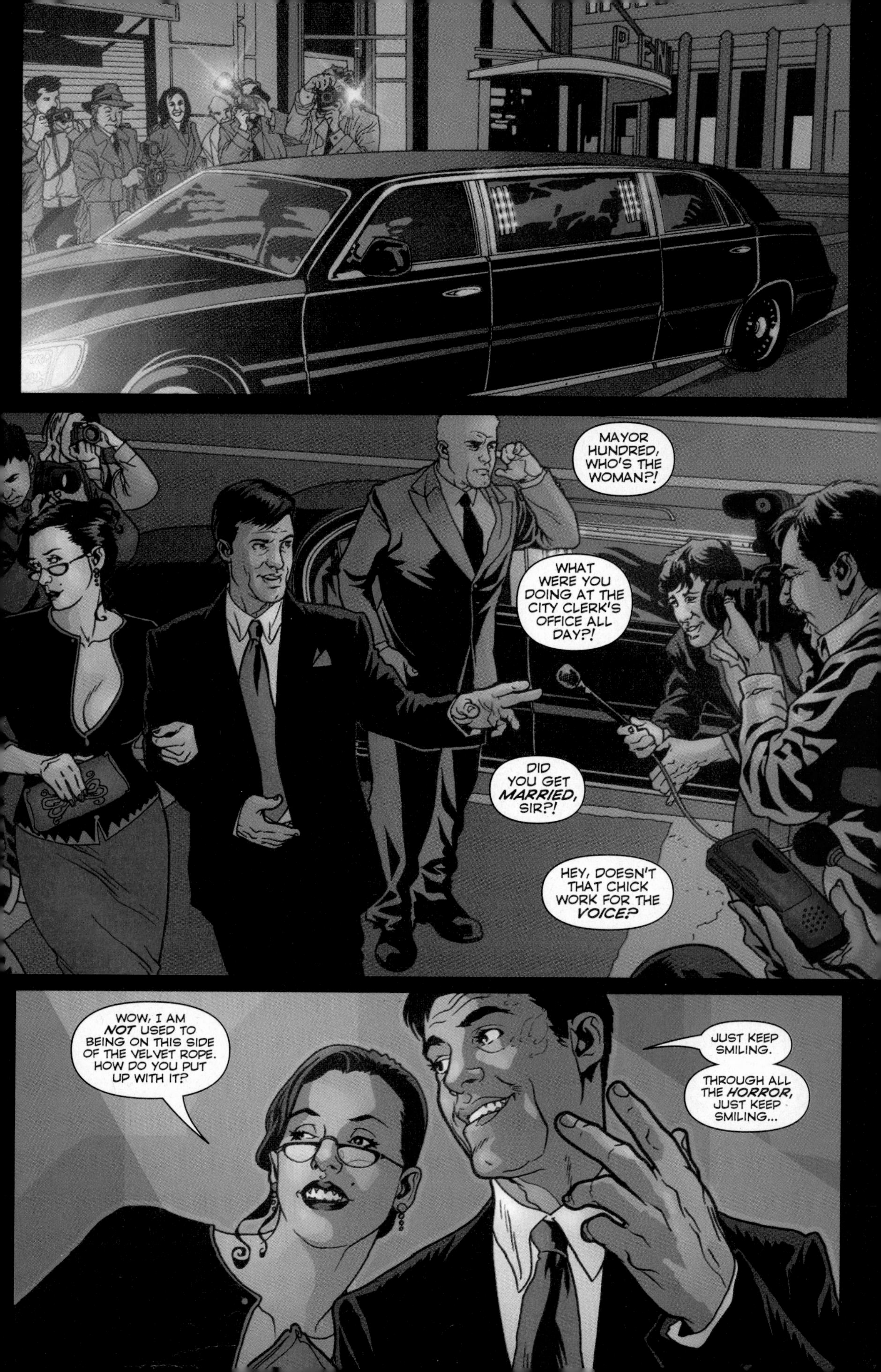
MAYOR HUNDRED, WHO'S THE WOMAN?!
WHAT WERE YOU DOING AT THE CITY CLERK'S OFFICE ALL DAY?!
DID YOU GET *MARRIED*, SIR?!
HEY, DOESN'T THAT CHICK WORK FOR THE *VOICE?*
WOW, I AM *NOT* USED TO BEING ON THIS SIDE OF THE VELVET ROPE. HOW DO YOU PUT UP WITH IT?
JUST KEEP SMILING.
THROUGH ALL THE *HORROR*, JUST KEEP SMILING...

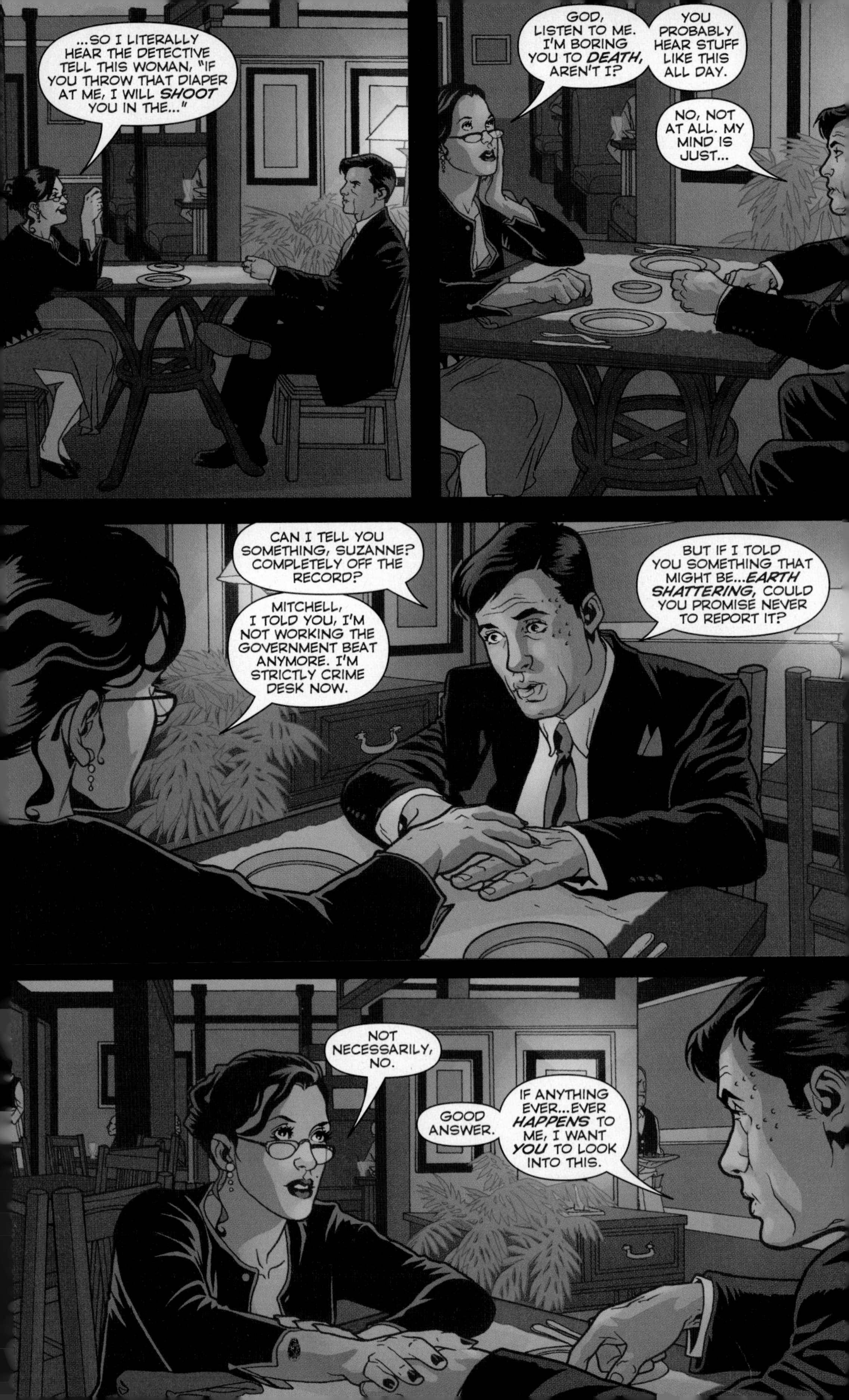
...SO I LITERALLY HEAR THE DETECTIVE TELL THIS WOMAN, "IF YOU THROW THAT DIAPER AT ME, I WILL SHOOT YOU IN THE..."
GOD, LISTEN TO ME. I'M BORING YOU TO DEATH, AREN'T I?
YOU PROBABLY HEAR STUFF LIKE THIS ALL DAY.
NO, NOT AT ALL. MY MIND IS JUST...
CAN I TELL YOU SOMETHING, SUZANNE? COMPLETELY OFF THE RECORD?
MITCHELL, I TOLD YOU, I'M NOT WORKING THE GOVERNMENT BEAT ANYMORE. I'M STRICTLY CRIME DESK NOW.
BUT IF I TOLD YOU SOMETHING THAT MIGHT BE...EARTH SHATTERING, COULD YOU PROMISE NEVER TO REPORT IT?
NOT NECESSARILY, NO.
GOOD ANSWER.
IF ANYTHING EVER...EVER HAPPENS TO ME, I WANT YOU TO LOOK INTO THIS.

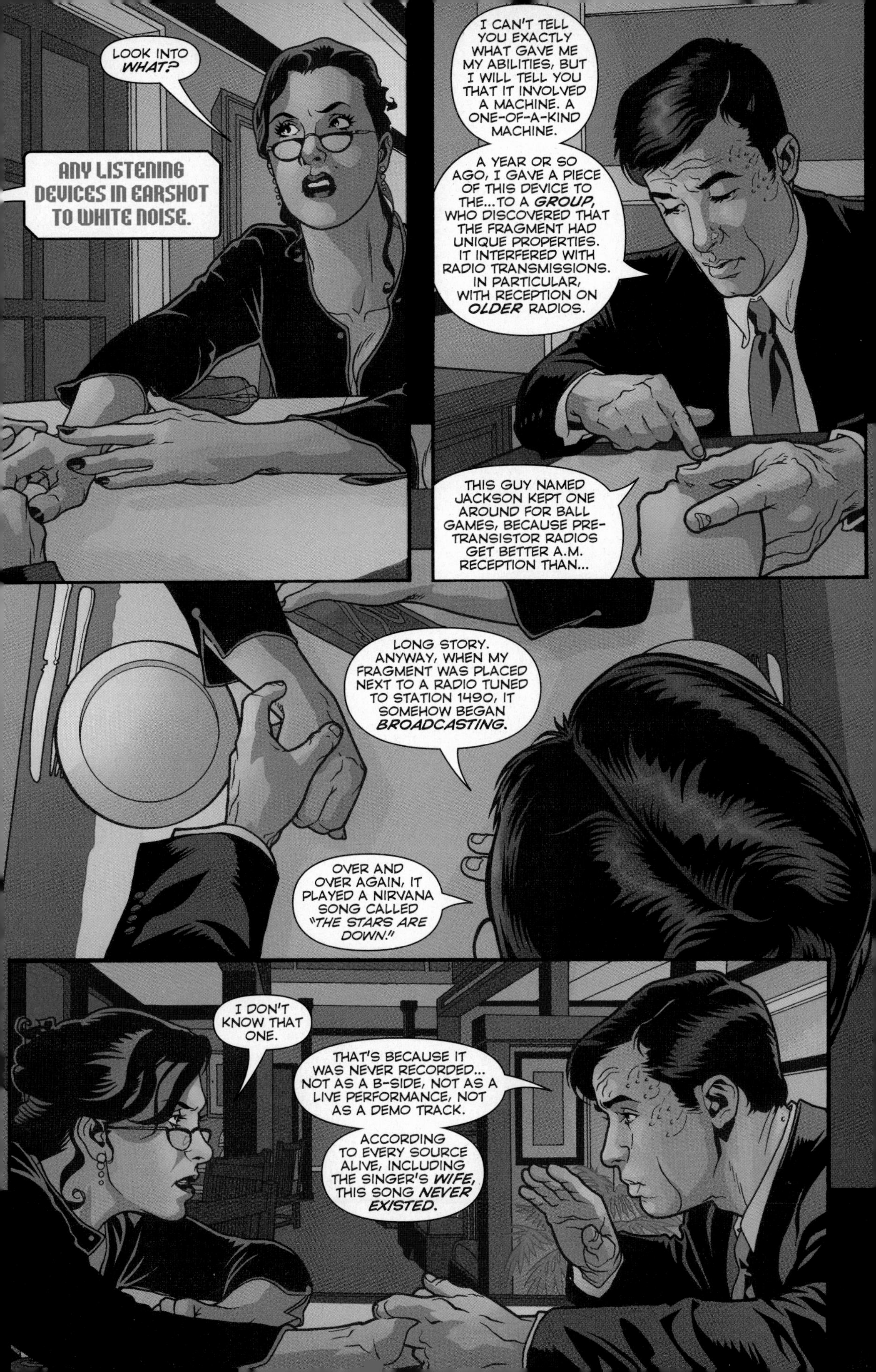

LOOK INTO *WHAT?*
ANY LISTENING DEVICES IN EARSHOT TO WHITE NOISE.
I CAN'T TELL YOU EXACTLY WHAT GAVE ME MY ABILITIES, BUT I WILL TELL YOU THAT IT INVOLVED A MACHINE. A ONE-OF-A-KIND MACHINE.
A YEAR OR SO AGO, I GAVE A PIECE OF THIS DEVICE TO THE...TO A *GROUP,* WHO DISCOVERED THAT THE FRAGMENT HAD UNIQUE PROPERTIES. IT INTERFERED WITH RADIO TRANSMISSIONS. IN PARTICULAR, WITH RECEPTION ON *OLDER* RADIOS.
THIS GUY NAMED JACKSON KEPT ONE AROUND FOR BALL GAMES, BECAUSE PRE-TRANSISTOR RADIOS GET BETTER A.M. RECEPTION THAN...
LONG STORY. ANYWAY, WHEN MY FRAGMENT WAS PLACED NEXT TO A RADIO TUNED TO STATION 1490, IT SOMEHOW BEGAN *BROADCASTING*.
OVER AND OVER AGAIN, IT PLAYED A NIRVANA SONG CALLED *"THE STARS ARE DOWN."*
I DON'T KNOW THAT ONE.
THAT'S BECAUSE IT WAS NEVER RECORDED... NOT AS A B-SIDE, NOT AS A LIVE PERFORMANCE, NOT AS A DEMO TRACK.
ACCORDING TO EVERY SOURCE ALIVE, INCLUDING THE SINGER'S *WIFE,* THIS SONG *NEVER EXISTED*.

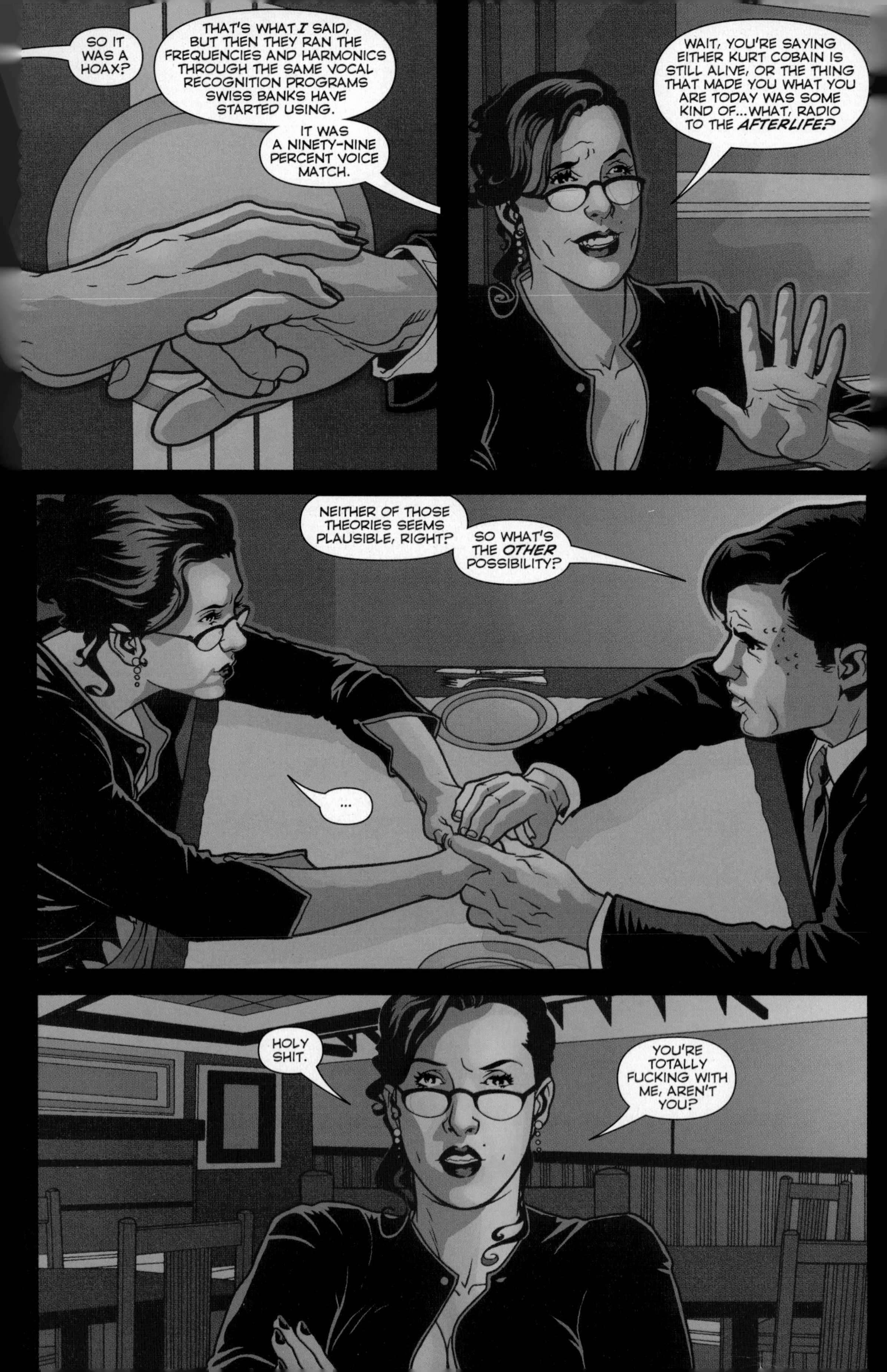
SO IT WAS A HOAX?
THAT'S WHAT I SAID, BUT THEN THEY RAN THE FREQUENCIES AND HARMONICS THROUGH THE SAME VOCAL RECOGNITION PROGRAMS SWISS BANKS HAVE STARTED USING.
IT WAS A NINETY-NINE PERCENT VOICE MATCH.
WAIT, YOU'RE SAYING EITHER KURT COBAIN IS STILL ALIVE, OR THE THING THAT MADE YOU WHAT YOU ARE TODAY WAS SOME KIND OF...WHAT, RADIO TO THE AFTERLIFE?
NEITHER OF THOSE THEORIES SEEMS PLAUSIBLE, RIGHT?
SO WHAT'S THE OTHER POSSIBILITY?
...
HOLY SHIT.
YOU'RE TOTALLY FUCKING WITH ME, AREN'T YOU?

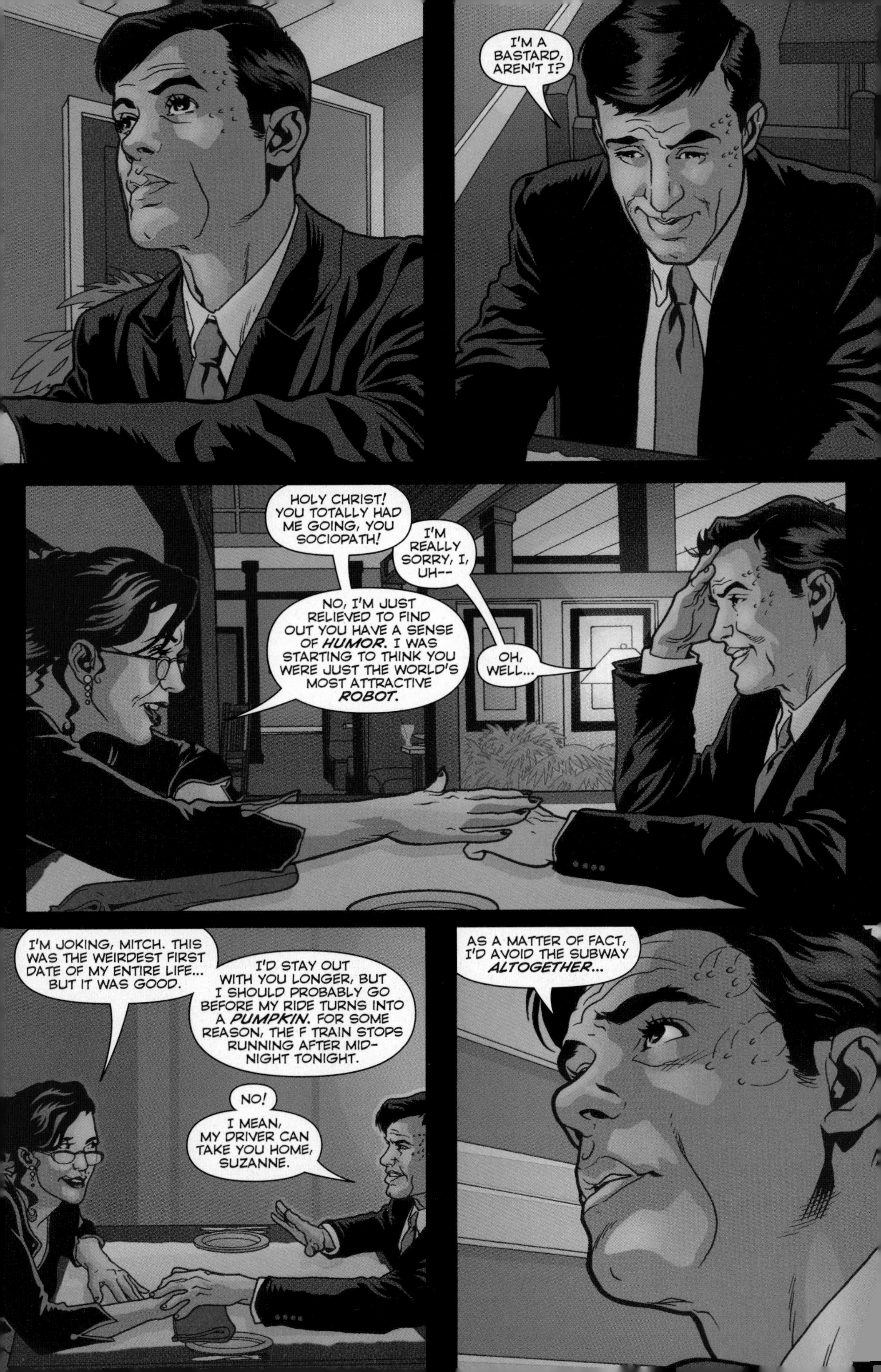
I'M A BASTARD, AREN'T I?
HOLY CHRIST! YOU TOTALLY HAD ME GOING, YOU SOCIOPATH!
I'M REALLY SORRY, I, UH--
NO, I'M JUST RELIEVED TO FIND OUT YOU HAVE A SENSE OF HUMOR. I WAS STARTING TO THINK YOU WERE JUST THE WORLD'S MOST ATTRACTIVE ROBOT.
OH, WELL...
I'M JOKING, MITCH. THIS WAS THE WEIRDEST FIRST DATE OF MY ENTIRE LIFE... BUT IT WAS GOOD.
I'D STAY OUT WITH YOU LONGER, BUT I SHOULD PROBABLY GO BEFORE MY RIDE TURNS INTO A PUMPKIN. FOR SOME REASON, THE F TRAIN STOPS RUNNING AFTER MID-NIGHT TONIGHT.
NO!
I MEAN, MY DRIVER CAN TAKE YOU HOME, SUZANNE.
AS A MATTER OF FACT, I'D AVOID THE SUBWAY ALTOGETHER...

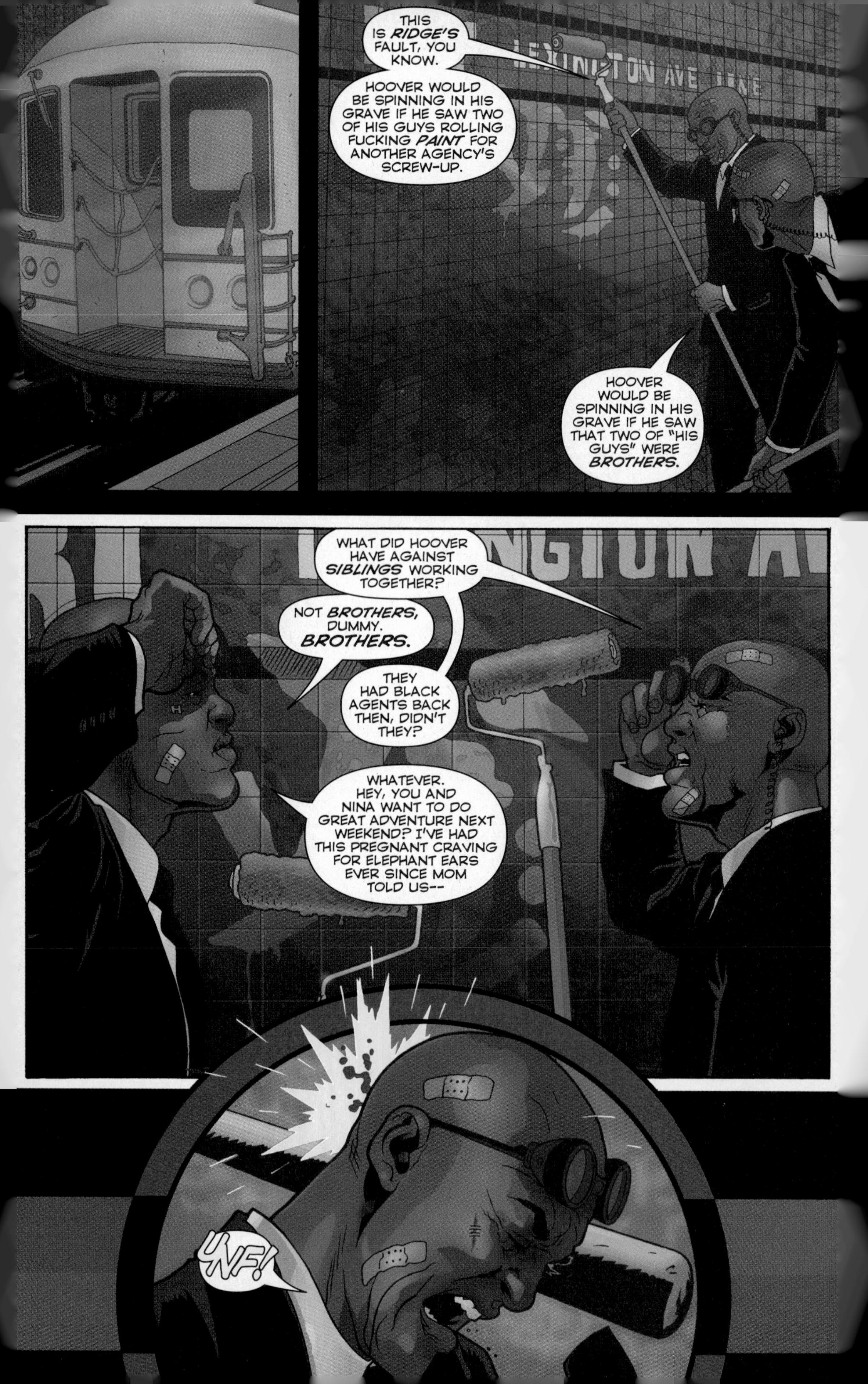
THIS IS *RIDGE'S* FAULT, YOU KNOW.
HOOVER WOULD BE SPINNING IN HIS GRAVE IF HE SAW TWO OF HIS GUYS ROLLING FUCKING *PAINT* FOR ANOTHER AGENCY'S SCREW-UP.
HOOVER WOULD BE SPINNING IN HIS GRAVE IF HE SAW THAT TWO OF "HIS GUYS" WERE *BROTHERS*.
WHAT DID HOOVER HAVE AGAINST *SIBLINGS* WORKING TOGETHER?
NOT *BROTHERS,* DUMMY. *BROTHERS*.
THEY HAD BLACK AGENTS BACK THEN, DIDN'T THEY?
WHATEVER. HEY, YOU AND NINA WANT TO DO GREAT ADVENTURE NEXT WEEKEND? I'VE HAD THIS PREGNANT CRAVING FOR ELEPHANT EARS EVER SINCE MOM TOLD US--
UNF!

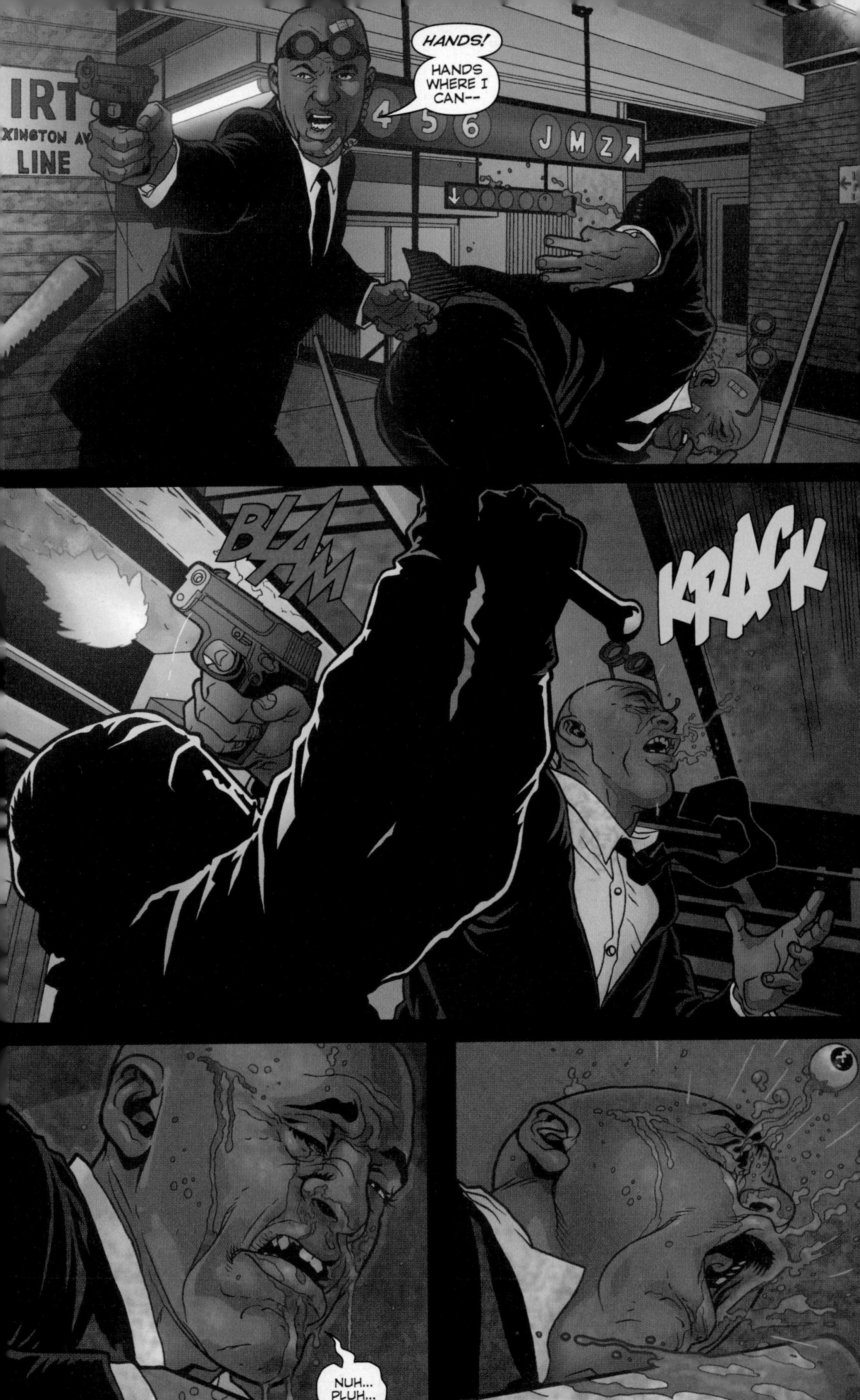
IRT
XINGTON AV
LINE
HANDS!
HANDS WHERE I CAN--
4 5 6
J M Z
BLAM
KRACK
NUH... PLUH...

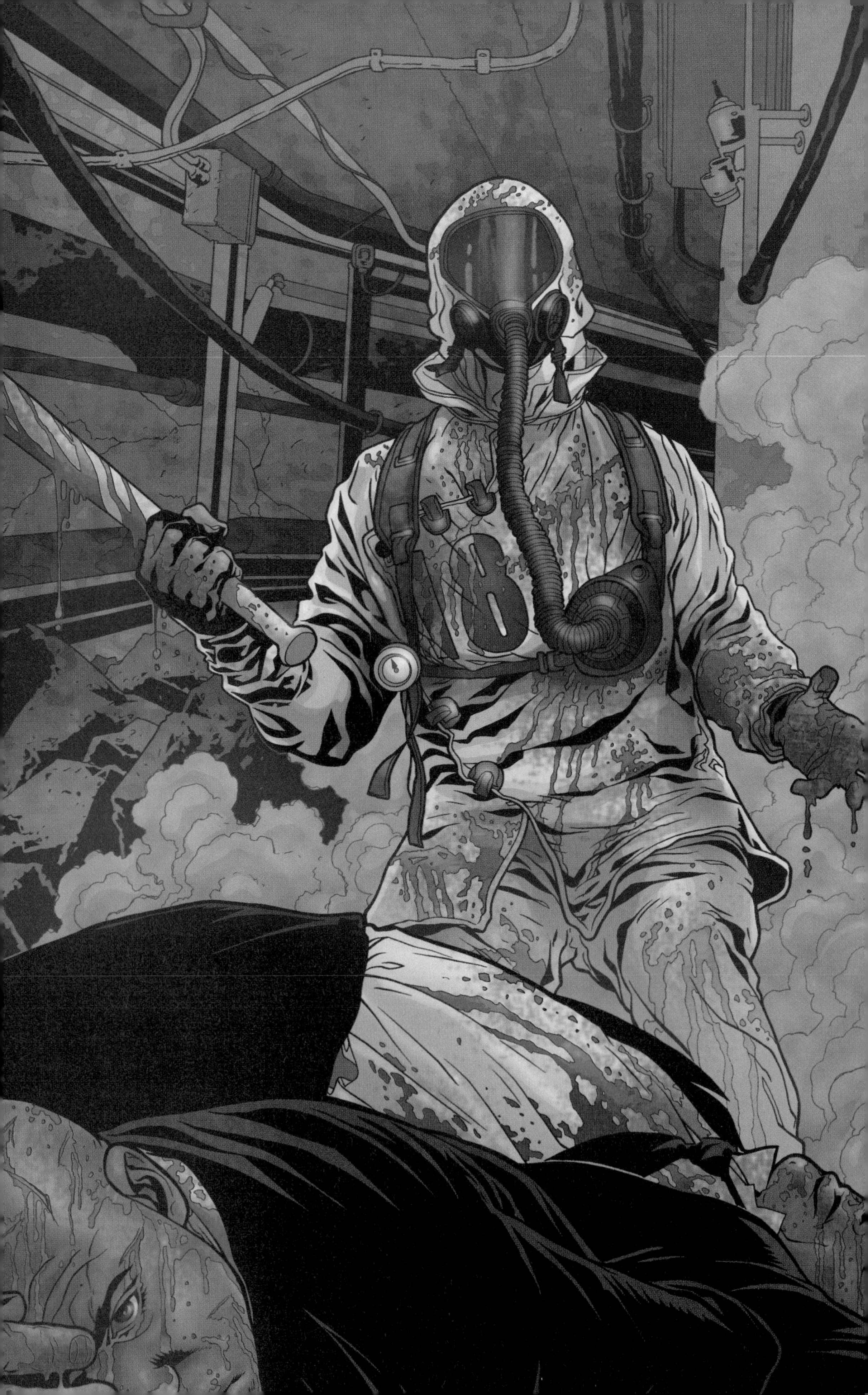

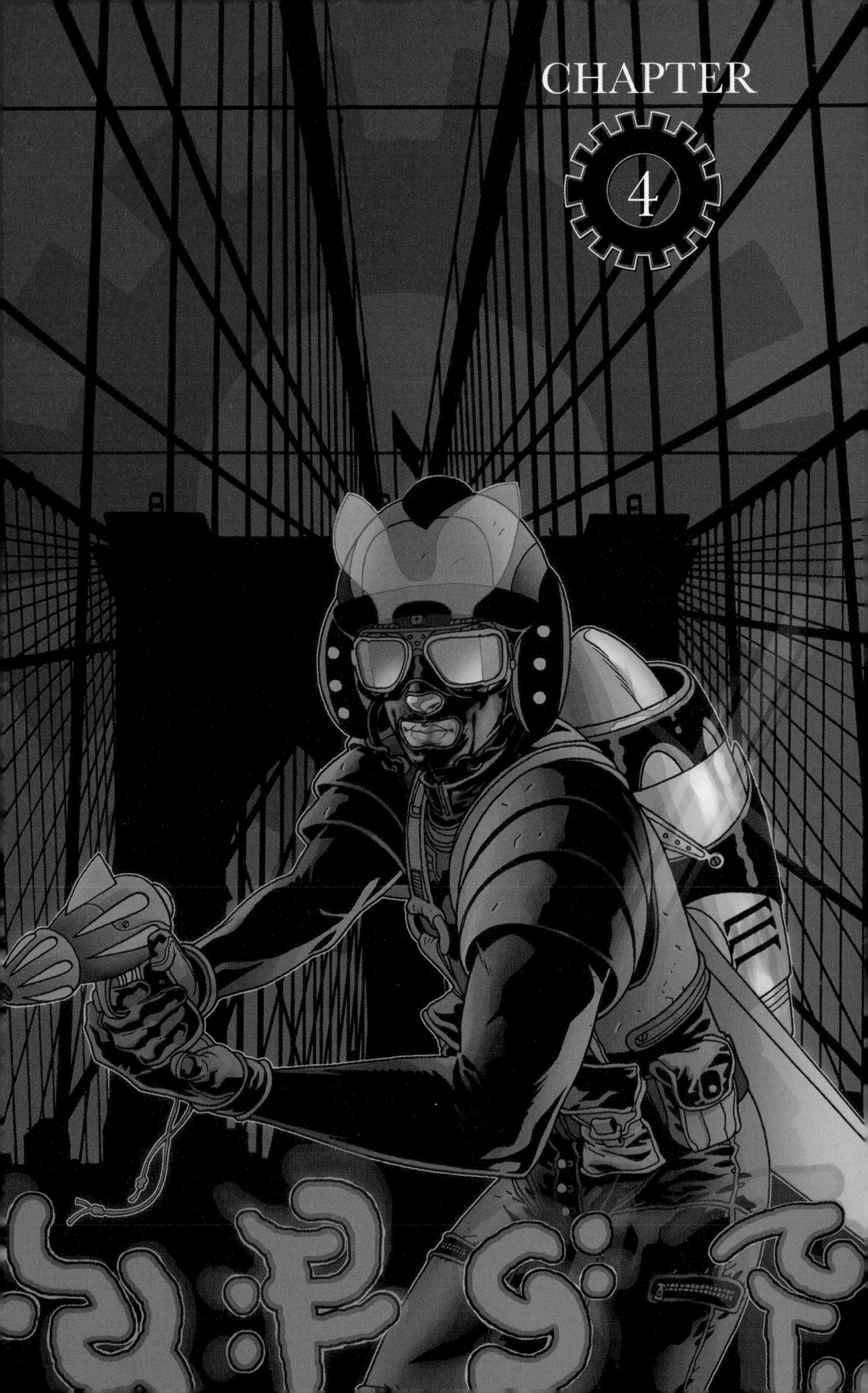
CHAPTER
4

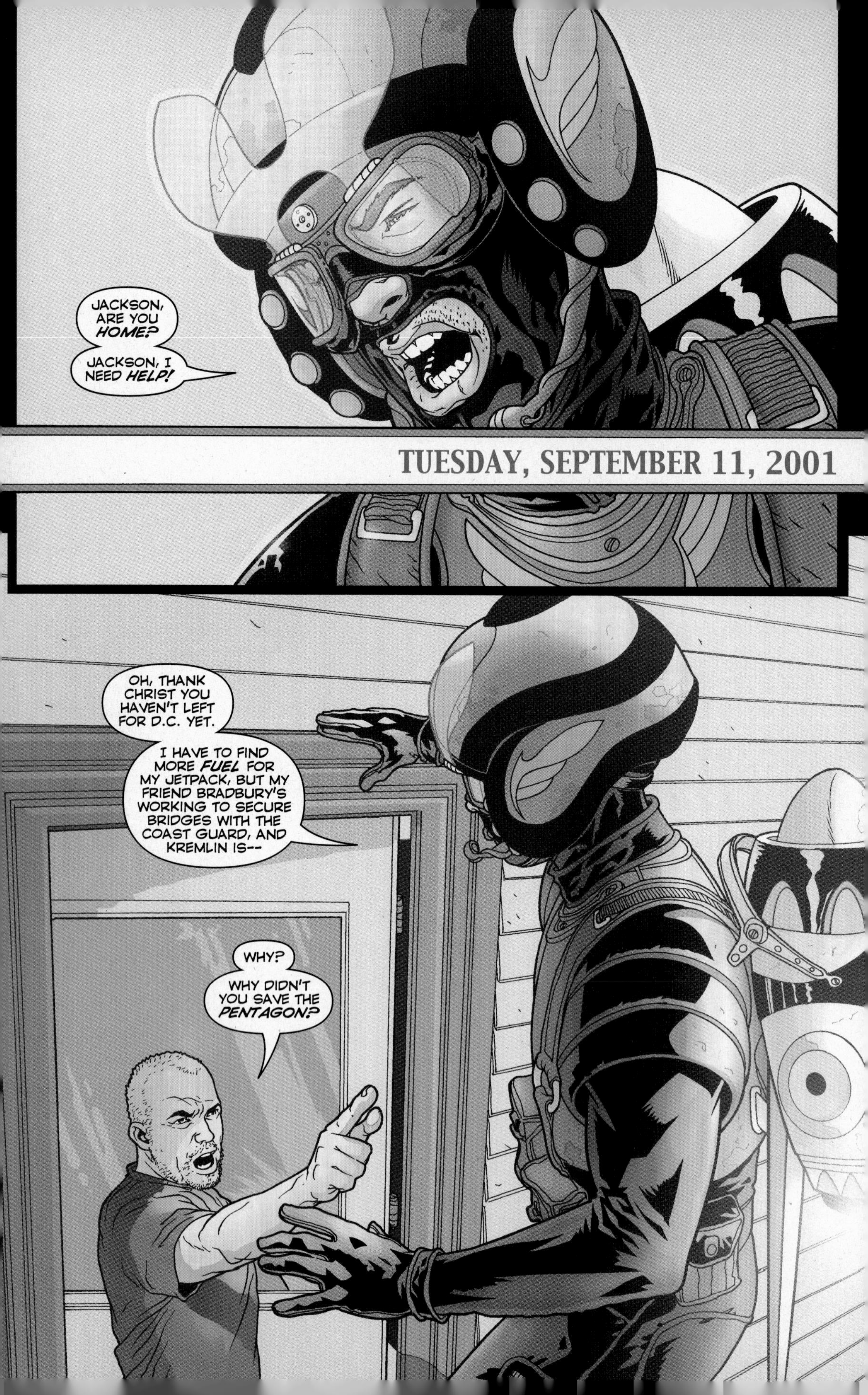
JACKSON, ARE YOU *HOME?*
JACKSON, I NEED *HELP!*
TUESDAY, SEPTEMBER 11, 2001
OH, THANK CHRIST YOU HAVEN'T LEFT FOR D.C. YET.
I HAVE TO FIND MORE *FUEL* FOR MY JETPACK, BUT MY FRIEND BRADBURY'S WORKING TO SECURE BRIDGES WITH THE COAST GUARD, AND KREMLIN IS--
WHY?
WHY DIDN'T YOU SAVE THE *PENTAGON?*

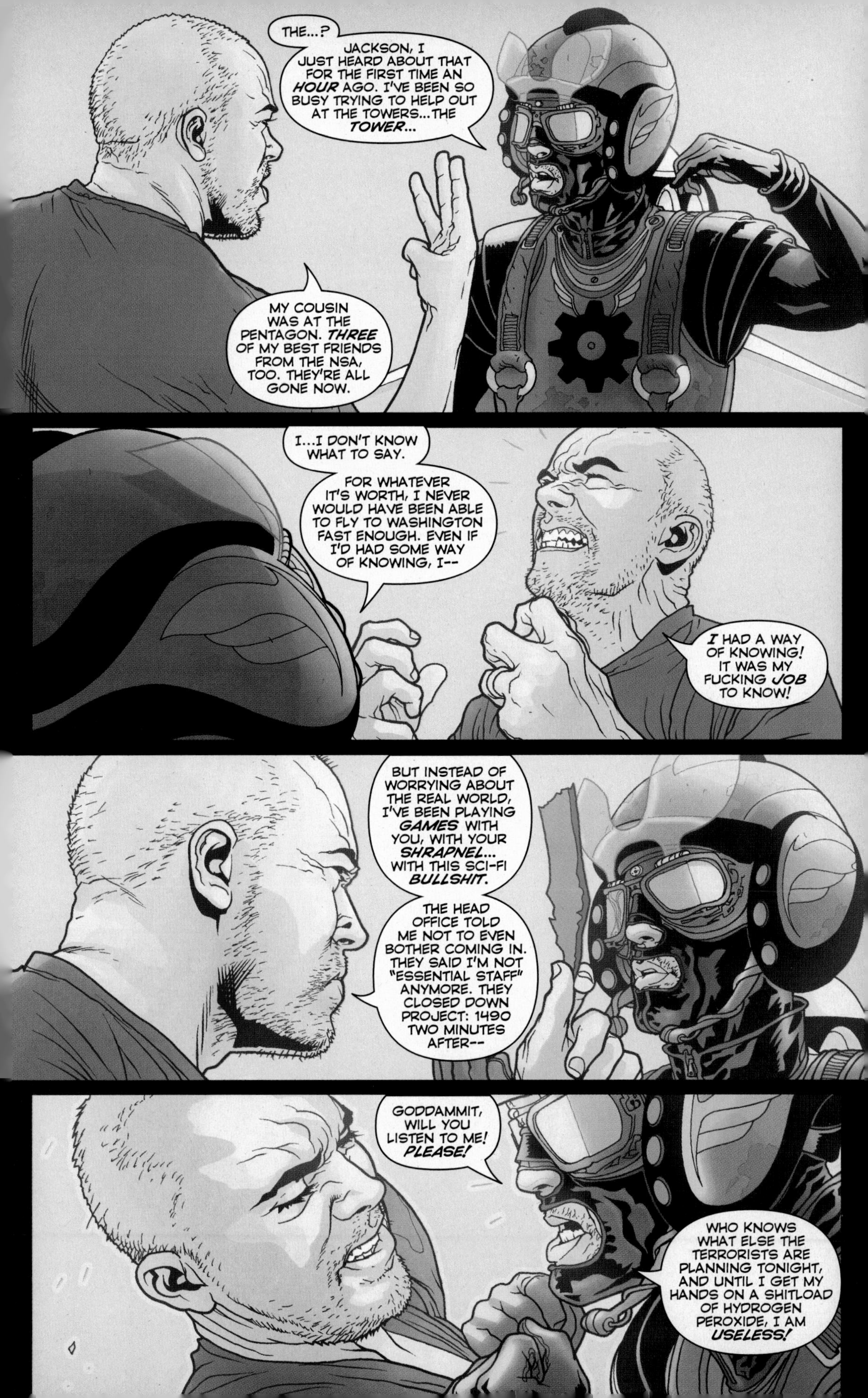
THE...?
JACKSON, I JUST HEARD ABOUT THAT FOR THE FIRST TIME AN HOUR AGO. I'VE BEEN SO BUSY TRYING TO HELP OUT AT THE TOWERS...THE TOWER...
MY COUSIN WAS AT THE PENTAGON. THREE OF MY BEST FRIENDS FROM THE NSA, TOO. THEY'RE ALL GONE NOW.
I...I DON'T KNOW WHAT TO SAY.
FOR WHATEVER IT'S WORTH, I NEVER WOULD HAVE BEEN ABLE TO FLY TO WASHINGTON FAST ENOUGH. EVEN IF I'D HAD SOME WAY OF KNOWING, I--
I HAD A WAY OF KNOWING! IT WAS MY FUCKING JOB TO KNOW!
BUT INSTEAD OF WORRYING ABOUT THE REAL WORLD, I'VE BEEN PLAYING GAMES WITH YOU, WITH YOUR SHRAPNEL... WITH THIS SCI-FI BULLSHIT.
THE HEAD OFFICE TOLD ME NOT TO EVEN BOTHER COMING IN. THEY SAID I'M NOT "ESSENTIAL STAFF" ANYMORE. THEY CLOSED DOWN PROJECT: 1490 TWO MINUTES AFTER--
GODDAMMIT, WILL YOU LISTEN TO ME! PLEASE!
WHO KNOWS WHAT ELSE THE TERRORISTS ARE PLANNING TONIGHT, AND UNTIL I GET MY HANDS ON A SHITLOAD OF HYDROGEN PEROXIDE, I AM USELESS!

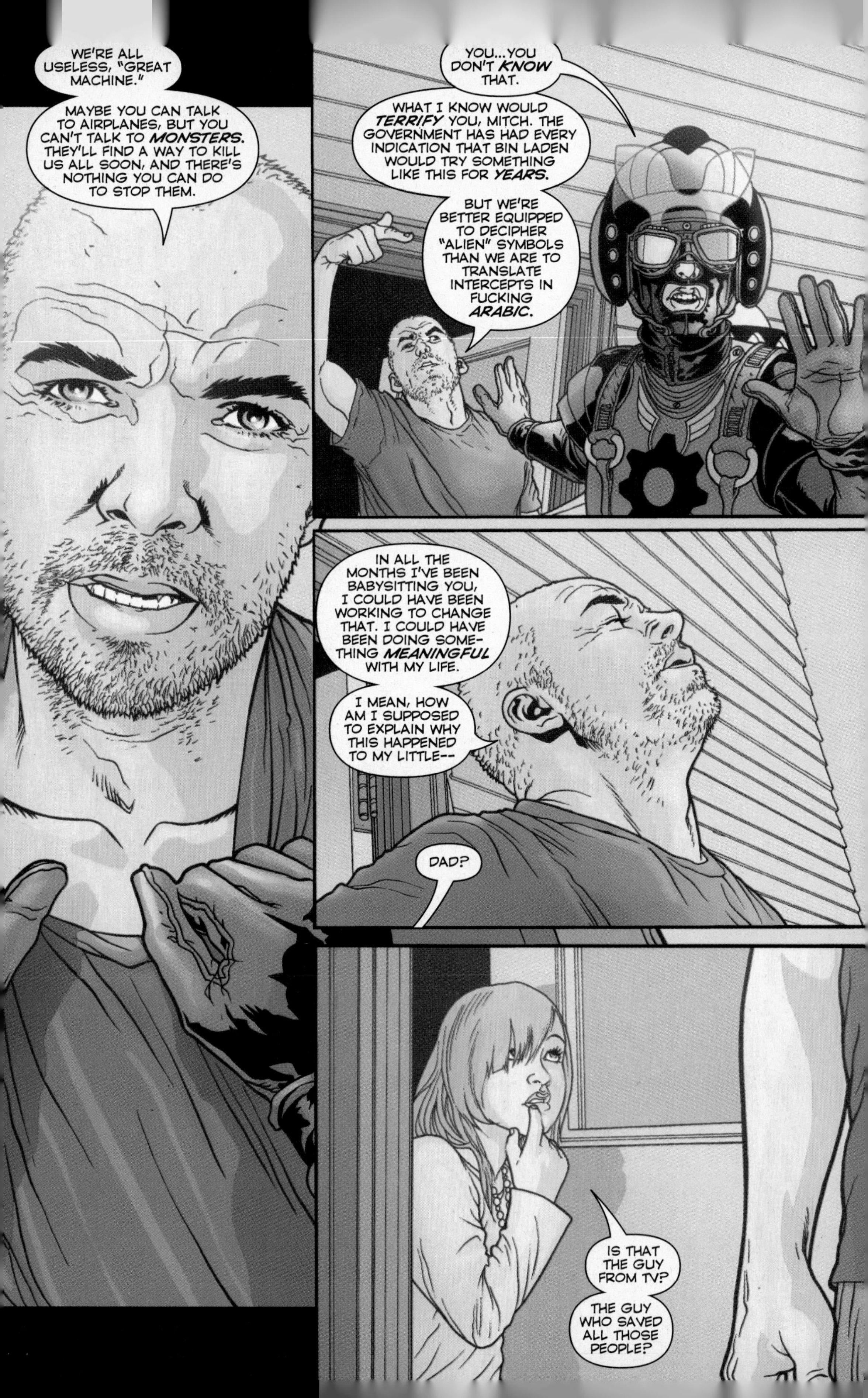
WE'RE ALL USELESS, "GREAT MACHINE."
MAYBE YOU CAN TALK TO AIRPLANES, BUT YOU CAN'T TALK TO *MONSTERS*. THEY'LL FIND A WAY TO KILL US ALL SOON, AND THERE'S NOTHING YOU CAN DO TO STOP THEM.
YOU...YOU DON'T *KNOW* THAT.
WHAT I KNOW WOULD *TERRIFY* YOU, MITCH. THE GOVERNMENT HAS HAD EVERY INDICATION THAT BIN LADEN WOULD TRY SOMETHING LIKE THIS FOR *YEARS*.
BUT WE'RE BETTER EQUIPPED TO DECIPHER "ALIEN" SYMBOLS THAN WE ARE TO TRANSLATE INTERCEPTS IN FUCKING *ARABIC*.
IN ALL THE MONTHS I'VE BEEN BABYSITTING YOU, I COULD HAVE BEEN WORKING TO CHANGE THAT. I COULD HAVE BEEN DOING SOMETHING *MEANINGFUL* WITH MY LIFE.
I MEAN, HOW AM I SUPPOSED TO EXPLAIN WHY THIS HAPPENED TO MY LITTLE--
DAD?
IS THAT THE GUY FROM TV?
THE GUY WHO SAVED ALL THOSE PEOPLE?

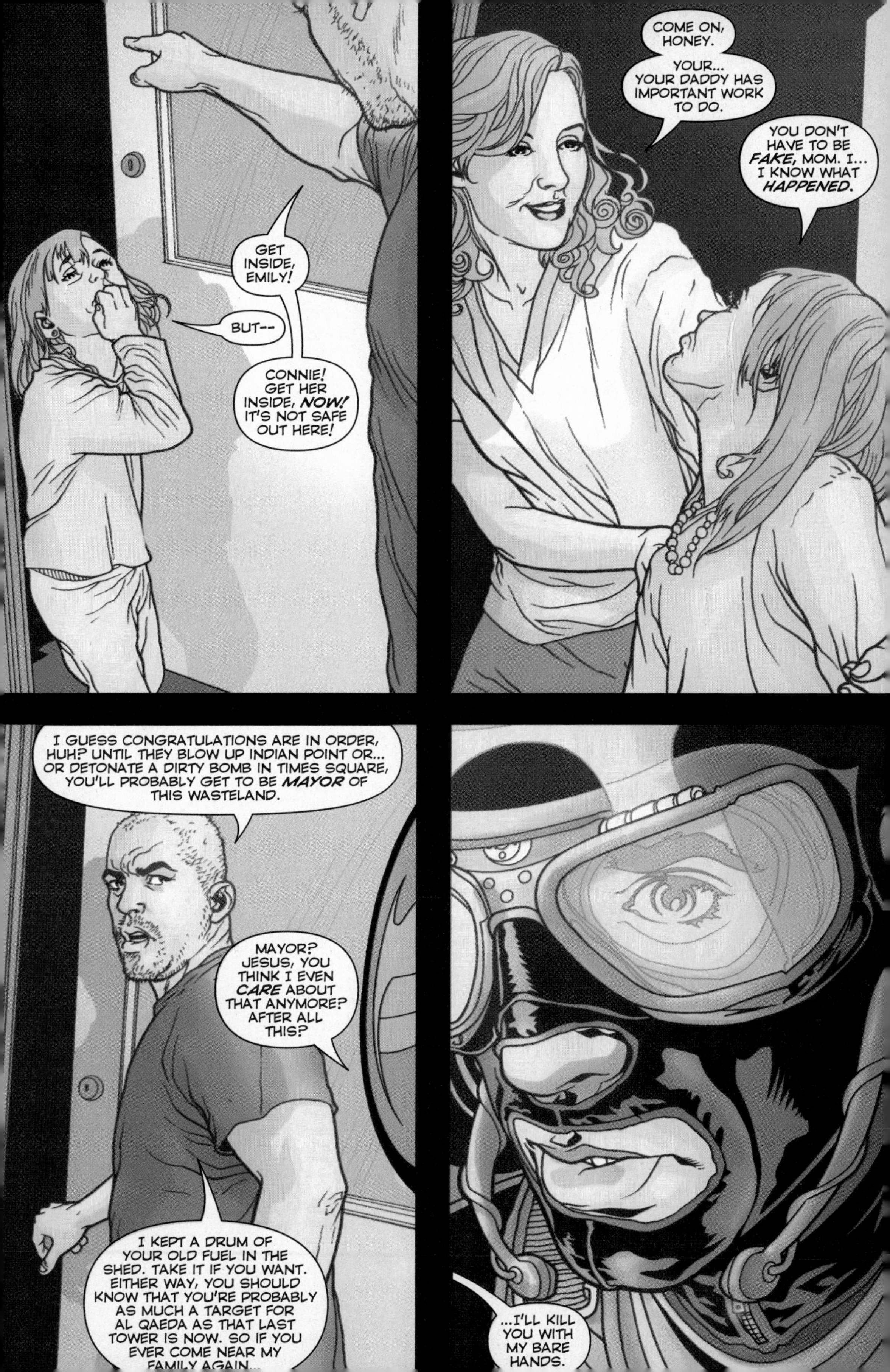
GET INSIDE, EMILY!
BUT--
CONNIE! GET HER INSIDE, NOW! IT'S NOT SAFE OUT HERE!
COME ON, HONEY.
YOUR... YOUR DADDY HAS IMPORTANT WORK TO DO.
YOU DON'T HAVE TO BE FAKE, MOM. I... I KNOW WHAT HAPPENED.
I GUESS CONGRATULATIONS ARE IN ORDER, HUH? UNTIL THEY BLOW UP INDIAN POINT OR... OR DETONATE A DIRTY BOMB IN TIMES SQUARE, YOU'LL PROBABLY GET TO BE MAYOR OF THIS WASTELAND.
MAYOR? JESUS, YOU THINK I EVEN CARE ABOUT THAT ANYMORE? AFTER ALL THIS?
I KEPT A DRUM OF YOUR OLD FUEL IN THE SHED. TAKE IT IF YOU WANT. EITHER WAY, YOU SHOULD KNOW THAT YOU'RE PROBABLY AS MUCH A TARGET FOR AL QAEDA AS THAT LAST TOWER IS NOW. SO IF YOU EVER COME NEAR MY FAMILY AGAIN...
...I'LL KILL YOU WITH MY BARE HANDS.

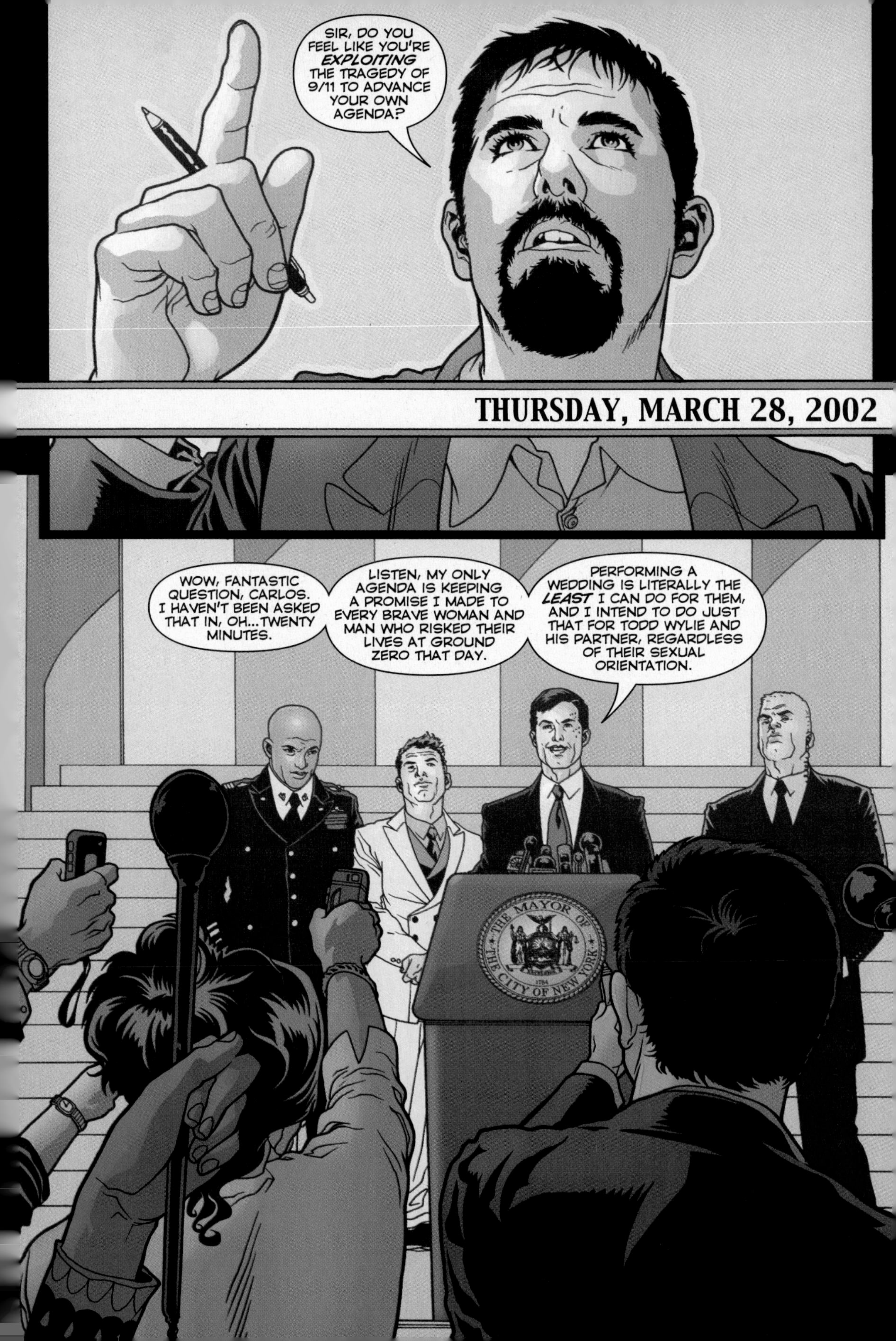
SIR, DO YOU FEEL LIKE YOU'RE *EXPLOITING* THE TRAGEDY OF 9/11 TO ADVANCE YOUR OWN AGENDA?
THURSDAY, MARCH 28, 2002
WOW, FANTASTIC QUESTION, CARLOS. I HAVEN'T BEEN ASKED THAT IN, OH...TWENTY MINUTES.
LISTEN, MY ONLY AGENDA IS KEEPING A PROMISE I MADE TO EVERY BRAVE WOMAN AND MAN WHO RISKED THEIR LIVES AT GROUND ZERO THAT DAY.
PERFORMING A WEDDING IS LITERALLY THE *LEAST* I CAN DO FOR THEM, AND I INTEND TO DO JUST THAT FOR TODD WYLIE AND HIS PARTNER, REGARDLESS OF THEIR SEXUAL ORIENTATION.
THE MAYOR OF THE CITY OF NEW YORK

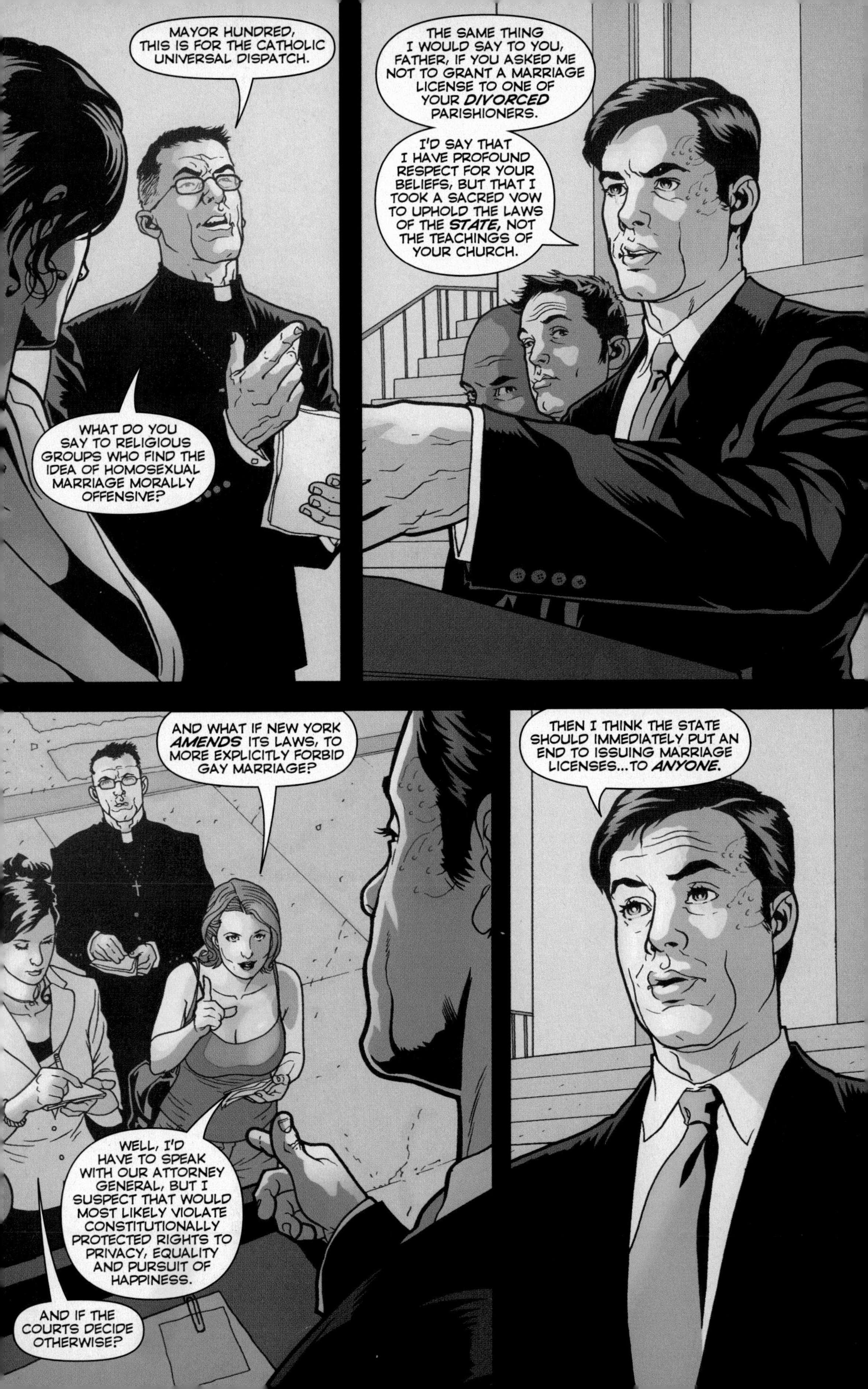
MAYOR HUNDRED, THIS IS FOR THE CATHOLIC UNIVERSAL DISPATCH.
WHAT DO YOU SAY TO RELIGIOUS GROUPS WHO FIND THE IDEA OF HOMOSEXUAL MARRIAGE MORALLY OFFENSIVE?
THE SAME THING I WOULD SAY TO YOU, FATHER, IF YOU ASKED ME NOT TO GRANT A MARRIAGE LICENSE TO ONE OF YOUR DIVORCED PARISHIONERS.
I'D SAY THAT I HAVE PROFOUND RESPECT FOR YOUR BELIEFS, BUT THAT I TOOK A SACRED VOW TO UPHOLD THE LAWS OF THE STATE, NOT THE TEACHINGS OF YOUR CHURCH.
AND WHAT IF NEW YORK AMENDS ITS LAWS, TO MORE EXPLICITLY FORBID GAY MARRIAGE?
WELL, I'D HAVE TO SPEAK WITH OUR ATTORNEY GENERAL, BUT I SUSPECT THAT WOULD MOST LIKELY VIOLATE CONSTITUTIONALLY PROTECTED RIGHTS TO PRIVACY, EQUALITY AND PURSUIT OF HAPPINESS.
AND IF THE COURTS DECIDE OTHERWISE?
THEN I THINK THE STATE SHOULD IMMEDIATELY PUT AN END TO ISSUING MARRIAGE LICENSES...TO ANYONE.

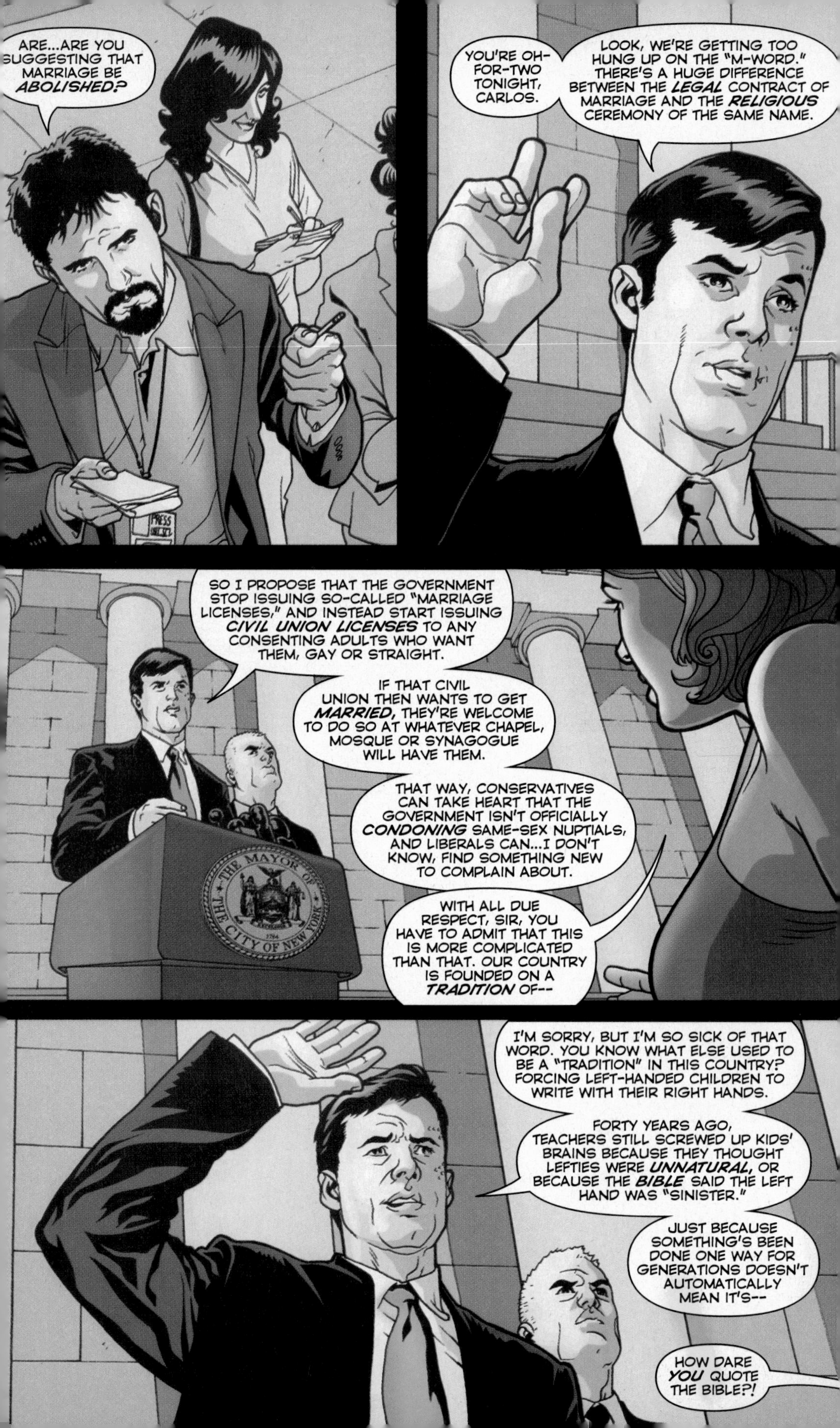
ARE...ARE YOU SUGGESTING THAT MARRIAGE BE ABOLISHED?
YOU'RE OH-FOR-TWO TONIGHT, CARLOS.
LOOK, WE'RE GETTING TOO HUNG UP ON THE "M-WORD." THERE'S A HUGE DIFFERENCE BETWEEN THE LEGAL CONTRACT OF MARRIAGE AND THE RELIGIOUS CEREMONY OF THE SAME NAME.
SO I PROPOSE THAT THE GOVERNMENT STOP ISSUING SO-CALLED "MARRIAGE LICENSES," AND INSTEAD START ISSUING CIVIL UNION LICENSES TO ANY CONSENTING ADULTS WHO WANT THEM, GAY OR STRAIGHT.
IF THAT CIVIL UNION THEN WANTS TO GET MARRIED, THEY'RE WELCOME TO DO SO AT WHATEVER CHAPEL, MOSQUE OR SYNAGOGUE WILL HAVE THEM.
THAT WAY, CONSERVATIVES CAN TAKE HEART THAT THE GOVERNMENT ISN'T OFFICIALLY CONDONING SAME-SEX NUPTIALS, AND LIBERALS CAN...I DON'T KNOW, FIND SOMETHING NEW TO COMPLAIN ABOUT.
THE MAYOR OF THE CITY OF NEW YORK
WITH ALL DUE RESPECT, SIR, YOU HAVE TO ADMIT THAT THIS IS MORE COMPLICATED THAN THAT. OUR COUNTRY IS FOUNDED ON A TRADITION OF--
I'M SORRY, BUT I'M SO SICK OF THAT WORD. YOU KNOW WHAT ELSE USED TO BE A "TRADITION" IN THIS COUNTRY? FORCING LEFT-HANDED CHILDREN TO WRITE WITH THEIR RIGHT HANDS.
FORTY YEARS AGO, TEACHERS STILL SCREWED UP KIDS' BRAINS BECAUSE THEY THOUGHT LEFTIES WERE UNNATURAL, OR BECAUSE THE BIBLE SAID THE LEFT HAND WAS "SINISTER."
JUST BECAUSE SOMETHING'S BEEN DONE ONE WAY FOR GENERATIONS DOESN'T AUTOMATICALLY MEAN IT'S--
HOW DARE YOU QUOTE THE BIBLE?!

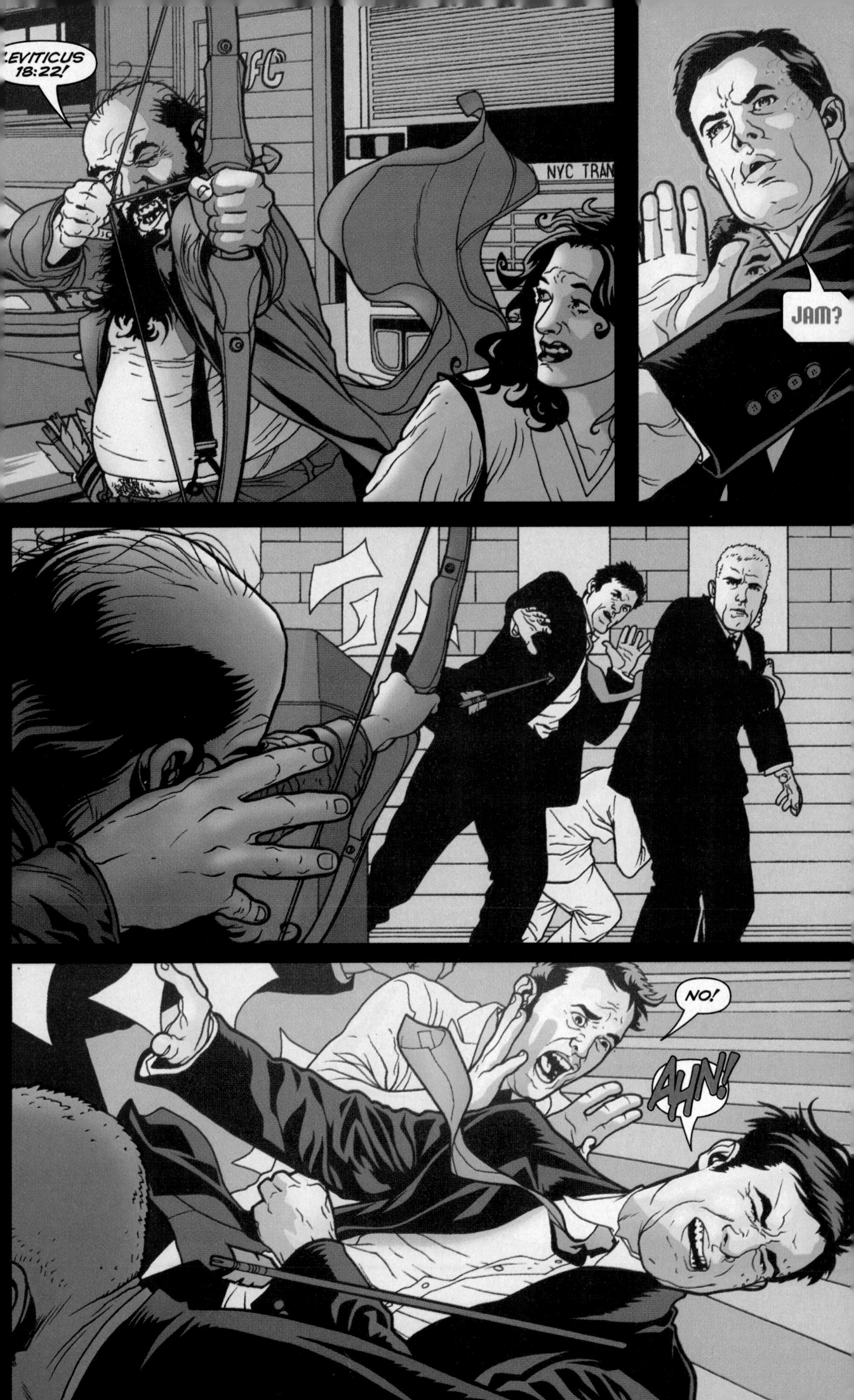
LEVITICUS 18:22!
JAM?
NO!
AHN!

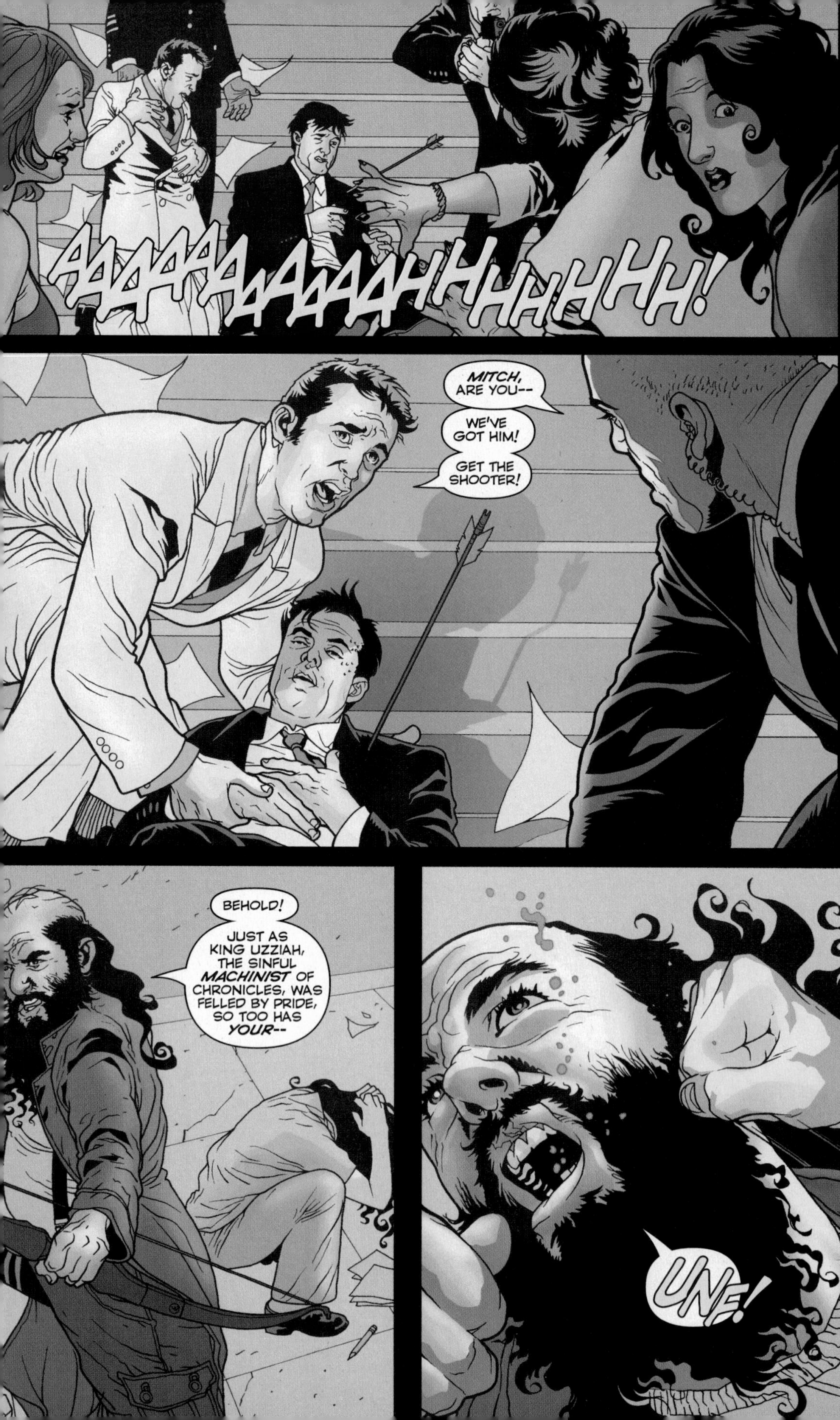
AAAAAAAAAAAHHHHHH!
MITCH, ARE YOU--
WE'VE GOT HIM!
GET THE SHOOTER!
BEHOLD!
JUST AS KING UZZIAH, THE SINFUL MACHINIST OF CHRONICLES, WAS FELLED BY PRIDE, SO TOO HAS YOUR--
UNF!

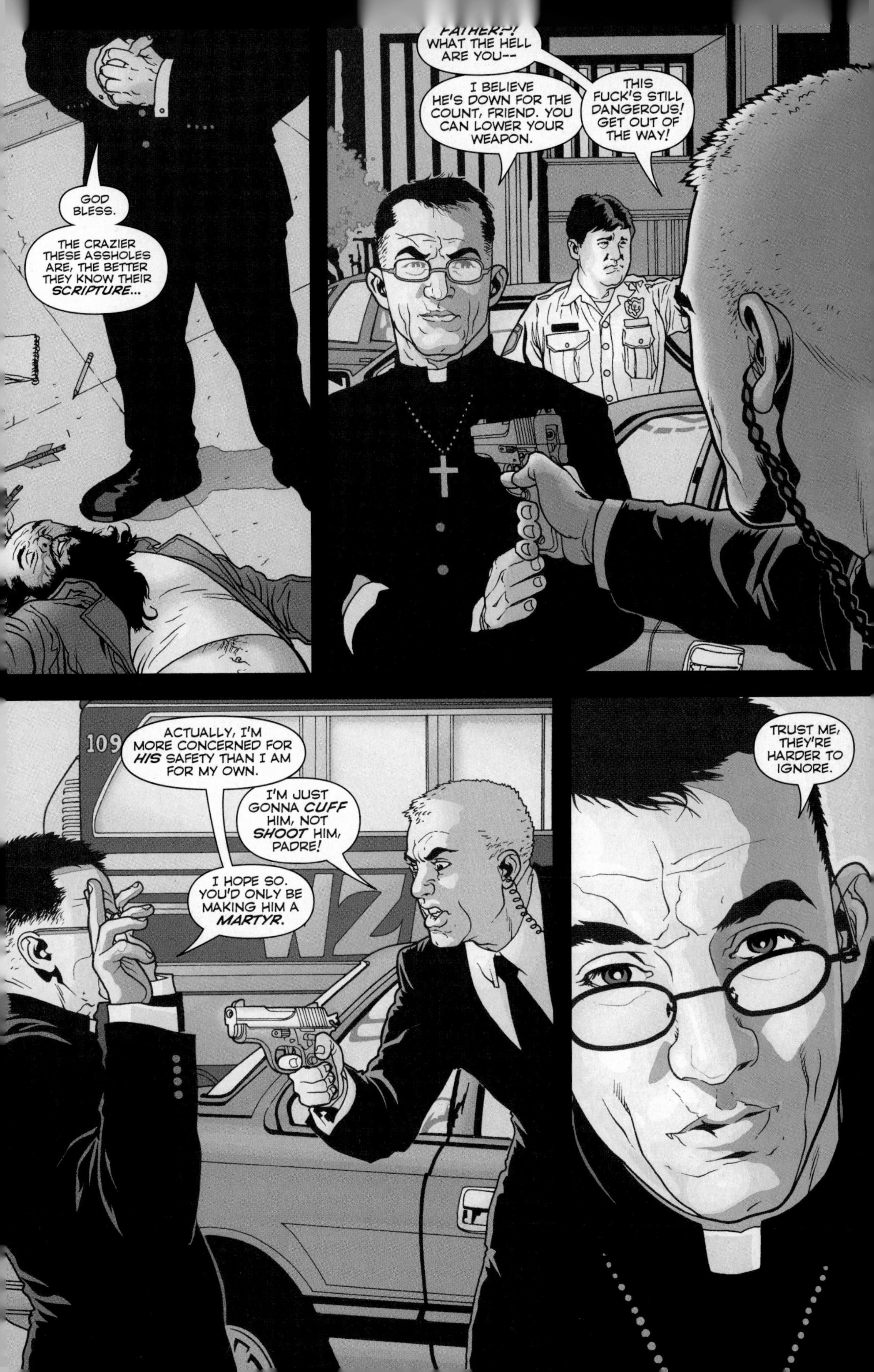
GOD BLESS.
THE CRAZIER THESE ASSHOLES ARE, THE BETTER THEY KNOW THEIR SCRIPTURE...
FATHER?! WHAT THE HELL ARE YOU--
I BELIEVE HE'S DOWN FOR THE COUNT, FRIEND. YOU CAN LOWER YOUR WEAPON.
THIS FUCK'S STILL DANGEROUS! GET OUT OF THE WAY!
ACTUALLY, I'M MORE CONCERNED FOR HIS SAFETY THAN I AM FOR MY OWN.
I'M JUST GONNA CUFF HIM, NOT SHOOT HIM, PADRE!
I HOPE SO. YOU'D ONLY BE MAKING HIM A MARTYR.
TRUST ME, THEY'RE HARDER TO IGNORE.

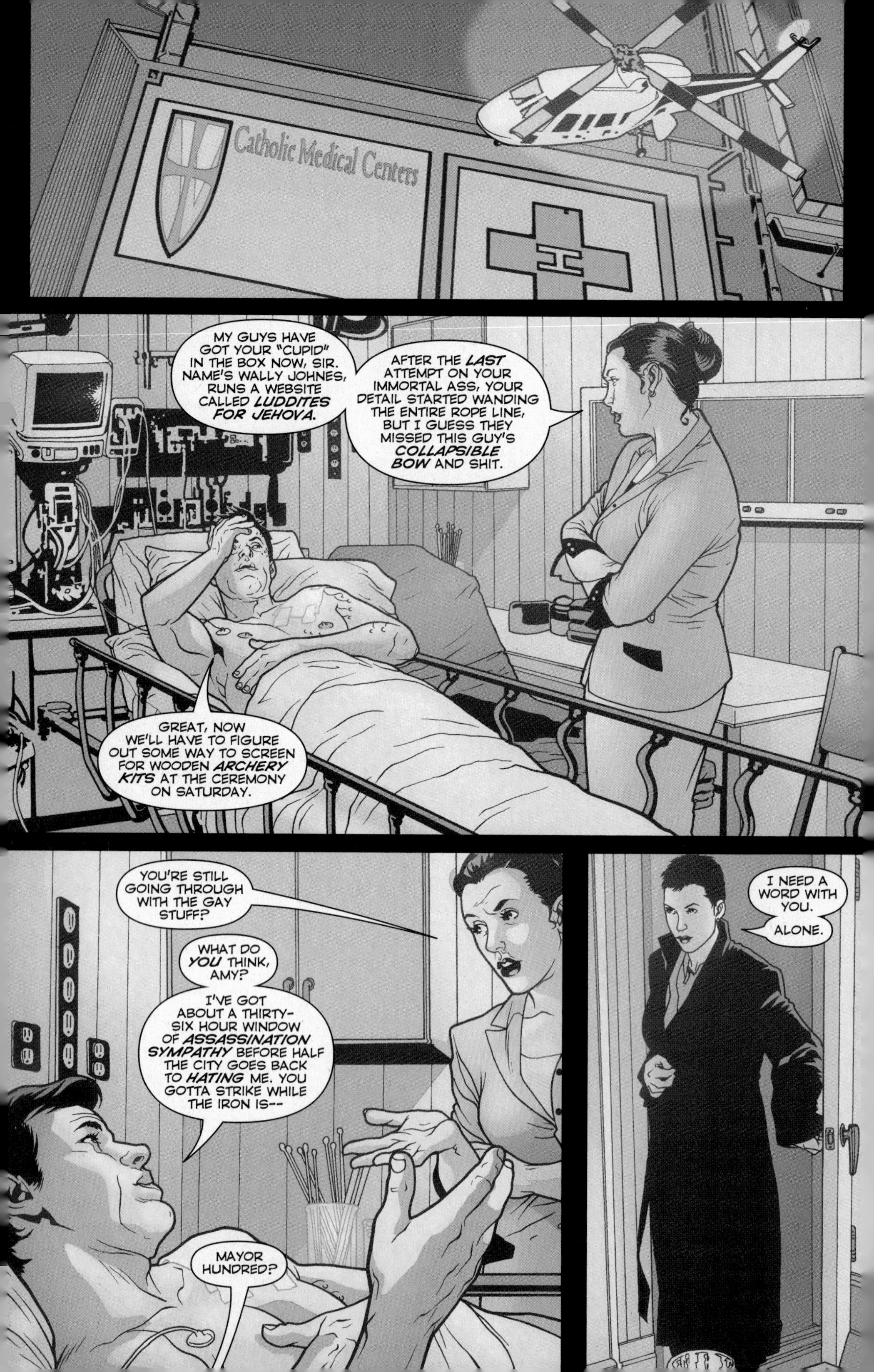
Catholic Medical Centers
MY GUYS HAVE GOT YOUR "CUPID" IN THE BOX NOW, SIR. NAME'S WALLY JOHNES, RUNS A WEBSITE CALLED LUDDITES FOR JEHOVA.
AFTER THE LAST ATTEMPT ON YOUR IMMORTAL ASS, YOUR DETAIL STARTED WANDING THE ENTIRE ROPE LINE, BUT I GUESS THEY MISSED THIS GUY'S COLLAPSIBLE BOW AND SHIT.
GREAT, NOW WE'LL HAVE TO FIGURE OUT SOME WAY TO SCREEN FOR WOODEN ARCHERY KITS AT THE CEREMONY ON SATURDAY.
YOU'RE STILL GOING THROUGH WITH THE GAY STUFF?
WHAT DO YOU THINK, AMY?
I'VE GOT ABOUT A THIRTY-SIX HOUR WINDOW OF ASSASSINATION SYMPATHY BEFORE HALF THE CITY GOES BACK TO HATING ME. YOU GOTTA STRIKE WHILE THE IRON IS--
MAYOR HUNDRED?
I NEED A WORD WITH YOU.
ALONE.

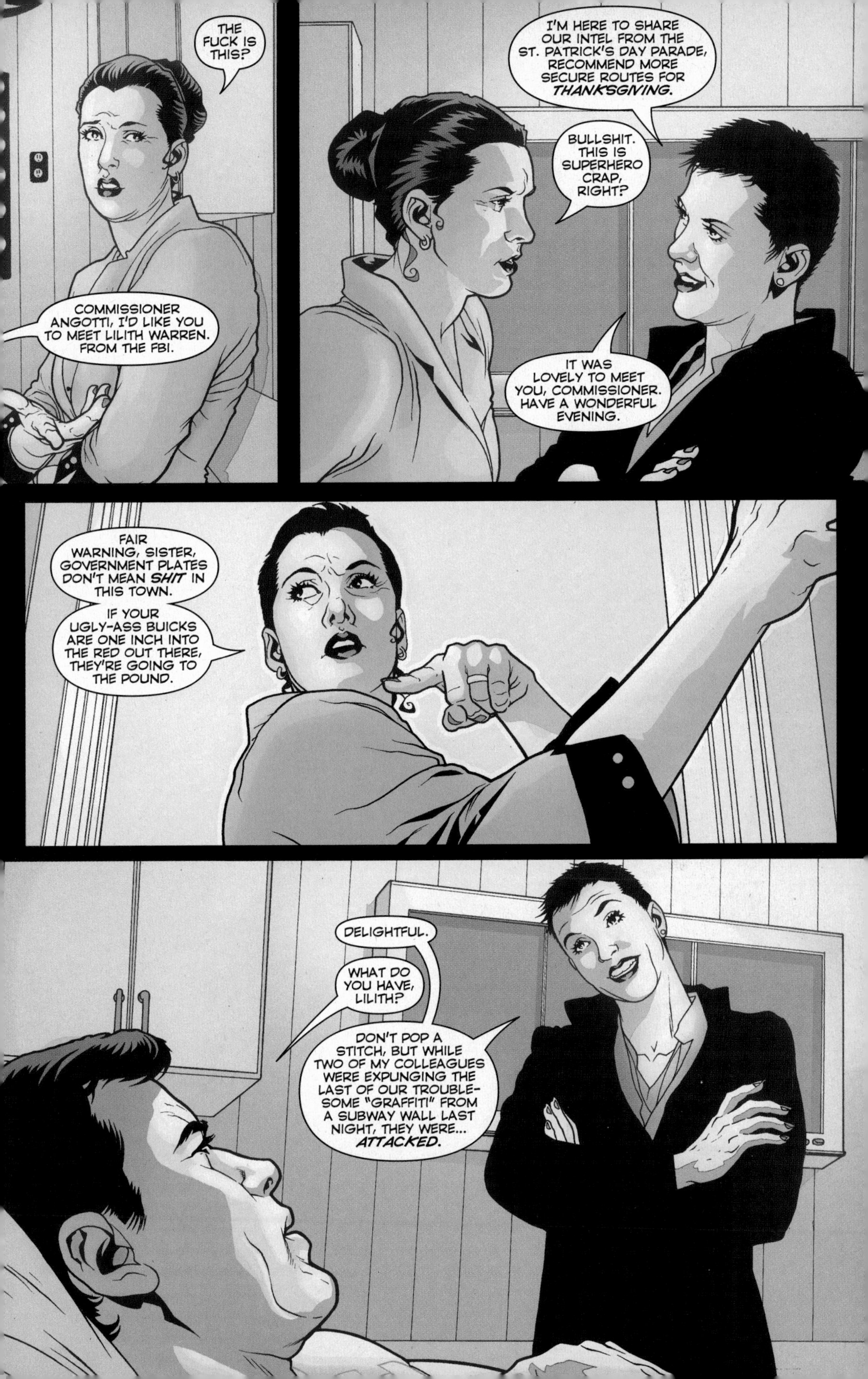
THE FUCK IS THIS?
COMMISSIONER ANGOTTI, I'D LIKE YOU TO MEET LILITH WARREN. FROM THE FBI.
I'M HERE TO SHARE OUR INTEL FROM THE ST. PATRICK'S DAY PARADE, RECOMMEND MORE SECURE ROUTES FOR THANKSGIVING.
BULLSHIT. THIS IS SUPERHERO CRAP, RIGHT?
IT WAS LOVELY TO MEET YOU, COMMISSIONER. HAVE A WONDERFUL EVENING.
FAIR WARNING, SISTER, GOVERNMENT PLATES DON'T MEAN SHIT IN THIS TOWN.
IF YOUR UGLY-ASS BUICKS ARE ONE INCH INTO THE RED OUT THERE, THEY'RE GOING TO THE POUND.
DELIGHTFUL.
WHAT DO YOU HAVE, LILITH?
DON'T POP A STITCH, BUT WHILE TWO OF MY COLLEAGUES WERE EXPUNGING THE LAST OF OUR TROUBLE-SOME "GRAFFITI" FROM A SUBWAY WALL LAST NIGHT, THEY WERE... ATTACKED.

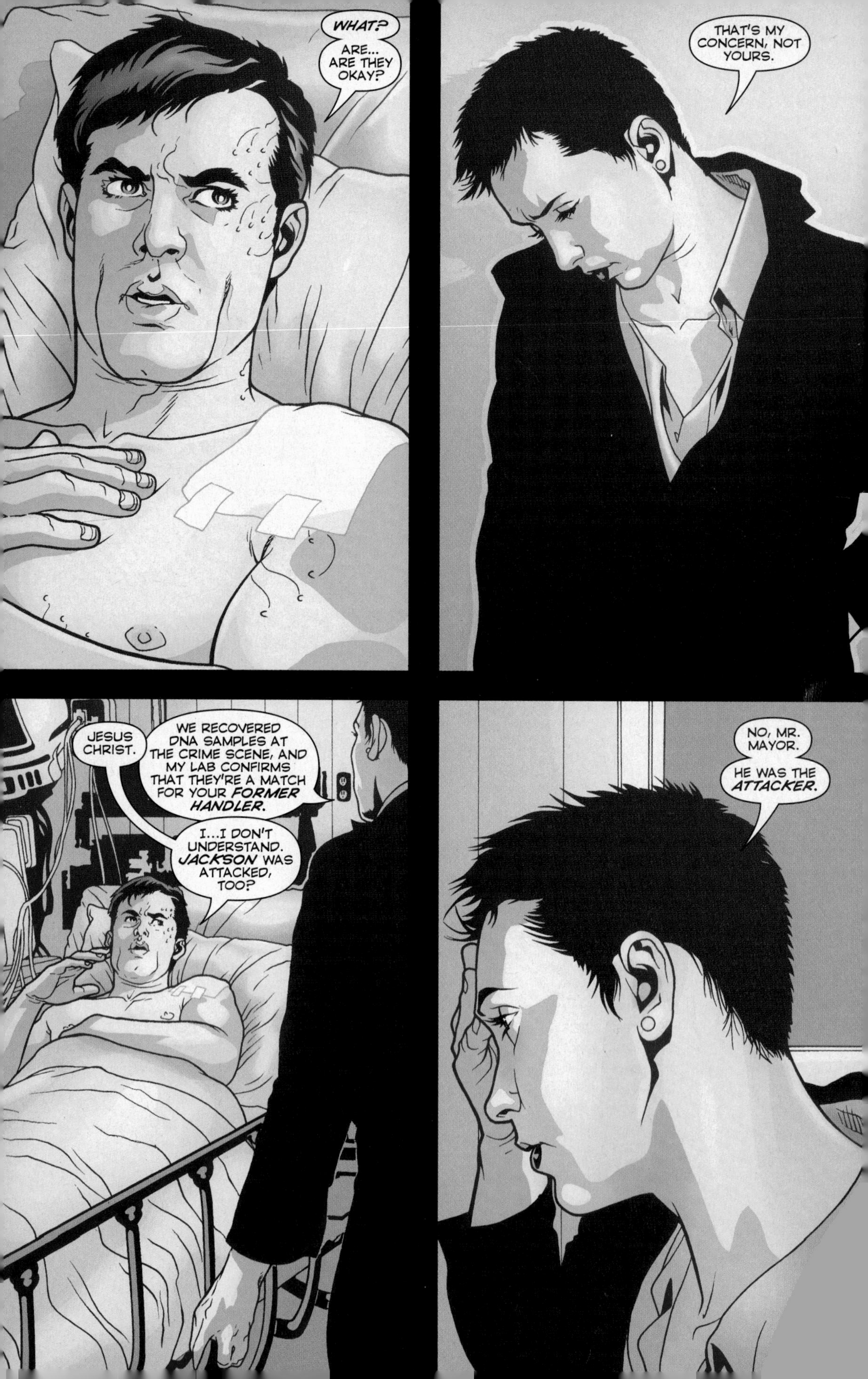
WHAT? ARE... ARE THEY OKAY?
THAT'S MY CONCERN, NOT YOURS.
WE RECOVERED DNA SAMPLES AT THE CRIME SCENE, AND MY LAB CONFIRMS THAT THEY'RE A MATCH FOR YOUR FORMER HANDLER.
JESUS CHRIST.
I...I DON'T UNDERSTAND. JACKSON WAS ATTACKED, TOO?
NO, MR. MAYOR.
HE WAS THE ATTACKER.

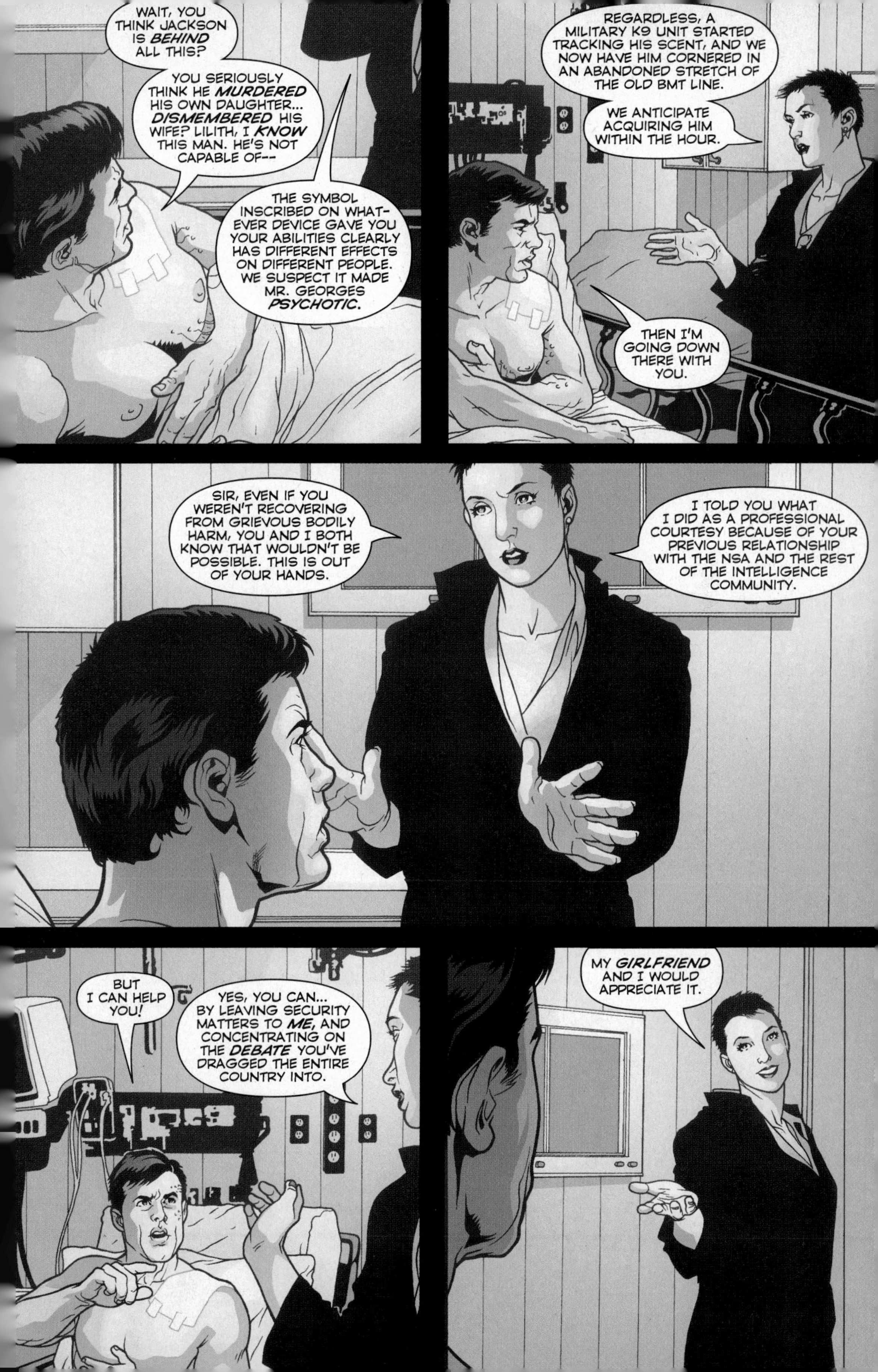

WAIT, YOU THINK JACKSON IS *BEHIND* ALL THIS?
YOU SERIOUSLY THINK HE *MURDERED* HIS OWN DAUGHTER... *DISMEMBERED* HIS WIFE? LILITH, I *KNOW* THIS MAN. HE'S NOT CAPABLE OF--
THE SYMBOL INSCRIBED ON WHAT-EVER DEVICE GAVE YOU YOUR ABILITIES CLEARLY HAS DIFFERENT EFFECTS ON DIFFERENT PEOPLE. WE SUSPECT IT MADE MR. GEORGES *PSYCHOTIC*.
REGARDLESS, A MILITARY K9 UNIT STARTED TRACKING HIS SCENT, AND WE NOW HAVE HIM CORNERED IN AN ABANDONED STRETCH OF THE OLD BMT LINE.
WE ANTICIPATE ACQUIRING HIM WITHIN THE HOUR.
THEN I'M GOING DOWN THERE WITH YOU.
SIR, EVEN IF YOU WEREN'T RECOVERING FROM GRIEVOUS BODILY HARM, YOU AND I BOTH KNOW THAT WOULDN'T BE POSSIBLE. THIS IS OUT OF YOUR HANDS.
I TOLD YOU WHAT I DID AS A PROFESSIONAL COURTESY BECAUSE OF YOUR PREVIOUS RELATIONSHIP WITH THE NSA AND THE REST OF THE INTELLIGENCE COMMUNITY.
BUT I CAN HELP YOU!
YES, YOU CAN... BY LEAVING SECURITY MATTERS TO *ME*, AND CONCENTRATING ON THE *DEBATE* YOU'VE DRAGGED THE ENTIRE COUNTRY INTO.
MY *GIRLFRIEND* AND I WOULD APPRECIATE IT.

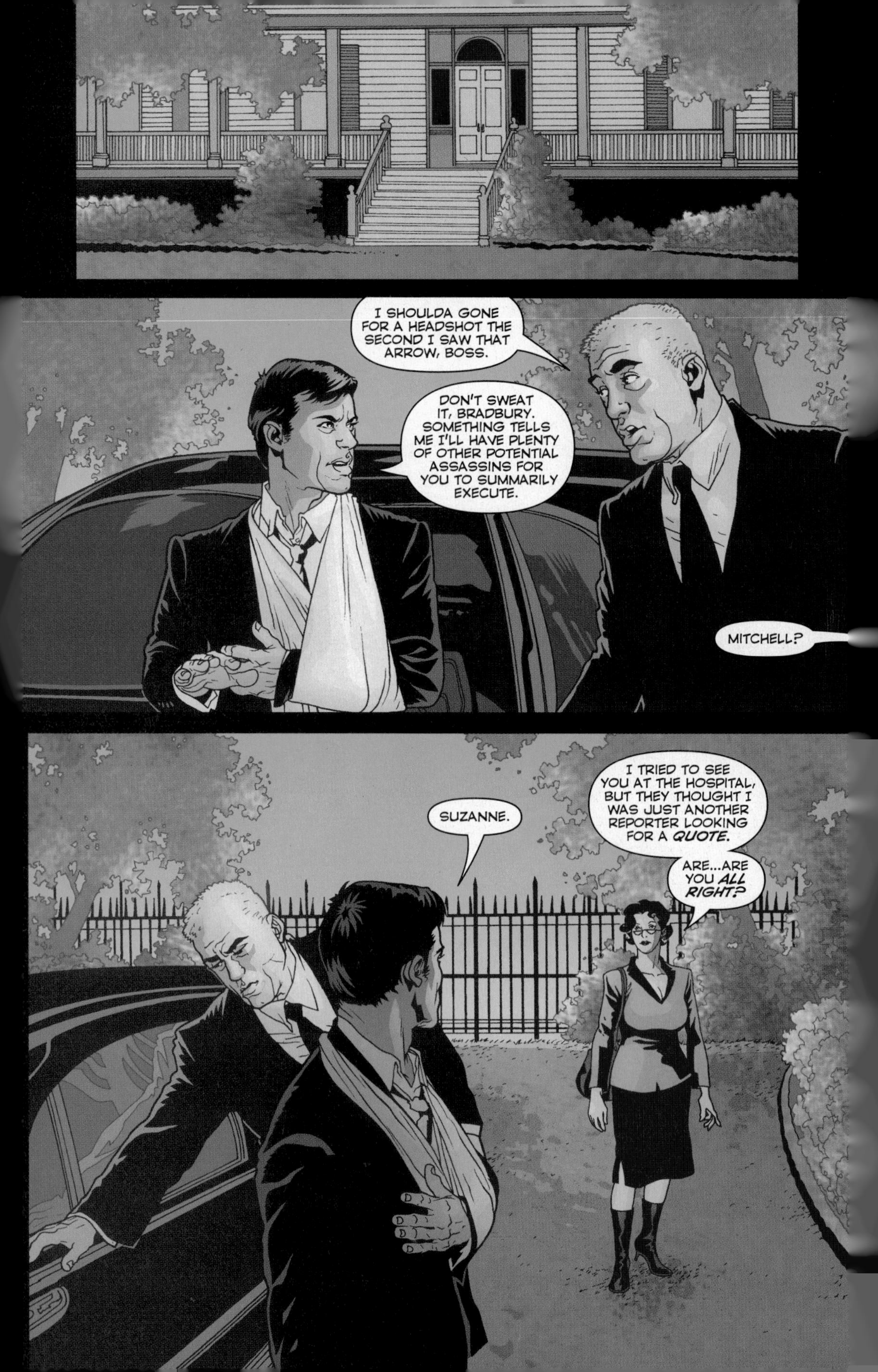
I SHOULDA GONE FOR A HEADSHOT THE SECOND I SAW THAT ARROW, BOSS.
DON'T SWEAT IT, BRADBURY. SOMETHING TELLS ME I'LL HAVE PLENTY OF OTHER POTENTIAL ASSASSINS FOR YOU TO SUMMARILY EXECUTE.
MITCHELL?
SUZANNE.
I TRIED TO SEE YOU AT THE HOSPITAL, BUT THEY THOUGHT I WAS JUST ANOTHER REPORTER LOOKING FOR A *QUOTE*.
ARE...ARE YOU *ALL RIGHT?*

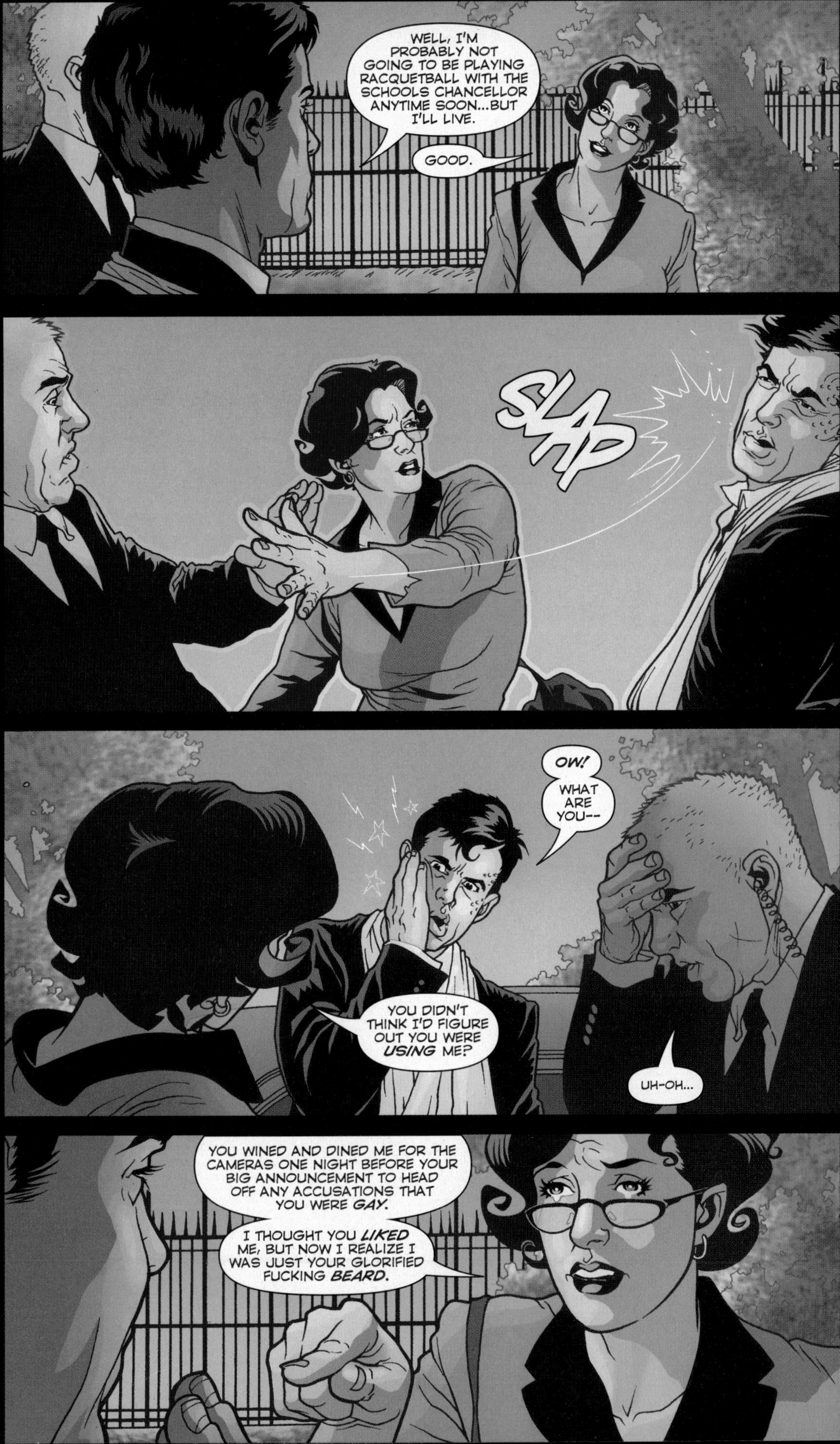
WELL, I'M PROBABLY NOT GOING TO BE PLAYING RACQUETBALL WITH THE SCHOOLS CHANCELLOR ANYTIME SOON...BUT I'LL LIVE.
GOOD.
SLAP
OW!
WHAT ARE YOU--
YOU DIDN'T THINK I'D FIGURE OUT YOU WERE USING ME?
UH-OH...
YOU WINED AND DINED ME FOR THE CAMERAS ONE NIGHT BEFORE YOUR BIG ANNOUNCEMENT TO HEAD OFF ANY ACCUSATIONS THAT YOU WERE GAY.
I THOUGHT YOU LIKED ME, BUT NOW I REALIZE I WAS JUST YOUR GLORIFIED FUCKING BEARD.

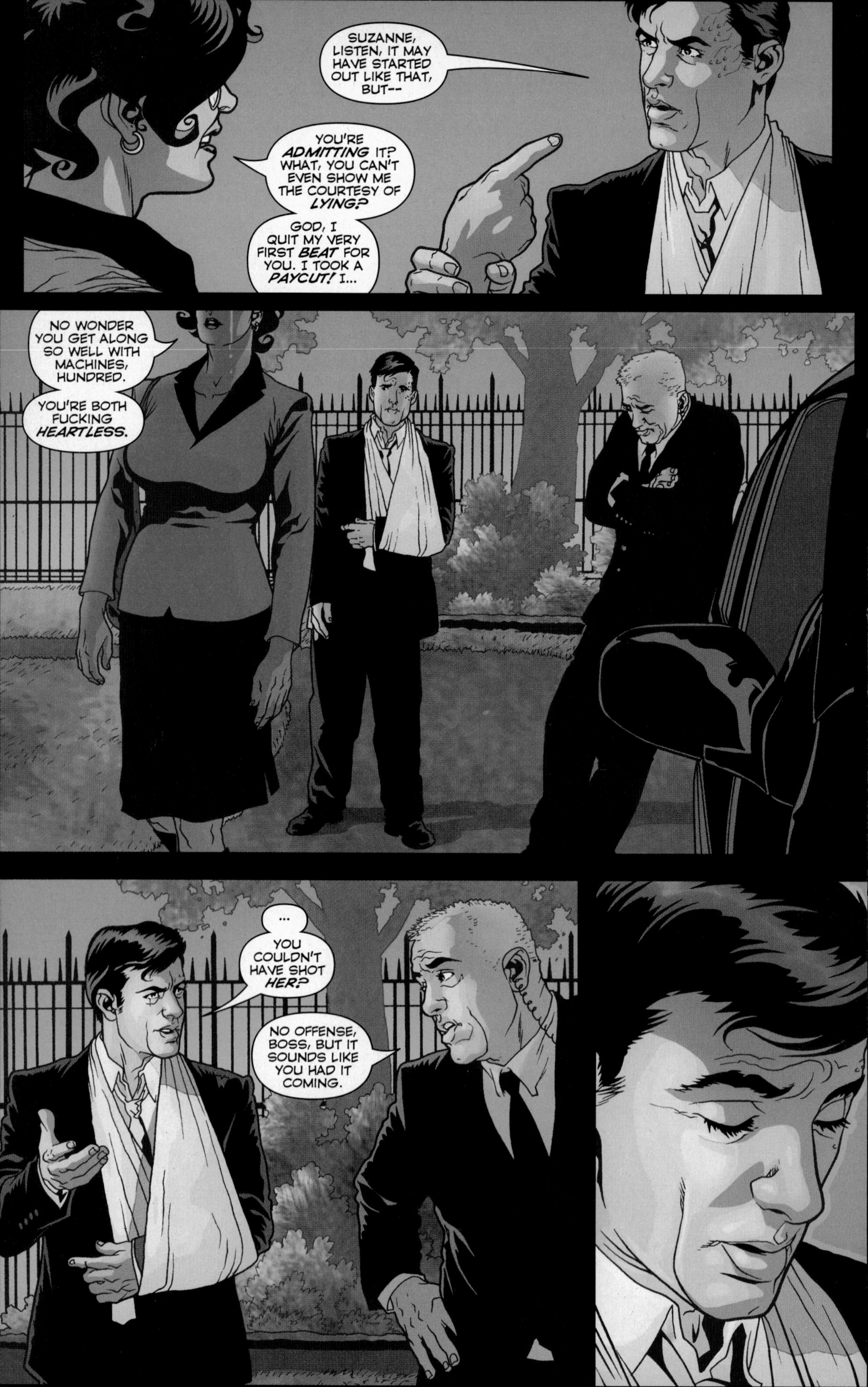
SUZANNE, LISTEN, IT MAY HAVE STARTED OUT LIKE THAT, BUT--
YOU'RE *ADMITTING* IT? WHAT, YOU CAN'T EVEN SHOW ME THE COURTESY OF *LYING?*
GOD, I QUIT MY VERY FIRST *BEAT* FOR YOU. I TOOK A *PAYCUT!* I...
NO WONDER YOU GET ALONG SO WELL WITH MACHINES, HUNDRED.
YOU'RE BOTH FUCKING *HEARTLESS.*
...
YOU COULDN'T HAVE SHOT *HER?*
NO OFFENSE, BOSS, BUT IT SOUNDS LIKE YOU HAD IT COMING.

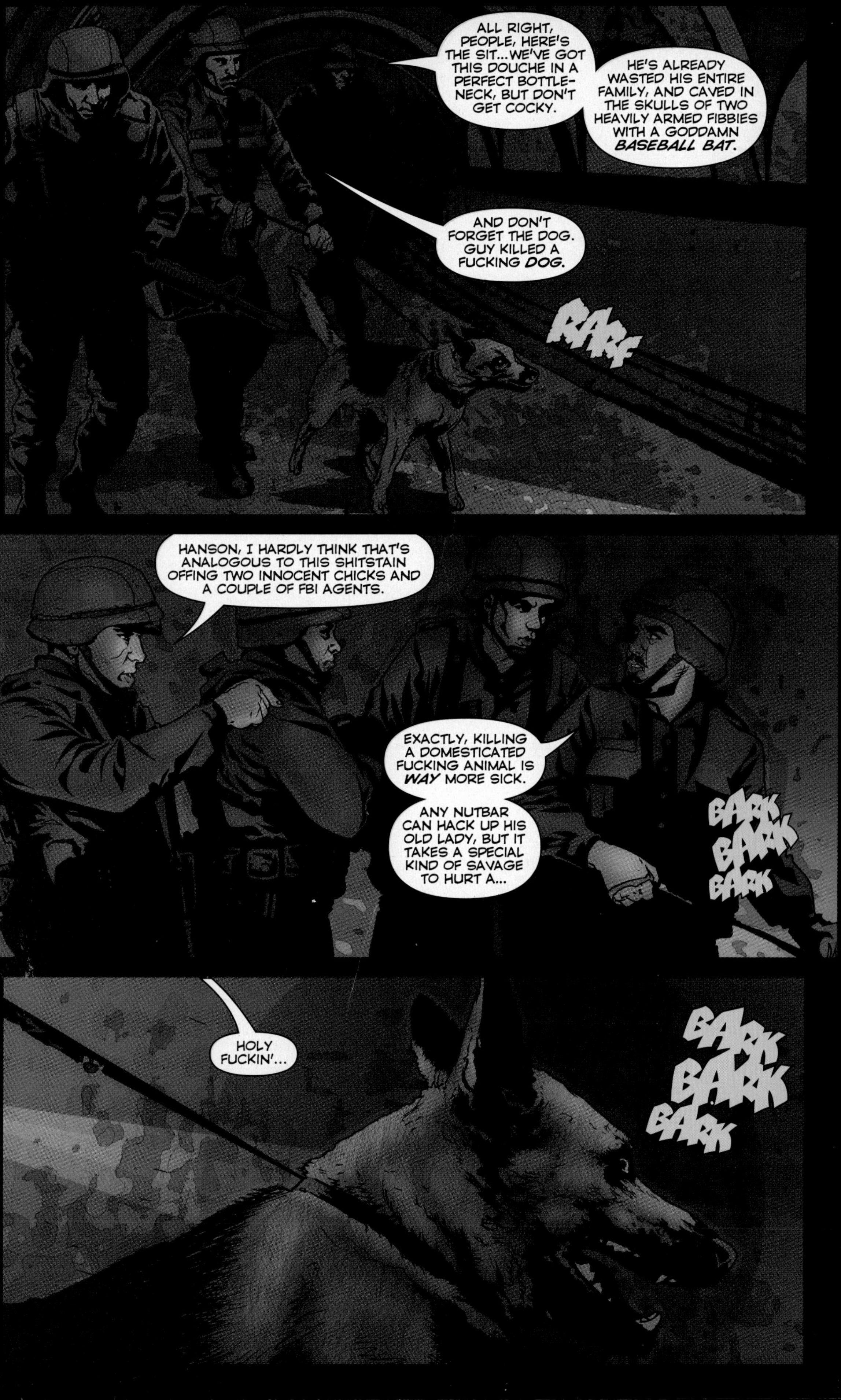
ALL RIGHT, PEOPLE, HERE'S THE SIT...WE'VE GOT THIS DOUCHE IN A PERFECT BOTTLE-NECK, BUT DON'T GET COCKY.
HE'S ALREADY WASTED HIS ENTIRE FAMILY, AND CAVED IN THE SKULLS OF TWO HEAVILY ARMED FIBBIES WITH A GODDAMN ***BASEBALL BAT.***
AND DON'T FORGET THE DOG. GUY KILLED A FUCKING ***DOG.***
RARF
HANSON, I HARDLY THINK THAT'S ANALOGOUS TO THIS SHITSTAIN OFFING TWO INNOCENT CHICKS AND A COUPLE OF FBI AGENTS.
EXACTLY, KILLING A DOMESTICATED FUCKING ANIMAL IS ***WAY*** MORE SICK.
ANY NUTBAR CAN HACK UP HIS OLD LADY, BUT IT TAKES A SPECIAL KIND OF SAVAGE TO HURT A...
BARK BARK BARK
HOLY FUCKIN'...
BARK BARK BARK

BARK
BARK
BARK
BARK
BARK
BARK

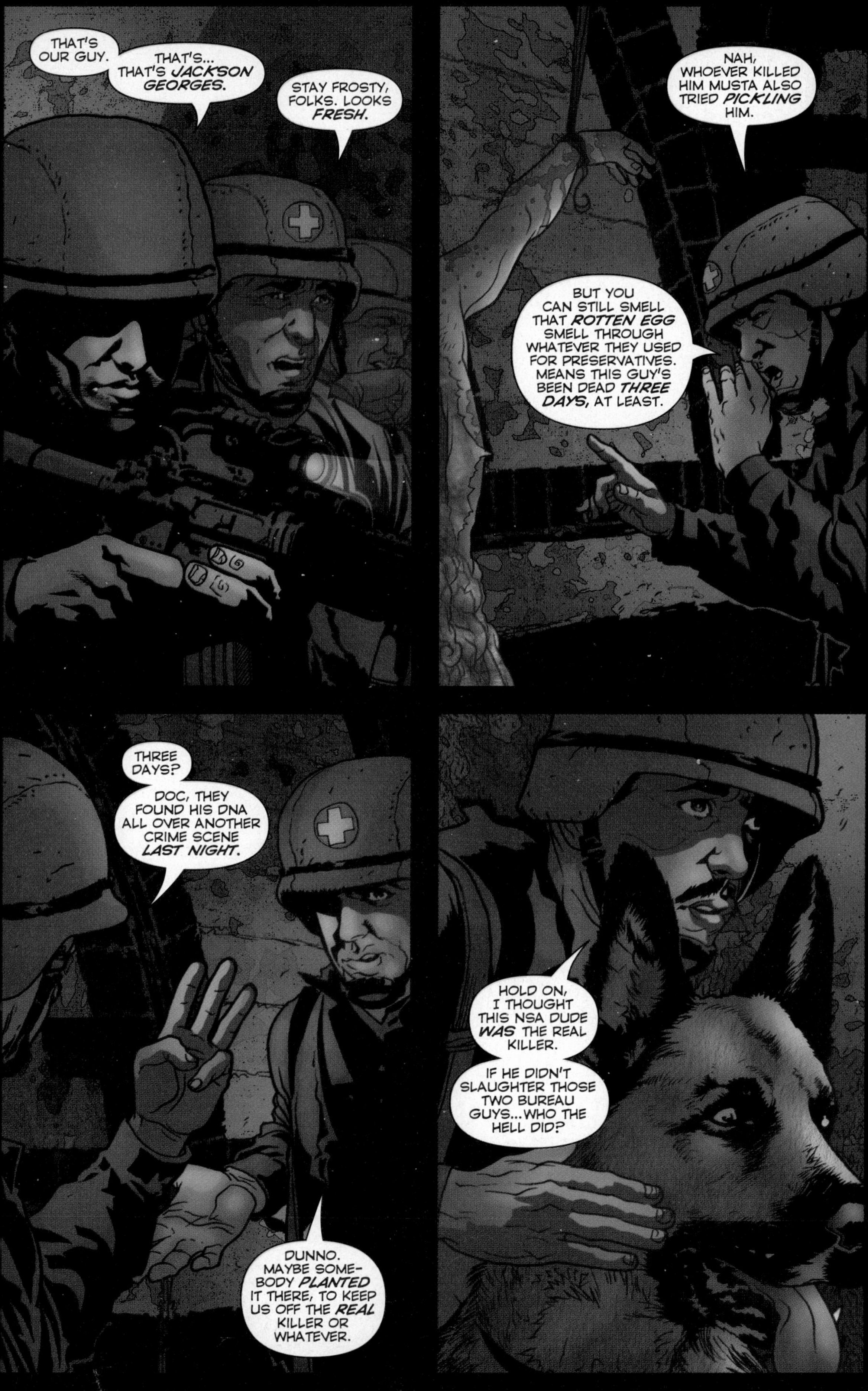

THAT'S OUR GUY.
THAT'S... THAT'S JACKSON GEORGES.
STAY FROSTY, FOLKS. LOOKS FRESH.
NAH, WHOEVER KILLED HIM MUSTA ALSO TRIED PICKLING HIM.
BUT YOU CAN STILL SMELL THAT ROTTEN EGG SMELL THROUGH WHATEVER THEY USED FOR PRESERVATIVES. MEANS THIS GUY'S BEEN DEAD THREE DAYS, AT LEAST.
THREE DAYS?
DOC, THEY FOUND HIS DNA ALL OVER ANOTHER CRIME SCENE LAST NIGHT.
DUNNO. MAYBE SOME-BODY PLANTED IT THERE, TO KEEP US OFF THE REAL KILLER OR WHATEVER.
HOLD ON, I THOUGHT THIS NSA DUDE WAS THE REAL KILLER.
IF HE DIDN'T SLAUGHTER THOSE TWO BUREAU GUYS... WHO THE HELL DID?

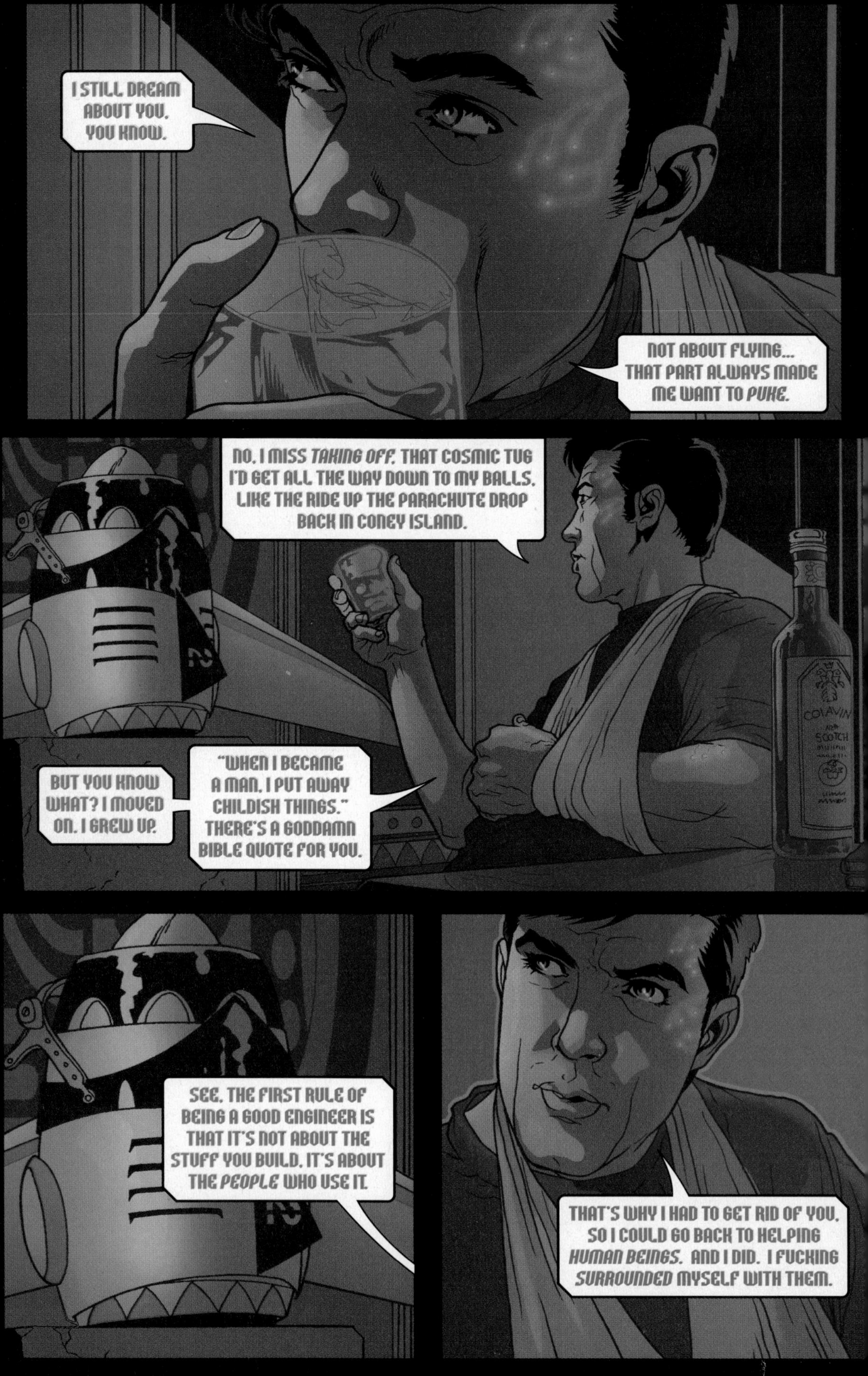
I STILL DREAM ABOUT YOU, YOU KNOW.
NOT ABOUT FLYING... THAT PART ALWAYS MADE ME WANT TO PUKE.
NO, I MISS TAKING OFF. THAT COSMIC TUG I'D GET ALL THE WAY DOWN TO MY BALLS. LIKE THE RIDE UP THE PARACHUTE DROP BACK IN CONEY ISLAND.
BUT YOU KNOW WHAT? I MOVED ON. I GREW UP.
"WHEN I BECAME A MAN, I PUT AWAY CHILDISH THINGS." THERE'S A GODDAMN BIBLE QUOTE FOR YOU.
COLAVIN
SCOTCH
SEE, THE FIRST RULE OF BEING A GOOD ENGINEER IS THAT IT'S NOT ABOUT THE STUFF YOU BUILD. IT'S ABOUT THE PEOPLE WHO USE IT.
THAT'S WHY I HAD TO GET RID OF YOU. SO I COULD GO BACK TO HELPING HUMAN BEINGS. AND I DID. I FUCKING SURROUNDED MYSELF WITH THEM.

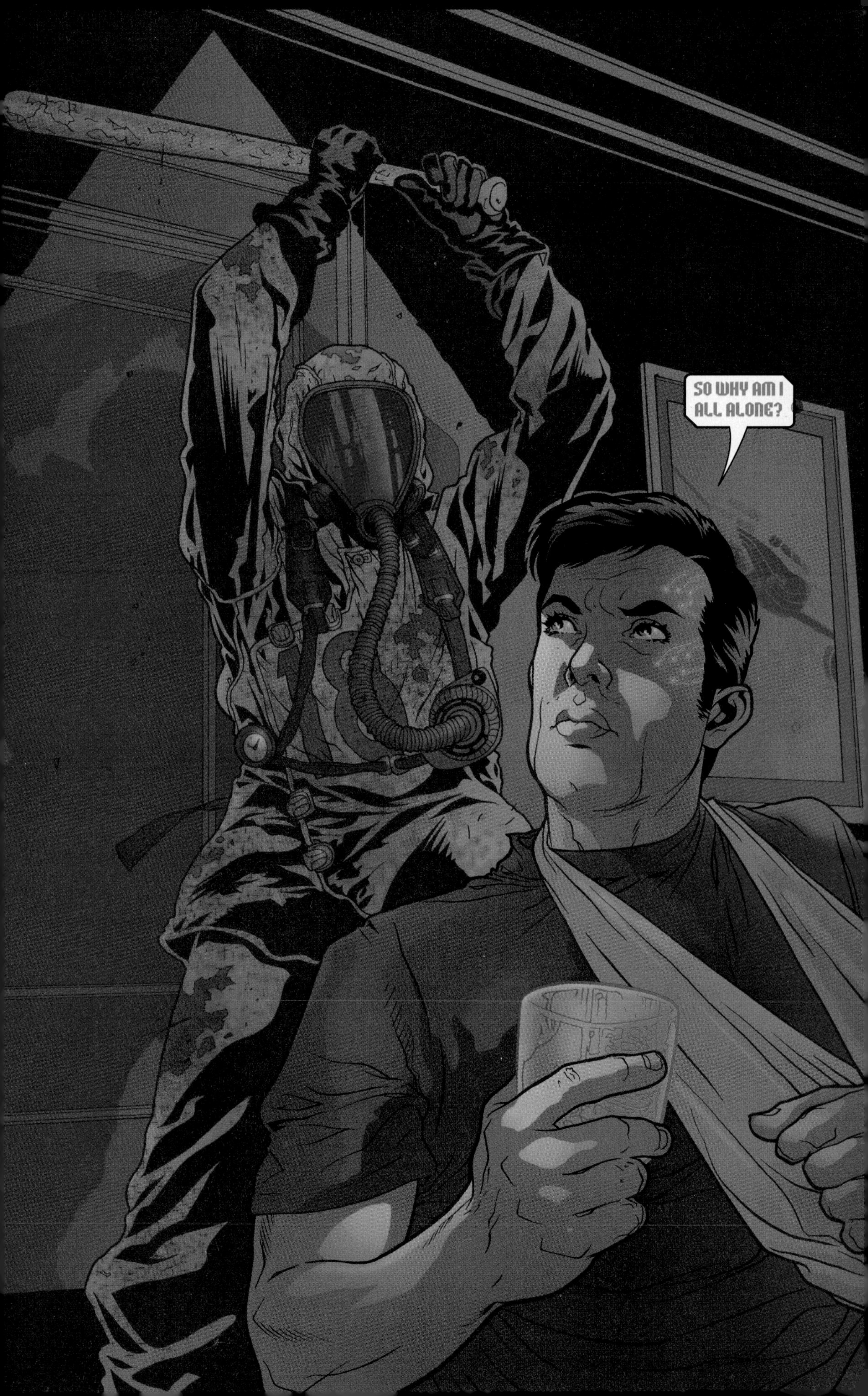
SO WHY AM I ALL ALONE?

# CHAPTER 5

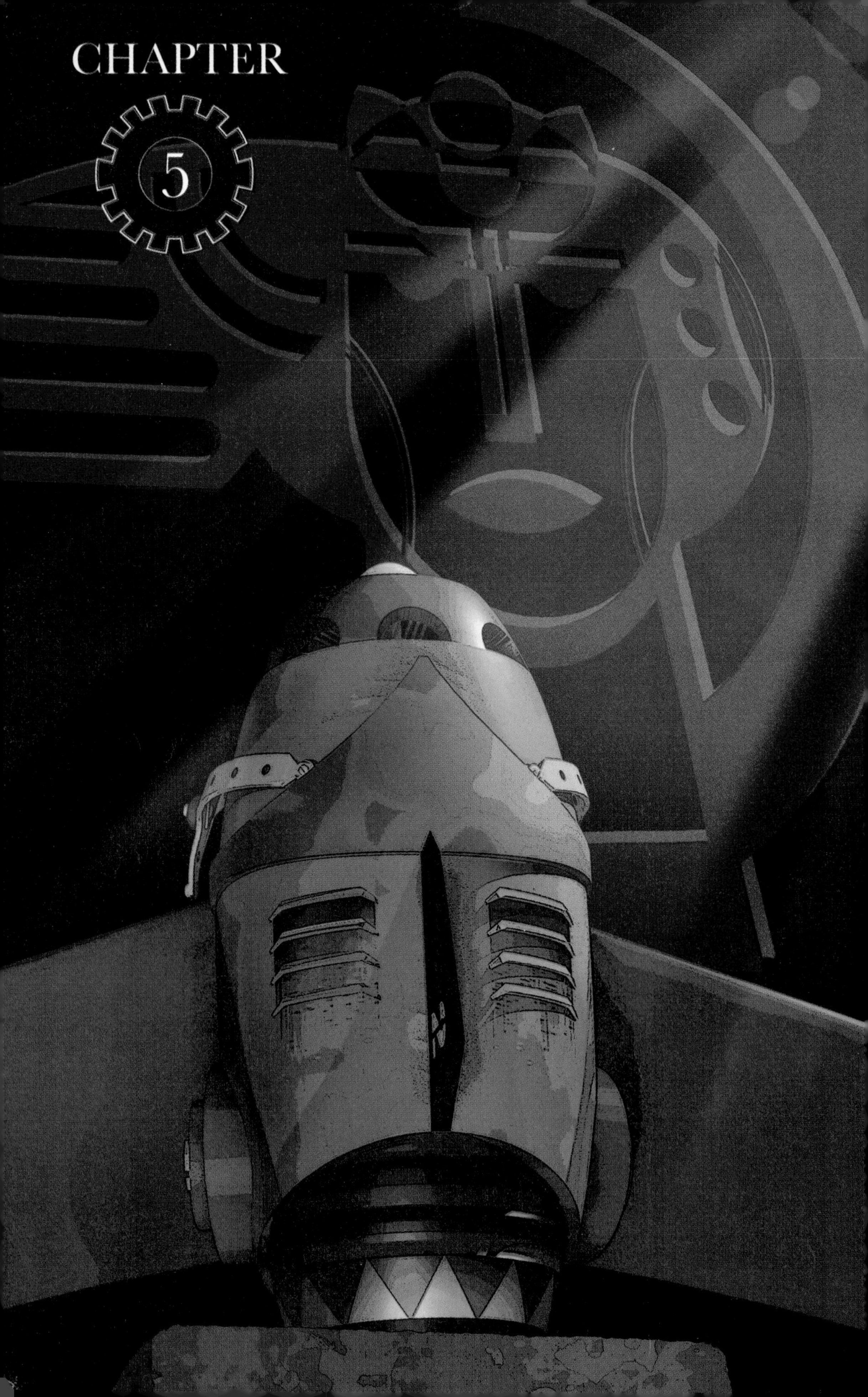

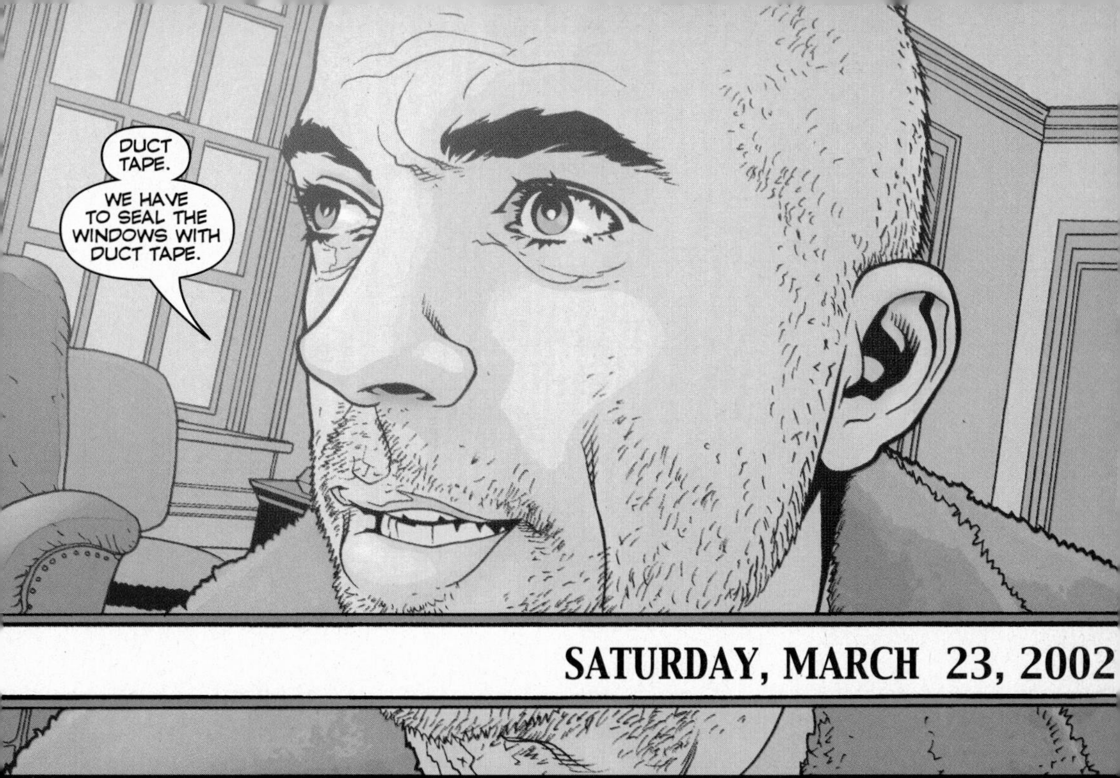
DUCT TAPE.
WE HAVE TO SEAL THE WINDOWS WITH DUCT TAPE.
SATURDAY, MARCH 23, 2002

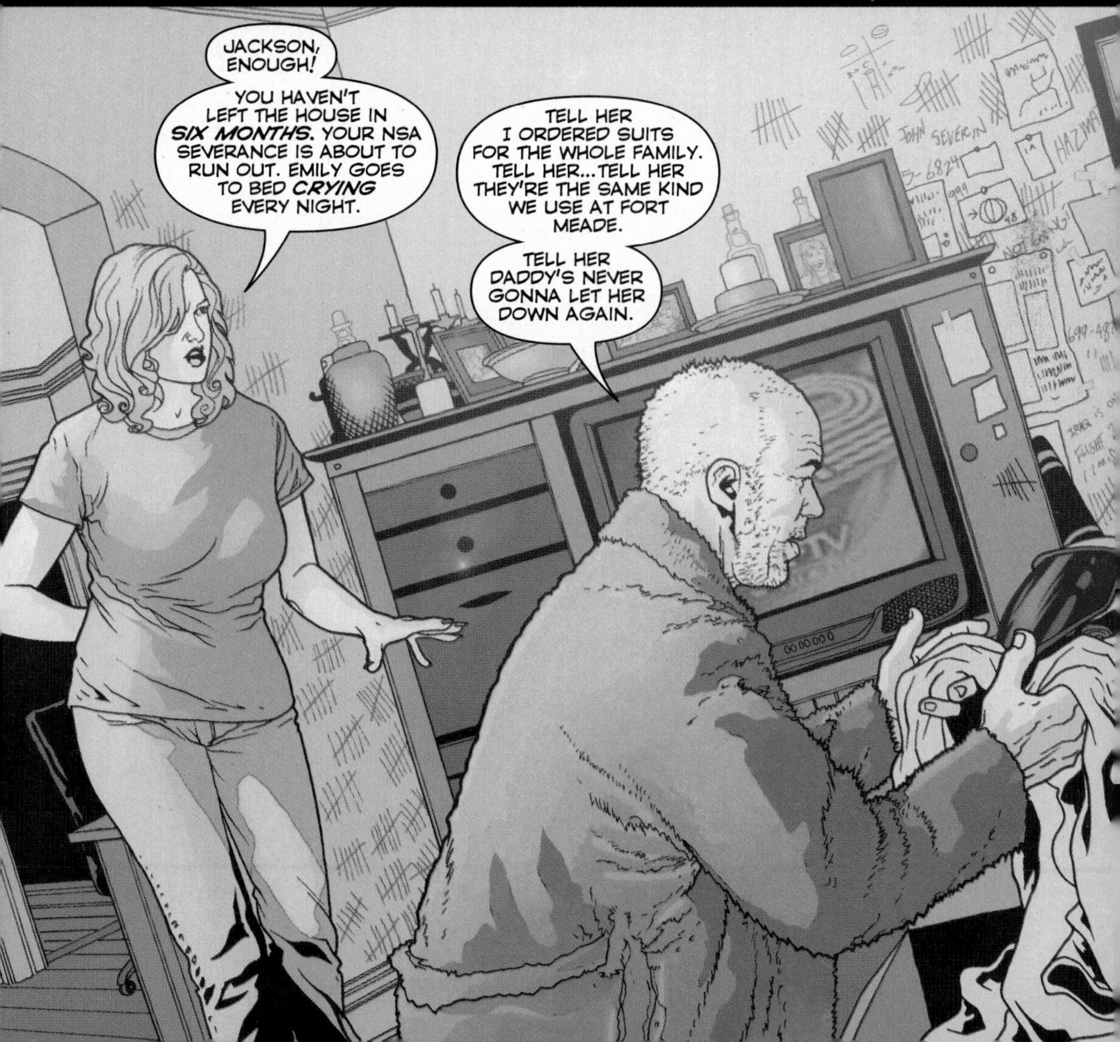
JACKSON, ENOUGH!
YOU HAVEN'T LEFT THE HOUSE IN *SIX MONTHS*. YOUR NSA SEVERANCE IS ABOUT TO RUN OUT. EMILY GOES TO BED *CRYING* EVERY NIGHT.
TELL HER I ORDERED SUITS FOR THE WHOLE FAMILY. TELL HER...TELL HER THEY'RE THE SAME KIND WE USE AT FORT MEADE.
TELL HER DADDY'S NEVER GONNA LET HER DOWN AGAIN.
JOHN SEVERIN

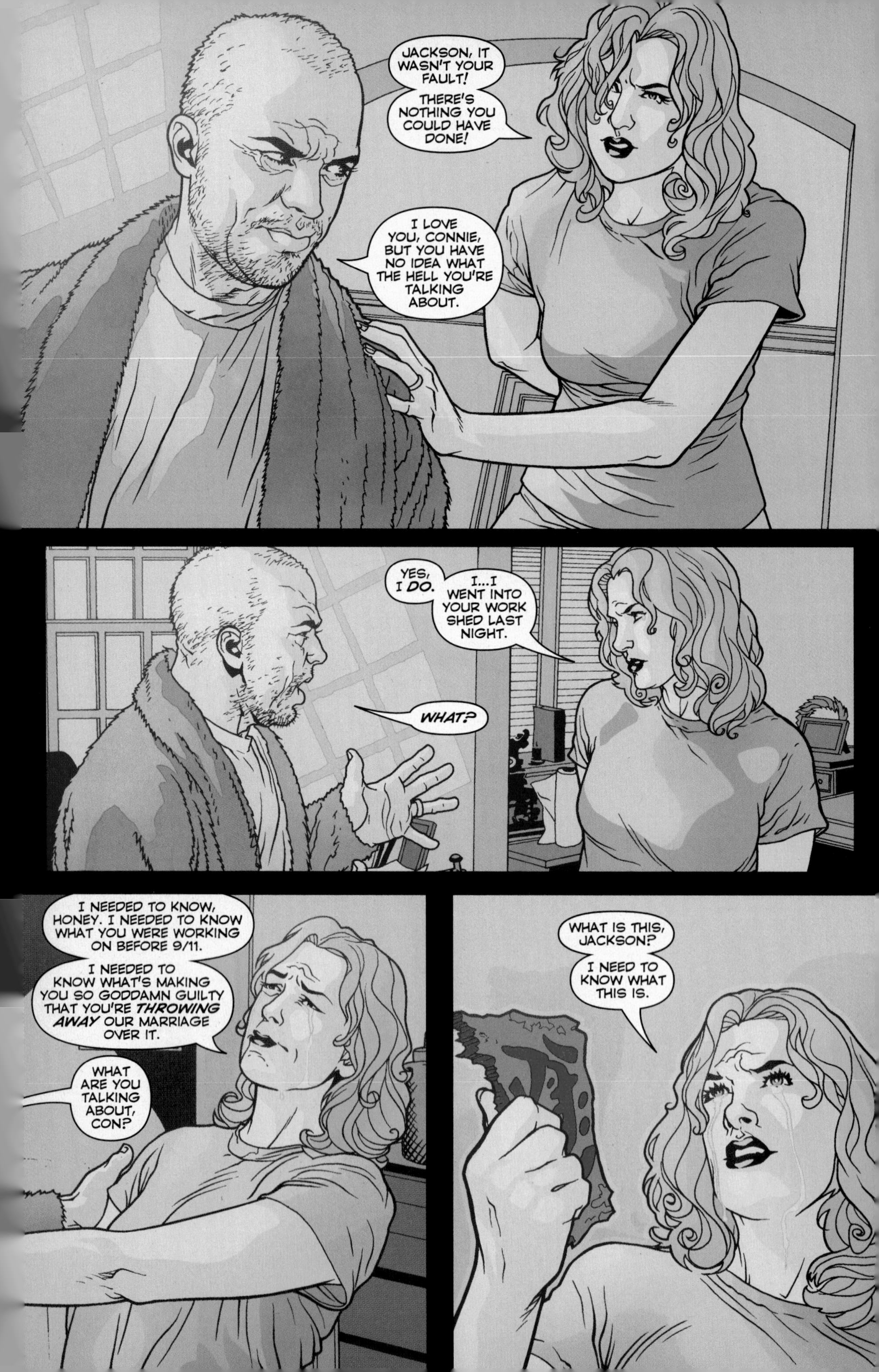
JACKSON, IT WASN'T YOUR FAULT!
THERE'S NOTHING YOU COULD HAVE DONE!
I LOVE YOU, CONNIE, BUT YOU HAVE NO IDEA WHAT THE HELL YOU'RE TALKING ABOUT.
YES, I DO.
I...I WENT INTO YOUR WORK SHED LAST NIGHT.
WHAT?
I NEEDED TO KNOW, HONEY. I NEEDED TO KNOW WHAT YOU WERE WORKING ON BEFORE 9/11.
I NEEDED TO KNOW WHAT'S MAKING YOU SO GODDAMN GUILTY THAT YOU'RE THROWING AWAY OUR MARRIAGE OVER IT.
WHAT ARE YOU TALKING ABOUT, CON?
WHAT IS THIS, JACKSON?
I NEED TO KNOW WHAT THIS IS.

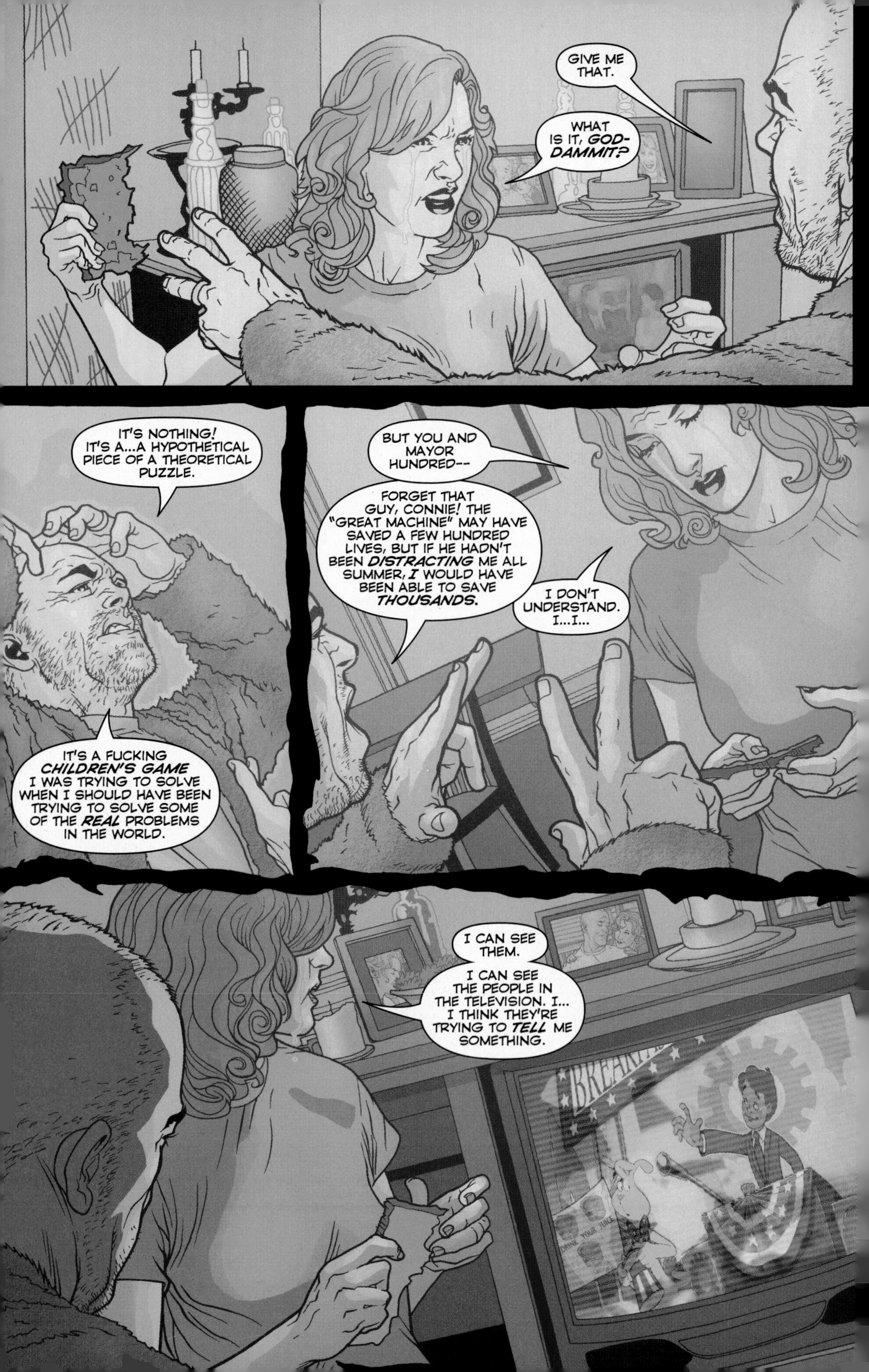
GIVE ME THAT.
WHAT IS IT, *GOD-DAMMIT?*
IT'S NOTHING! IT'S A...A HYPOTHETICAL PIECE OF A THEORETICAL PUZZLE.
IT'S A FUCKING *CHILDREN'S GAME* I WAS TRYING TO SOLVE WHEN I SHOULD HAVE BEEN TRYING TO SOLVE SOME OF THE *REAL* PROBLEMS IN THE WORLD.
BUT YOU AND MAYOR HUNDRED--
FORGET THAT GUY, CONNIE! THE "GREAT MACHINE" MAY HAVE SAVED A FEW HUNDRED LIVES, BUT IF HE HADN'T BEEN *DISTRACTING* ME ALL SUMMER, *I* WOULD HAVE BEEN ABLE TO SAVE *THOUSANDS.*
I DON'T UNDERSTAND. I...I...
I CAN SEE THEM.
I CAN SEE THE PEOPLE IN THE TELEVISION. I... I THINK THEY'RE TRYING TO *TELL* ME SOMETHING.

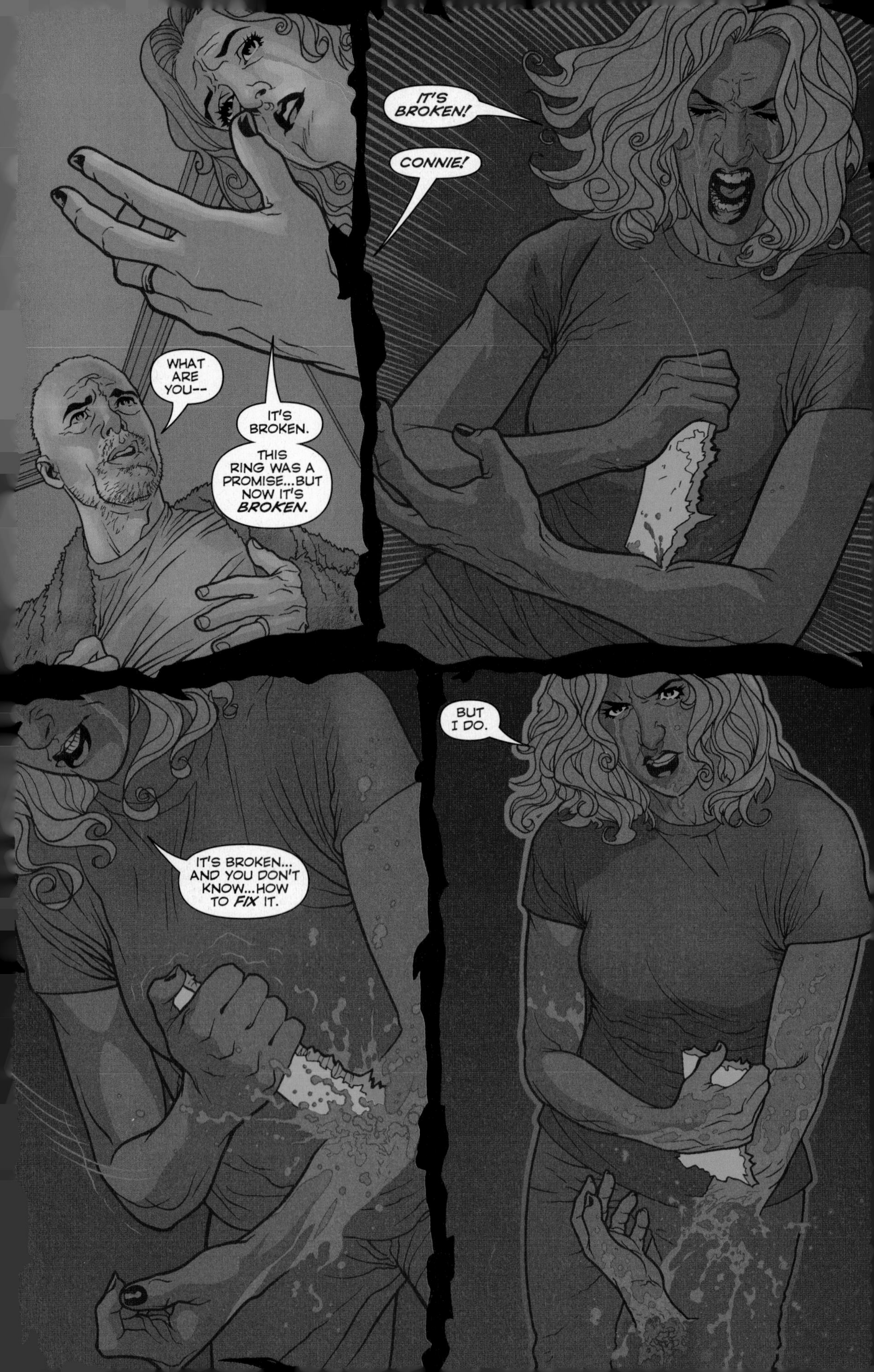

WHAT ARE YOU--
IT'S BROKEN.
THIS RING WAS A PROMISE...BUT NOW IT'S *BROKEN.*
*IT'S BROKEN!*
CONNIE!
IT'S BROKEN... AND YOU DON'T KNOW...HOW TO *FIX* IT.
BUT I DO.

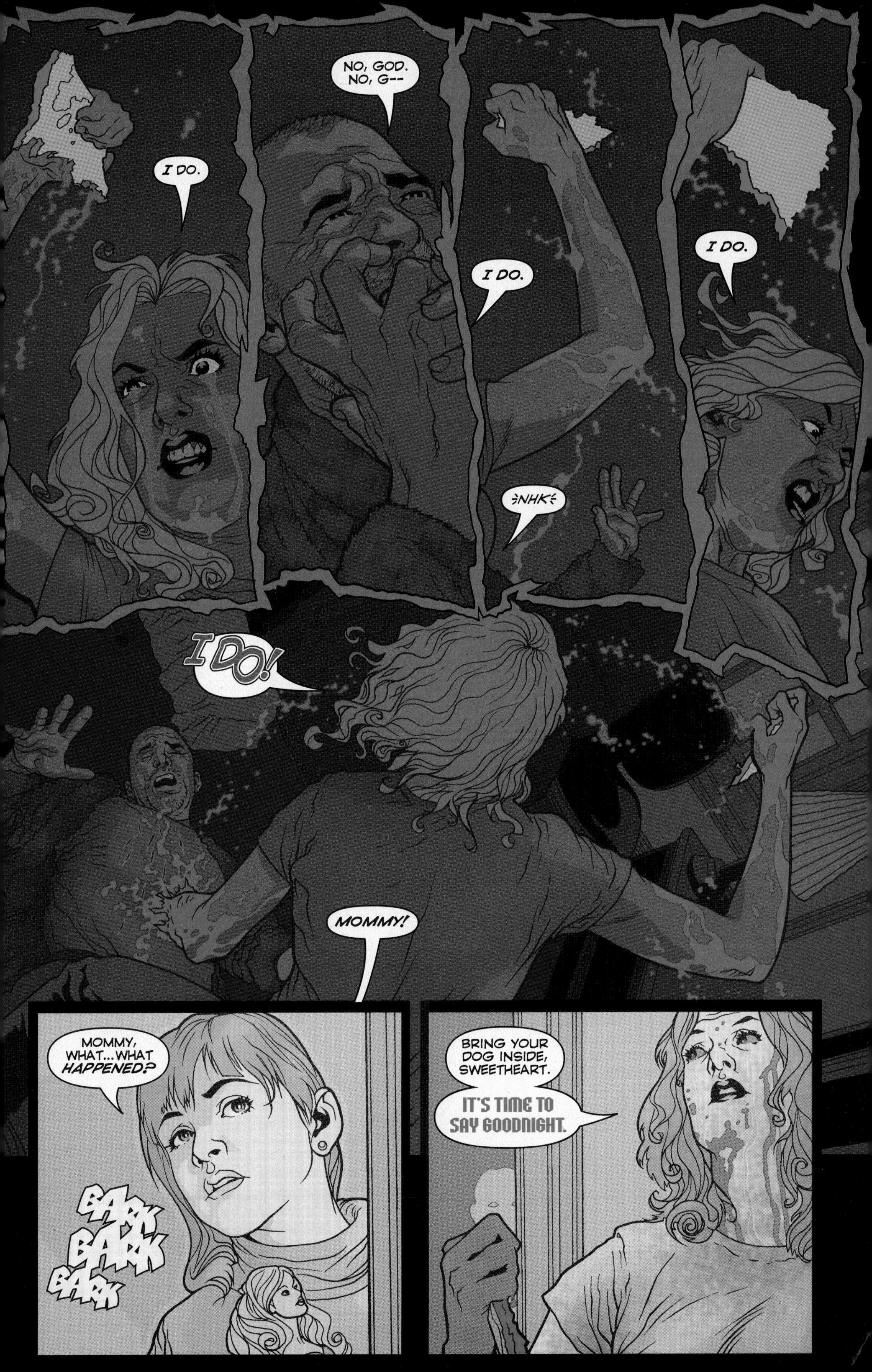
I DO.
NO, GOD. NO, G--
I DO.
NHK
I DO.
I DO!
MOMMY!
MOMMY, WHAT...WHAT HAPPENED?
BARK BARK BARK
BRING YOUR DOG INSIDE, SWEETHEART.
IT'S TIME TO SAY GOODNIGHT.

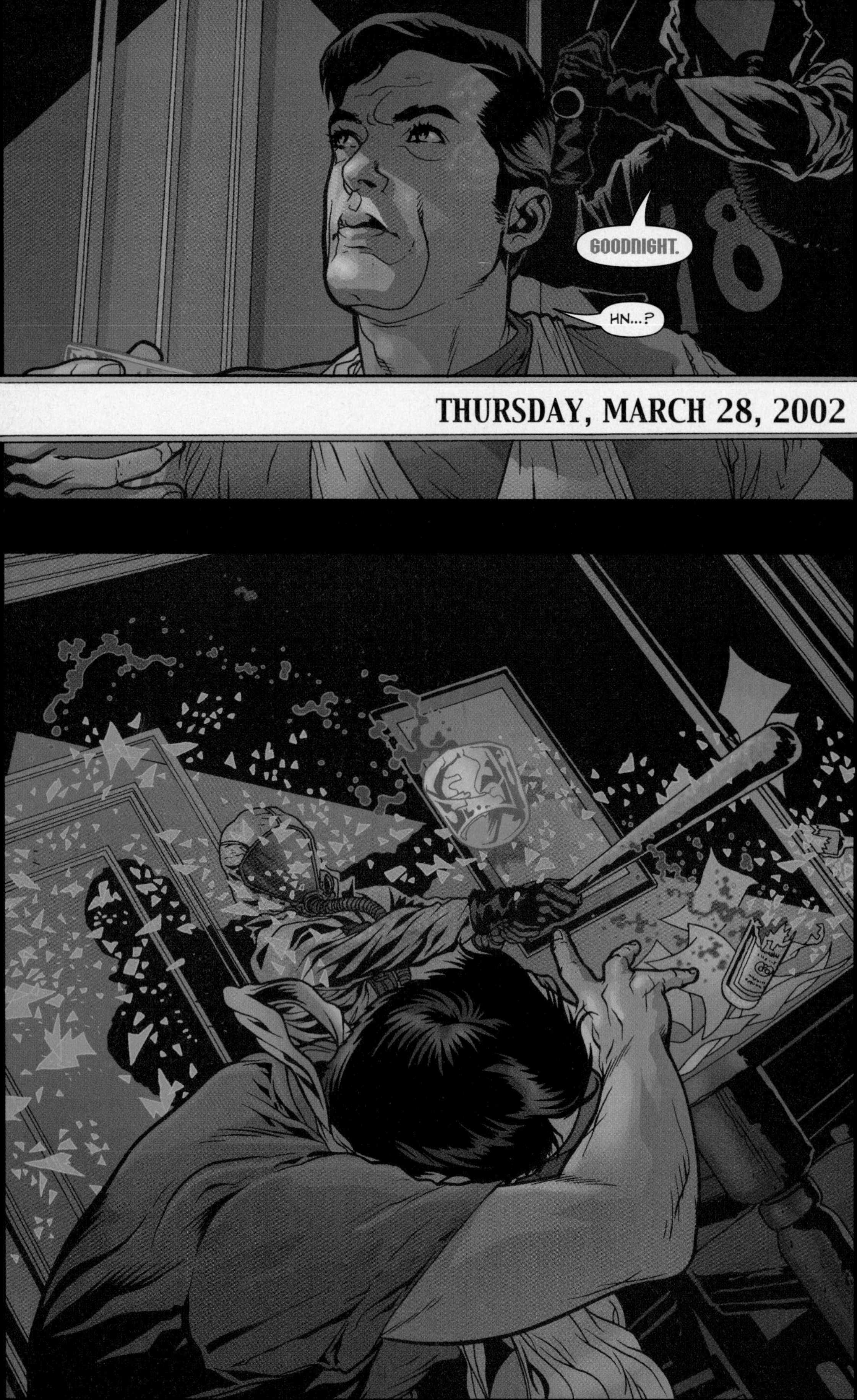
GOODNIGHT.
HN...?
THURSDAY, MARCH 28, 2002

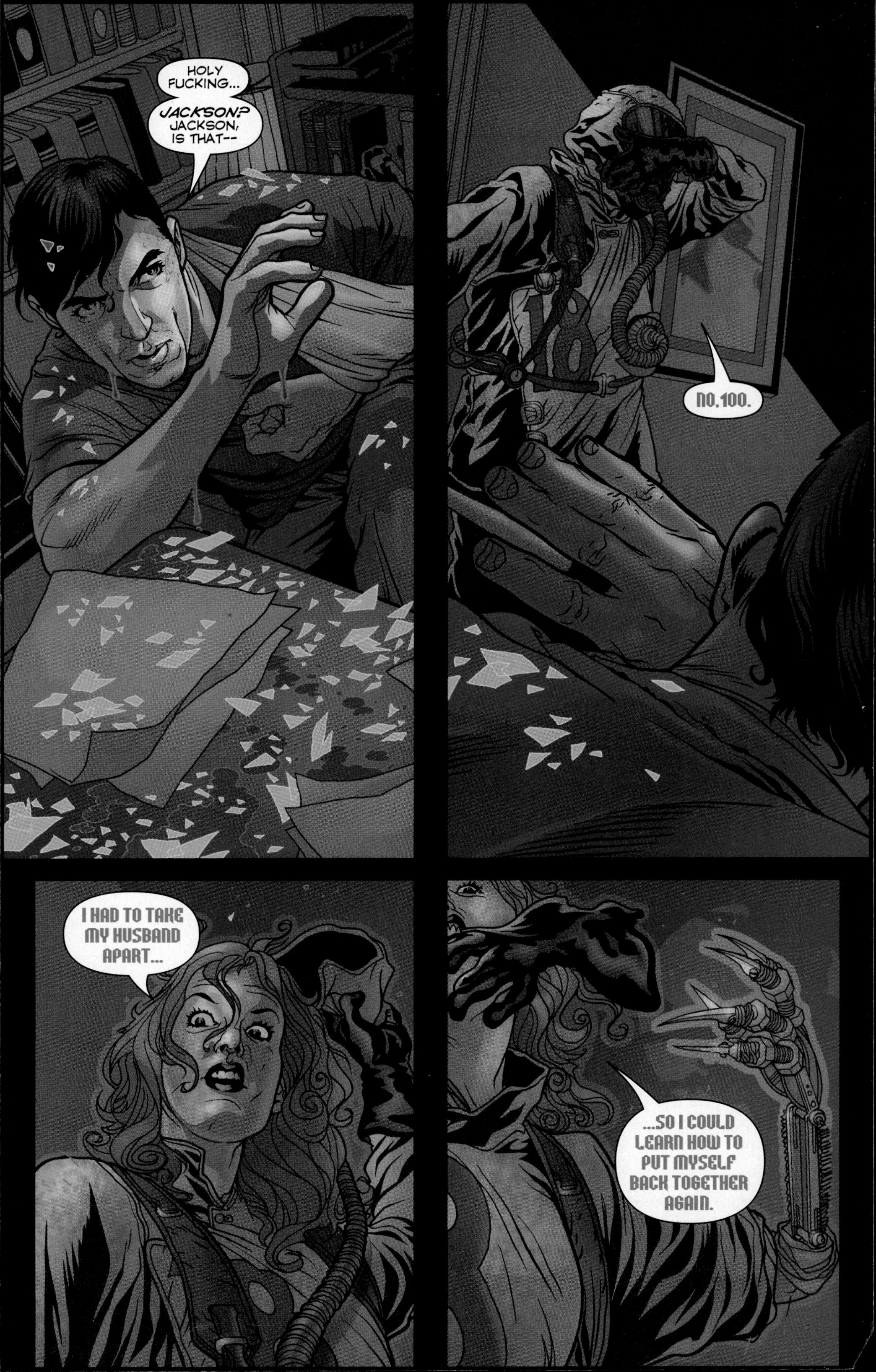
HOLY FUCKING...
JACKSON? JACKSON, IS THAT--
NO.100.
I HAD TO TAKE MY HUSBAND APART...
...SO I COULD LEARN HOW TO PUT MYSELF BACK TOGETHER AGAIN.

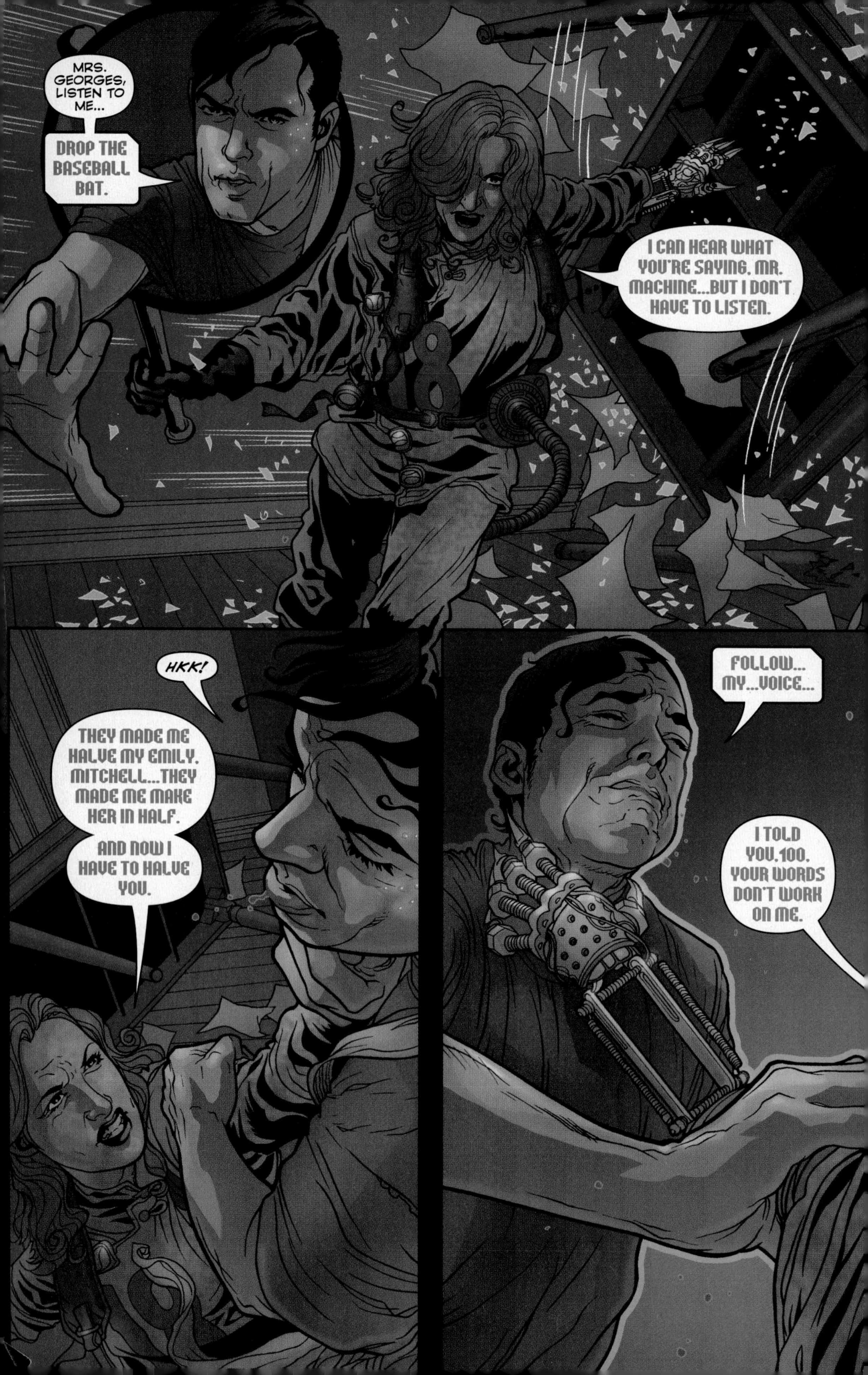
MRS. GEORGES, LISTEN TO ME...
DROP THE BASEBALL BAT.
I CAN HEAR WHAT YOU'RE SAYING, MR. MACHINE...BUT I DON'T HAVE TO LISTEN.
HKK!
THEY MADE ME HALVE MY EMILY, MITCHELL...THEY MADE ME MAKE HER IN HALF.
AND NOW I HAVE TO HALVE YOU.
FOLLOW... MY...VOICE...
I TOLD YOU, TOO. YOUR WORDS DON'T WORK ON ME.

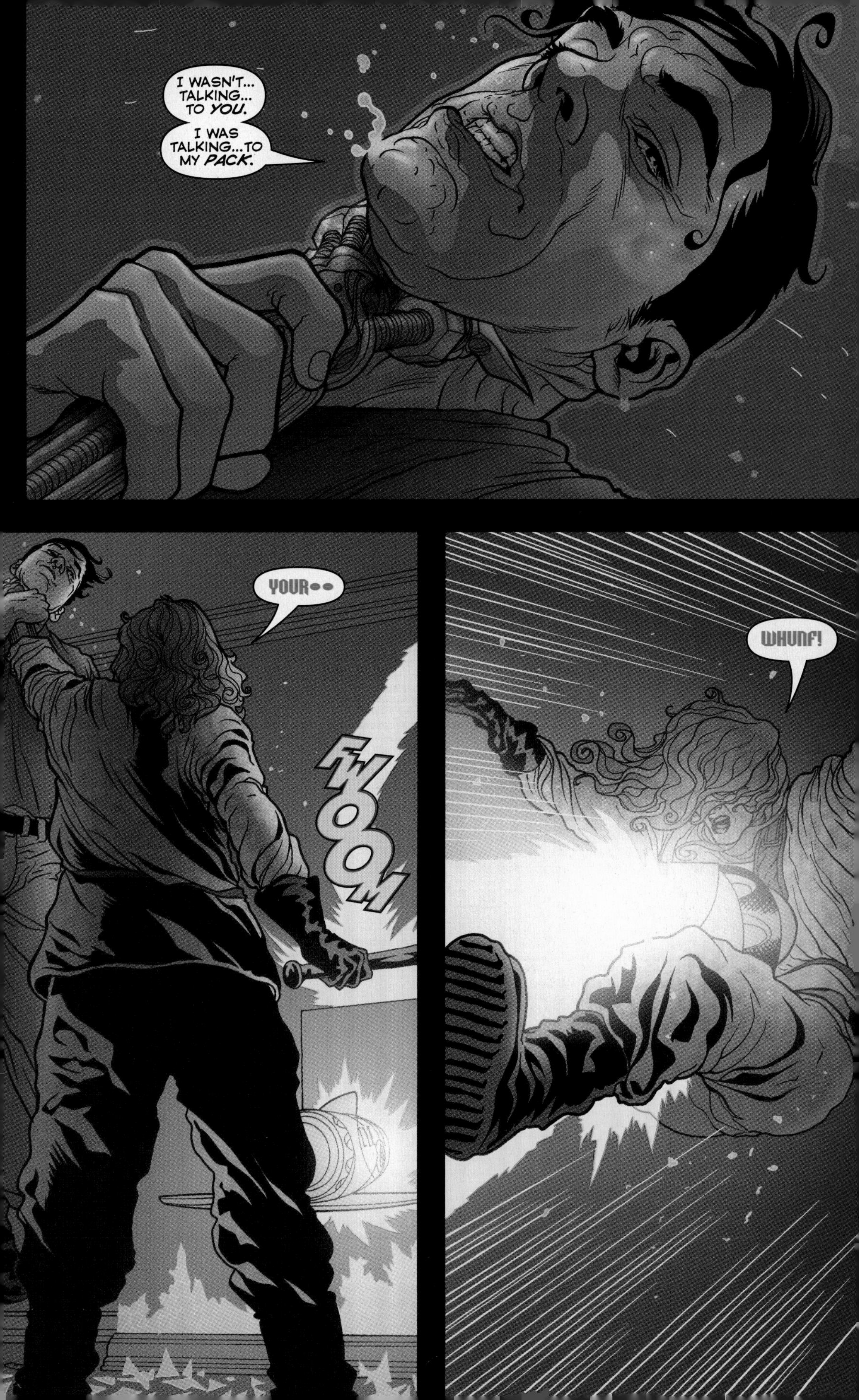
I WASN'T... TALKING... TO *YOU*.
I WAS TALKING...TO MY *PACK*.
YOUR..
FWOOOM
WHUNF!

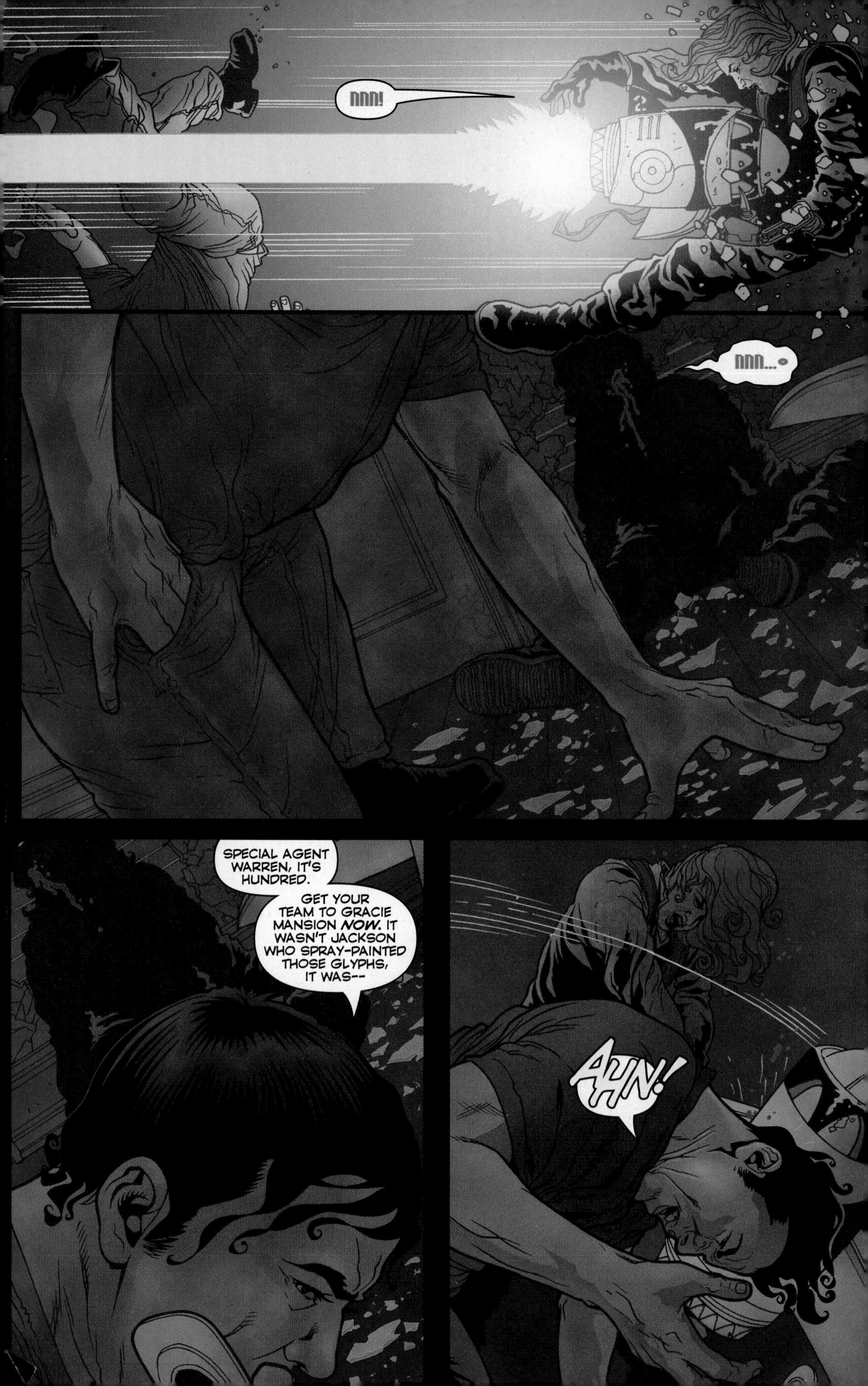
NNN!
NNN...
SPECIAL AGENT WARREN, IT'S HUNDRED.
GET YOUR TEAM TO GRACIE MANSION *NOW.* IT WASN'T JACKSON WHO SPRAY-PAINTED THOSE GLYPHS, IT WAS--
AHN!

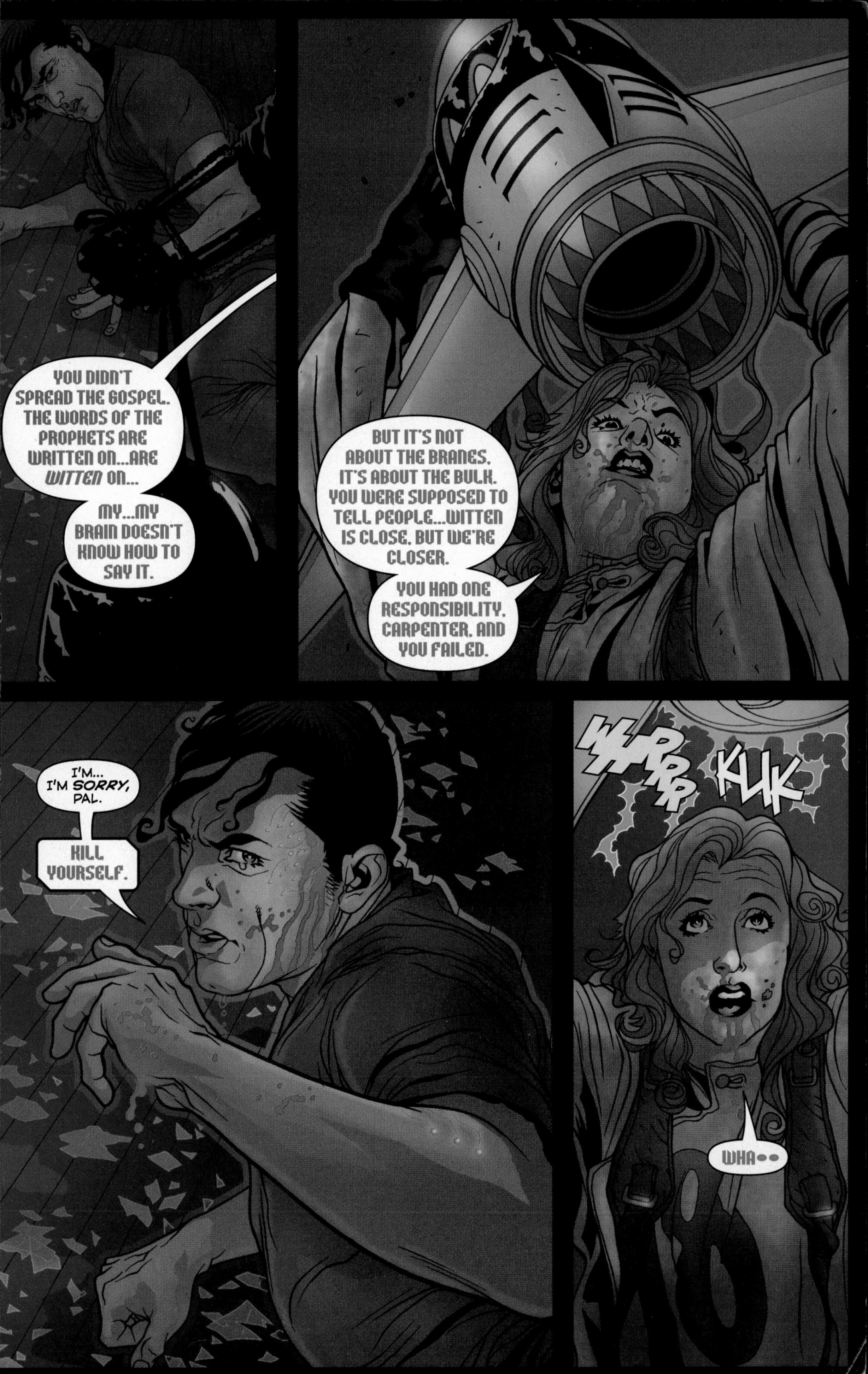
YOU DIDN'T SPREAD THE GOSPEL. THE WORDS OF THE PROPHETS ARE WRITTEN ON...ARE *WITTEN* ON...
MY...MY BRAIN DOESN'T KNOW HOW TO SAY IT.
BUT IT'S NOT ABOUT THE BRANES, IT'S ABOUT THE BULK. YOU WERE SUPPOSED TO TELL PEOPLE...WITTEN IS CLOSE, BUT WE'RE CLOSER.
YOU HAD ONE RESPONSIBILITY, CARPENTER, AND YOU FAILED.
I'M... I'M *SORRY,* PAL.
KILL YOURSELF.
WHRRR KLIK
WHA..

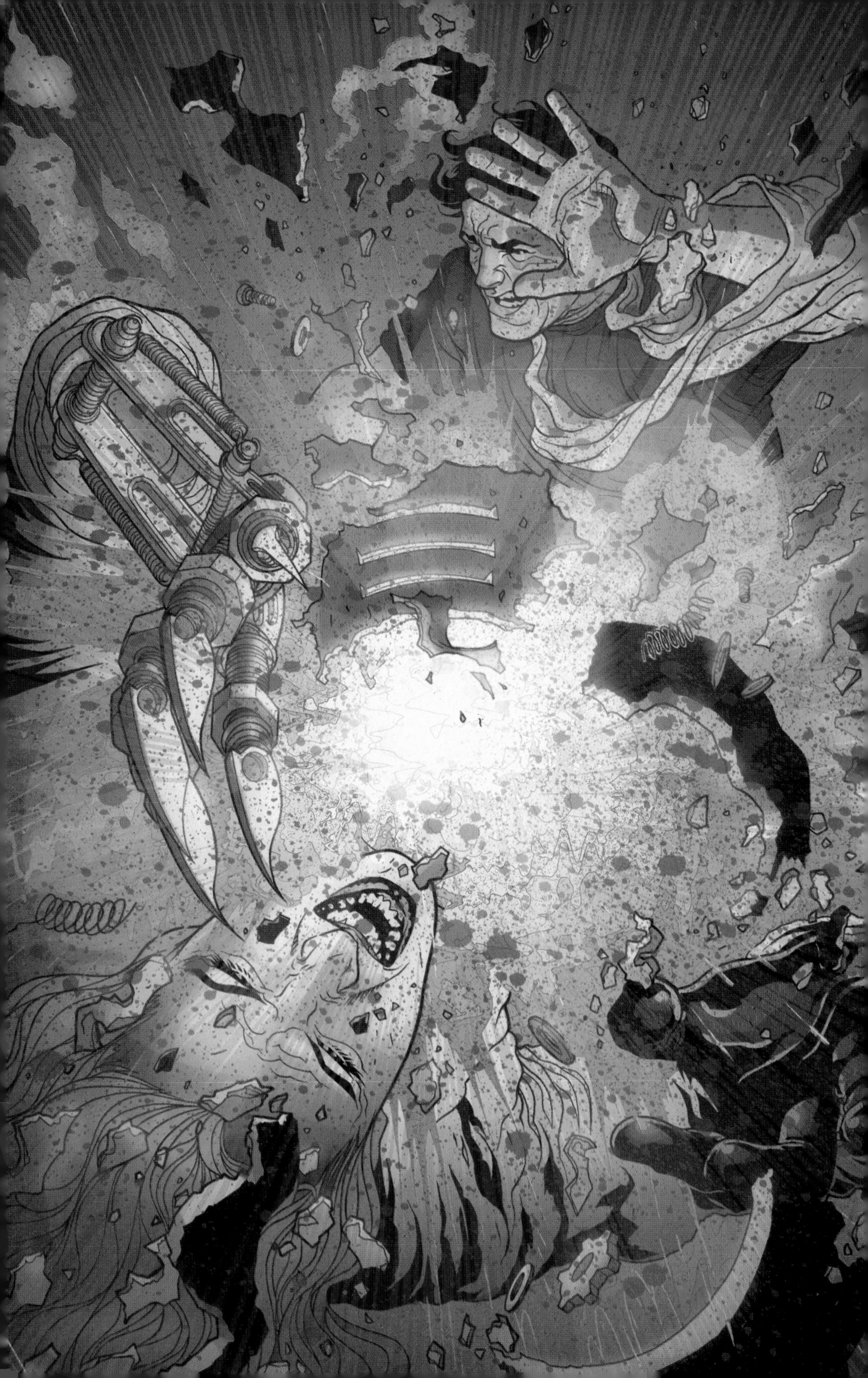

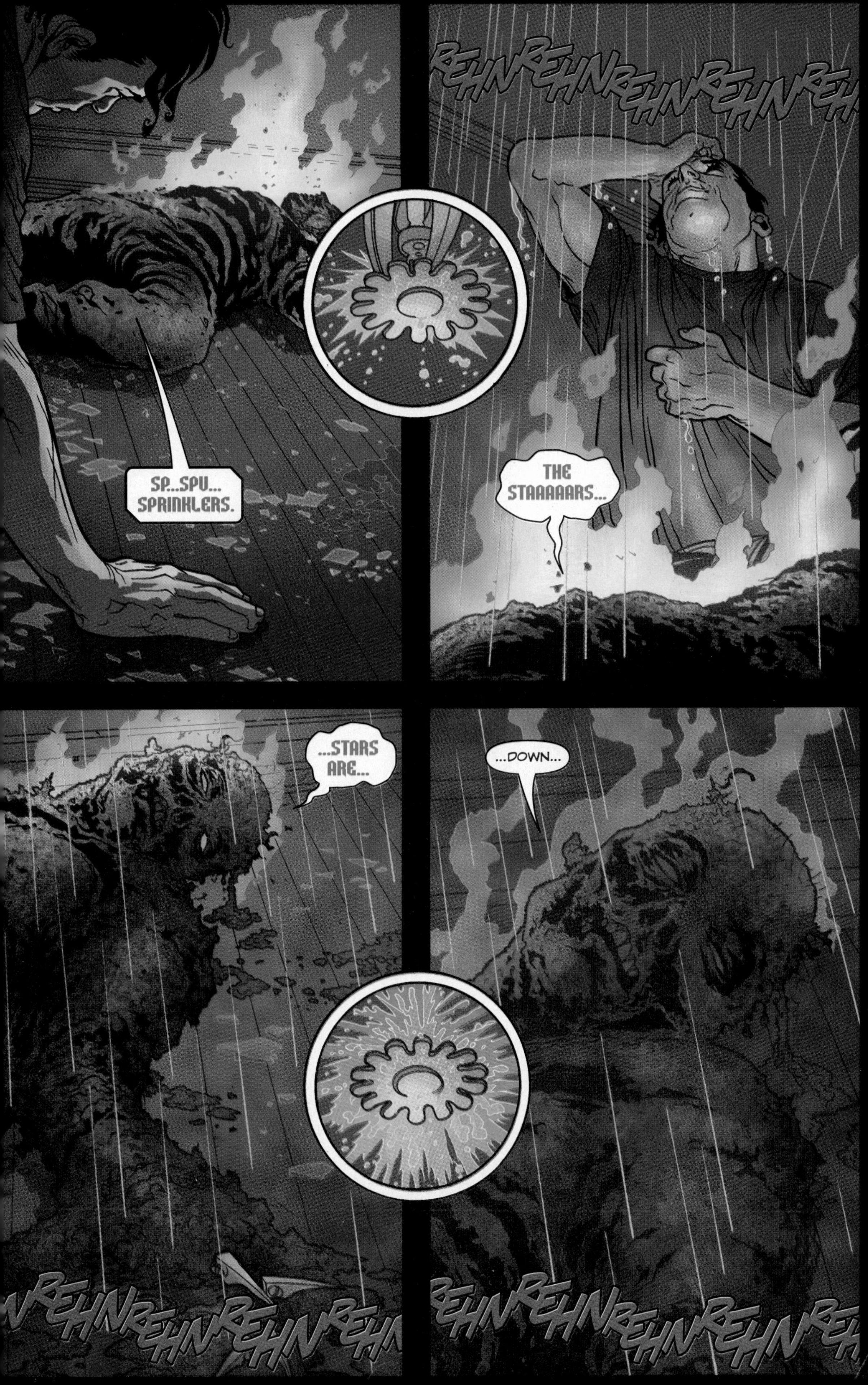
SP...SPU...
SPRINKLERS.
REHNREHNREHNREHNREHNREH
THE
STAAAAARS...
...STARS
ARE...
...DOWN...
REHNREHNREHNREHN
REHNREHNREHNREHNREH

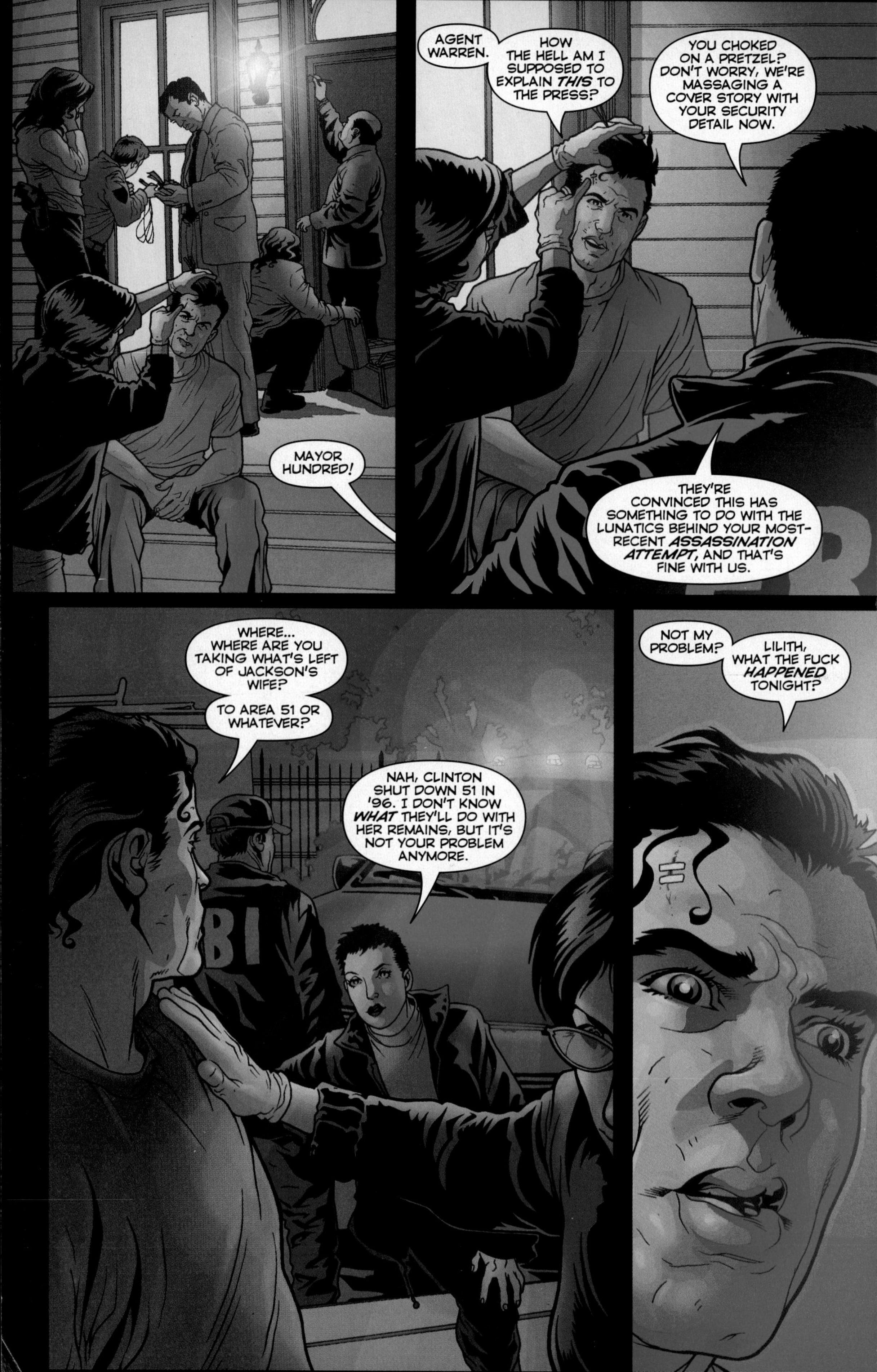
MAYOR HUNDRED!
AGENT WARREN.
HOW THE HELL AM I SUPPOSED TO EXPLAIN THIS TO THE PRESS?
YOU CHOKED ON A PRETZEL? DON'T WORRY, WE'RE MASSAGING A COVER STORY WITH YOUR SECURITY DETAIL NOW.
THEY'RE CONVINCED THIS HAS SOMETHING TO DO WITH THE LUNATICS BEHIND YOUR MOST-RECENT ASSASSINATION ATTEMPT, AND THAT'S FINE WITH US.
WHERE... WHERE ARE YOU TAKING WHAT'S LEFT OF JACKSON'S WIFE?
TO AREA 51 OR WHATEVER?
NAH, CLINTON SHUT DOWN 51 IN '96. I DON'T KNOW WHAT THEY'LL DO WITH HER REMAINS, BUT IT'S NOT YOUR PROBLEM ANYMORE.
NOT MY PROBLEM?
LILITH, WHAT THE FUCK HAPPENED TONIGHT?
FBI

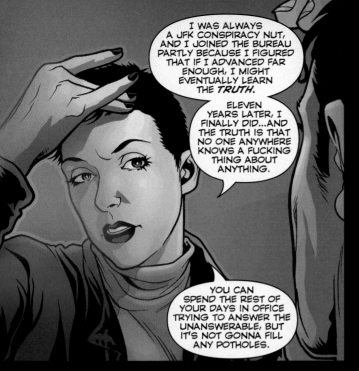

I WAS ALWAYS A JFK CONSPIRACY NUT, AND I JOINED THE BUREAU PARTLY BECAUSE I FIGURED THAT IF I ADVANCED FAR ENOUGH, I MIGHT EVENTUALLY LEARN THE *TRUTH*.

ELEVEN YEARS LATER, I FINALLY DID...AND THE TRUTH IS THAT NO ONE ANYWHERE KNOWS A FUCKING THING ABOUT ANYTHING.

YOU CAN SPEND THE REST OF YOUR DAYS IN OFFICE TRYING TO ANSWER THE UNANSWERABLE, BUT IT'S NOT GONNA FILL ANY POTHOLES.

MY GOD.

IN LESS THAN FORTY-EIGHT HOURS, I'M MARRYING TWO MEN ON THIS EXACT SPOT...AND MOST PEOPLE WILL THINK *THAT'S* THE STRANGEST THING GOING ON IN THIS COUNTRY.

IGNORANCE IS BLISS, HUH?

SPEAKING OF WHICH, IS THAT THE HARLEM RIVER OR THE EAST RIVER OUT THERE? I'VE GOT A BET WITH THE CHOPPER PILOT WHO BROUGHT ME OVER.

WHAT? NO, IT'S... IT'S BOTH. THEY CONVERGE RIGHT IN FRONT OF THE RESIDENCE.

THE CURRENTS ARE BRUTAL, USUALLY TAKE DOWN A BOAT OR TWO EVERY FEW YEARS. THEY CALL IT *HELL GATE*.

YEAH...I GUESS THEY WOULD.

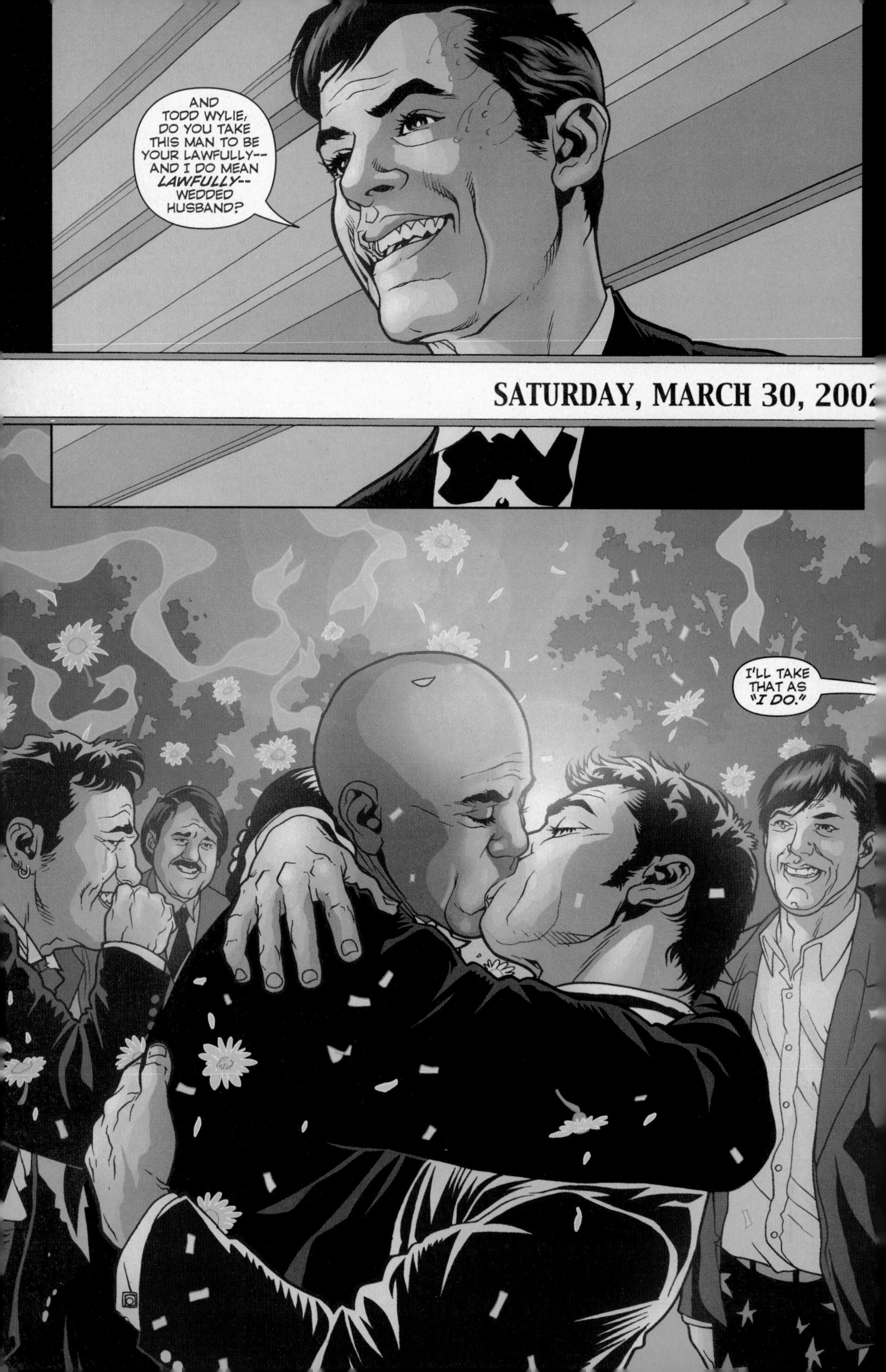
AND TODD WYLIE, DO YOU TAKE THIS MAN TO BE YOUR LAWFULLY-- AND I DO MEAN *LAWFULLY*-- WEDDED HUSBAND?
SATURDAY, MARCH 30, 200
I'LL TAKE THAT AS *"I DO."*

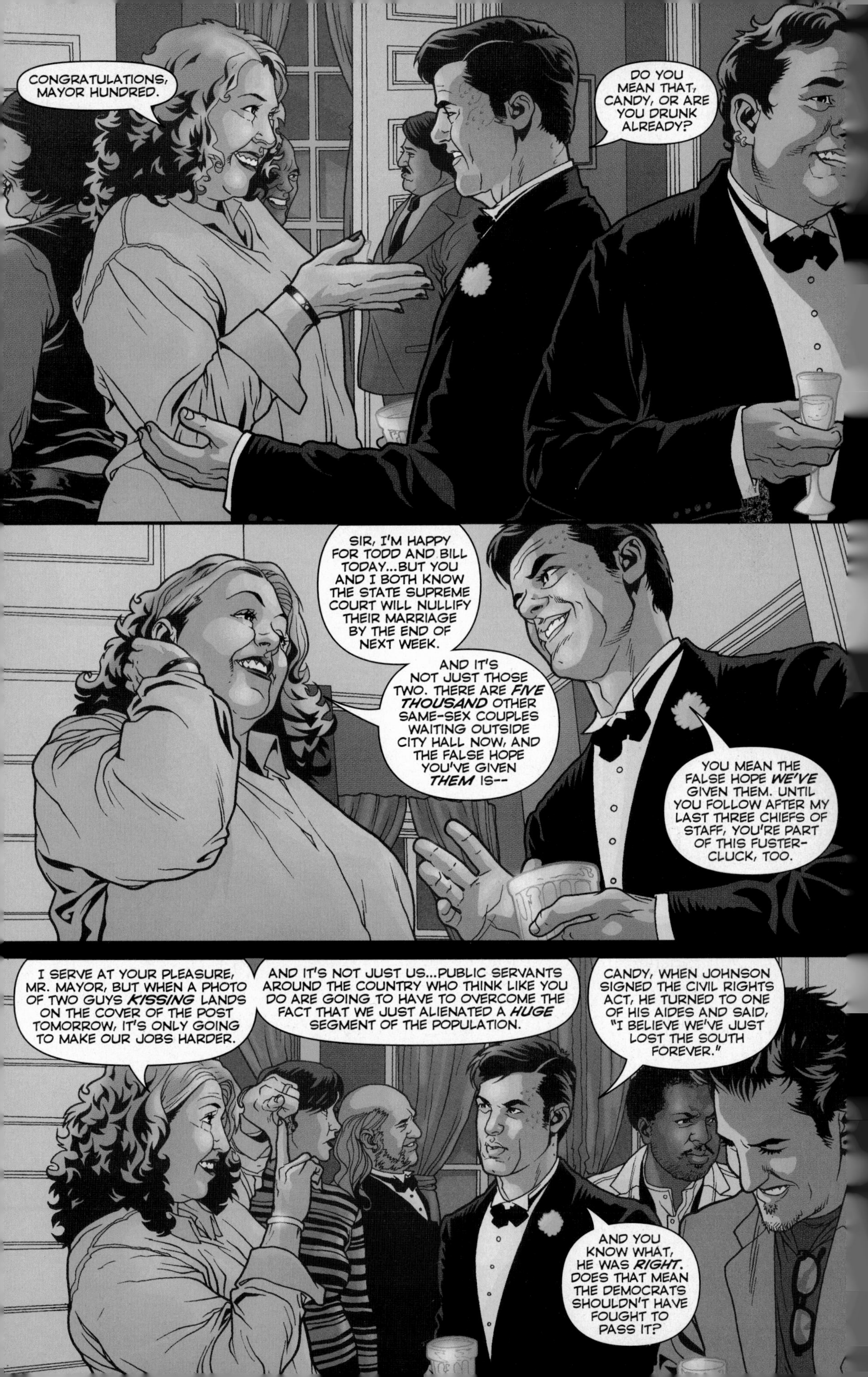
CONGRATULATIONS, MAYOR HUNDRED.
DO YOU MEAN THAT, CANDY, OR ARE YOU DRUNK ALREADY?
SIR, I'M HAPPY FOR TODD AND BILL TODAY...BUT YOU AND I BOTH KNOW THE STATE SUPREME COURT WILL NULLIFY THEIR MARRIAGE BY THE END OF NEXT WEEK.
AND IT'S NOT JUST THOSE TWO. THERE ARE FIVE THOUSAND OTHER SAME-SEX COUPLES WAITING OUTSIDE CITY HALL NOW, AND THE FALSE HOPE YOU'VE GIVEN THEM IS--
YOU MEAN THE FALSE HOPE WE'VE GIVEN THEM. UNTIL YOU FOLLOW AFTER MY LAST THREE CHIEFS OF STAFF, YOU'RE PART OF THIS FUSTER-CLUCK, TOO.
I SERVE AT YOUR PLEASURE, MR. MAYOR, BUT WHEN A PHOTO OF TWO GUYS KISSING LANDS ON THE COVER OF THE POST TOMORROW, IT'S ONLY GOING TO MAKE OUR JOBS HARDER.
AND IT'S NOT JUST US...PUBLIC SERVANTS AROUND THE COUNTRY WHO THINK LIKE YOU DO ARE GOING TO HAVE TO OVERCOME THE FACT THAT WE JUST ALIENATED A HUGE SEGMENT OF THE POPULATION.
CANDY, WHEN JOHNSON SIGNED THE CIVIL RIGHTS ACT, HE TURNED TO ONE OF HIS AIDES AND SAID, "I BELIEVE WE'VE JUST LOST THE SOUTH FOREVER."
AND YOU KNOW WHAT, HE WAS RIGHT. DOES THAT MEAN THE DEMOCRATS SHOULDN'T HAVE FOUGHT TO PASS IT?

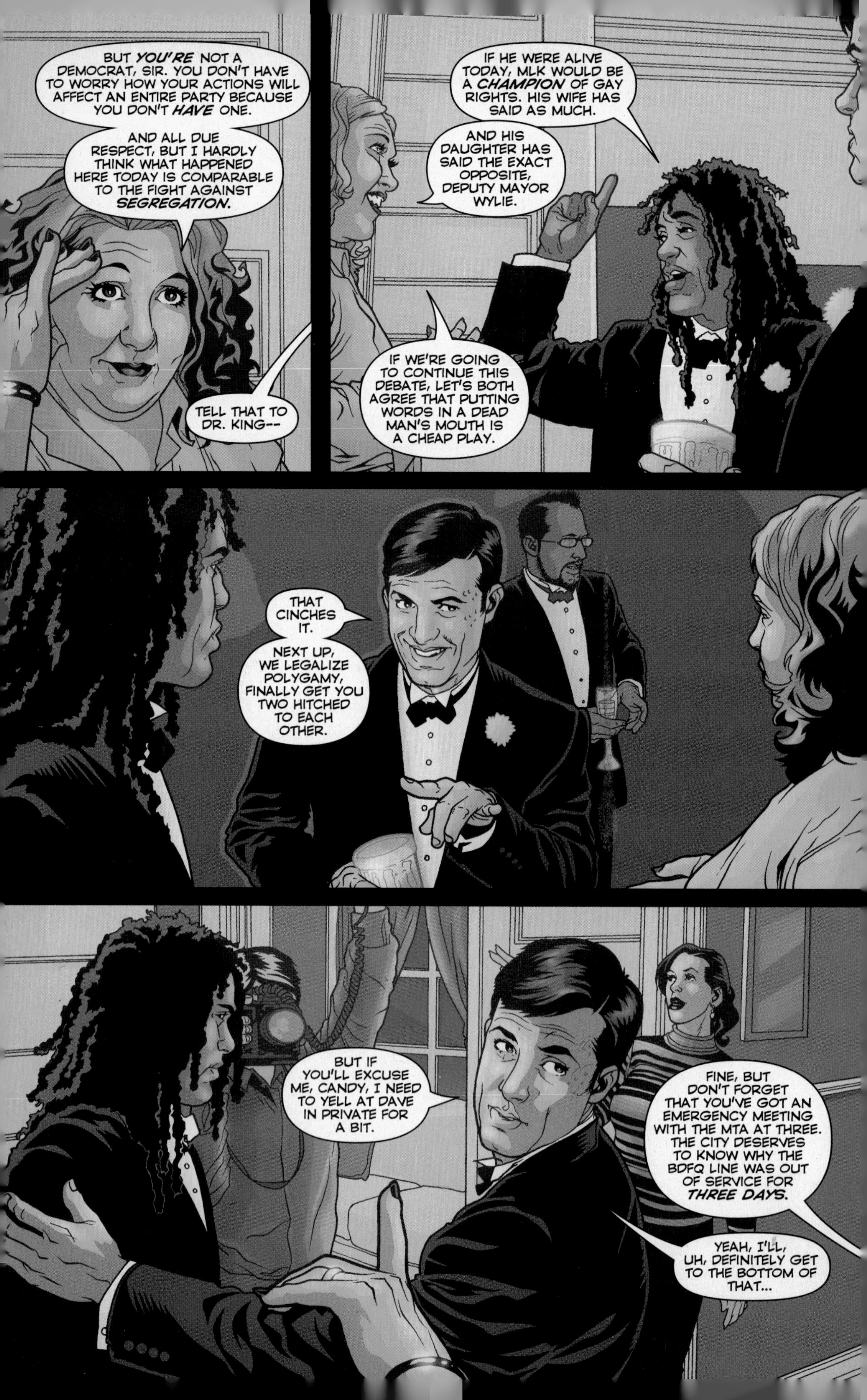
BUT YOU'RE NOT A DEMOCRAT, SIR. YOU DON'T HAVE TO WORRY HOW YOUR ACTIONS WILL AFFECT AN ENTIRE PARTY BECAUSE YOU DON'T HAVE ONE.
AND ALL DUE RESPECT, BUT I HARDLY THINK WHAT HAPPENED HERE TODAY IS COMPARABLE TO THE FIGHT AGAINST SEGREGATION.
TELL THAT TO DR. KING--
IF HE WERE ALIVE TODAY, MLK WOULD BE A CHAMPION OF GAY RIGHTS. HIS WIFE HAS SAID AS MUCH.
AND HIS DAUGHTER HAS SAID THE EXACT OPPOSITE, DEPUTY MAYOR WYLIE.
IF WE'RE GOING TO CONTINUE THIS DEBATE, LET'S BOTH AGREE THAT PUTTING WORDS IN A DEAD MAN'S MOUTH IS A CHEAP PLAY.
THAT CINCHES IT.
NEXT UP, WE LEGALIZE POLYGAMY, FINALLY GET YOU TWO HITCHED TO EACH OTHER.
BUT IF YOU'LL EXCUSE ME, CANDY, I NEED TO YELL AT DAVE IN PRIVATE FOR A BIT.
FINE, BUT DON'T FORGET THAT YOU'VE GOT AN EMERGENCY MEETING WITH THE MTA AT THREE. THE CITY DESERVES TO KNOW WHY THE BDFQ LINE WAS OUT OF SERVICE FOR THREE DAYS.
YEAH, I'LL, UH, DEFINITELY GET TO THE BOTTOM OF THAT...

SIR, I CAN'T BEGIN TO THANK YOU ENOUGH FOR WHAT YOU DID FOR MY BROTHER TODAY. I--

YEAH, YEAH, SAVE IT FOR MY EULOGY. I HEARD THROUGH THE GRAPEVINE THAT YOU'RE PULLING THE KIDS OUT OF HORACE MANN. IS THAT *TRUE?*

I *KNEW* I SHOULDN'T HAVE TOLD JOURNAL...

JESUS, DAVE, IS YOUR *FAMILY* ALL RIGHT WITH THIS?

I DECIDED IT *WASN'T* RIGHT FOR ME TO FIGHT AGAINST SCHOOL VOUCHERS WHILE SENDING MY OWN KIDS TO A PRIVATE INSTITUTION, OKAY? MAYBE YOU HAD A *POINT.*

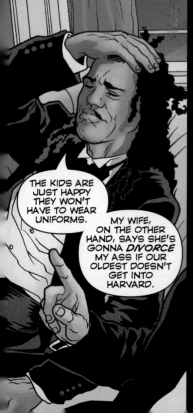

LISTEN, I ADMIRE YOUR PRINCIPLES, BUT YOU CAN'T RISK HURTING YOUR *MARRIAGE* OVER THIS.

RISK IS WHAT MARRIAGE IS ALL ABOUT, SIR.

SOMEDAY, YOU'LL SEE WHAT I MEAN.

THE KIDS ARE JUST HAPPY THEY WON'T HAVE TO WEAR UNIFORMS. MY WIFE, ON THE OTHER HAND, SAYS SHE'S GONNA *DIVORCE* MY ASS IF OUR OLDEST DOESN'T GET INTO HARVARD.

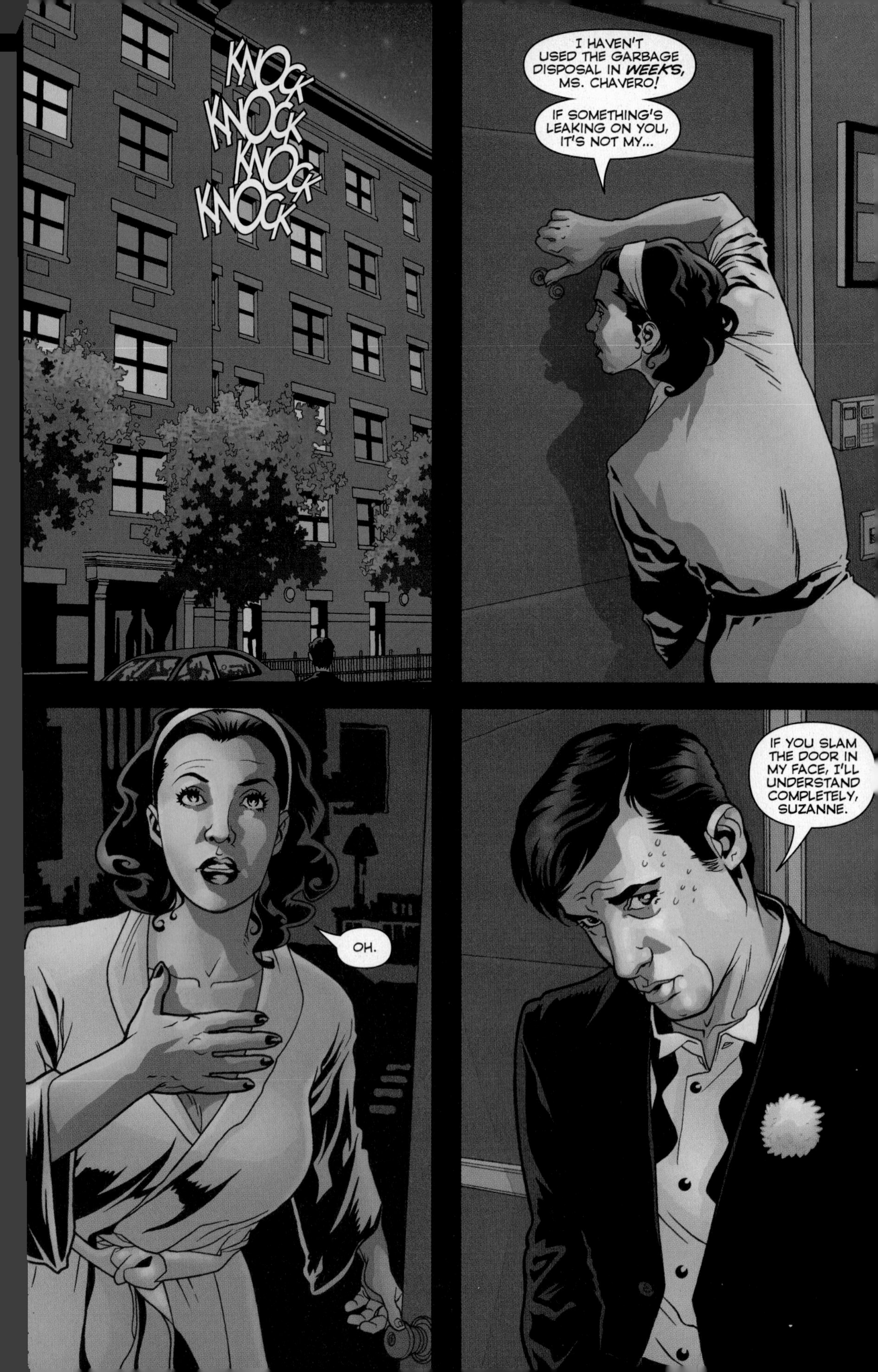
KNOCK KNOCK KNOCK KNOCK
I HAVEN'T USED THE GARBAGE DISPOSAL IN *WEEKS*, MS. CHAVERO!
IF SOMETHING'S LEAKING ON YOU, IT'S NOT MY...
OH.
IF YOU SLAM THE DOOR IN MY FACE, I'LL UNDERSTAND COMPLETELY, SUZANNE.

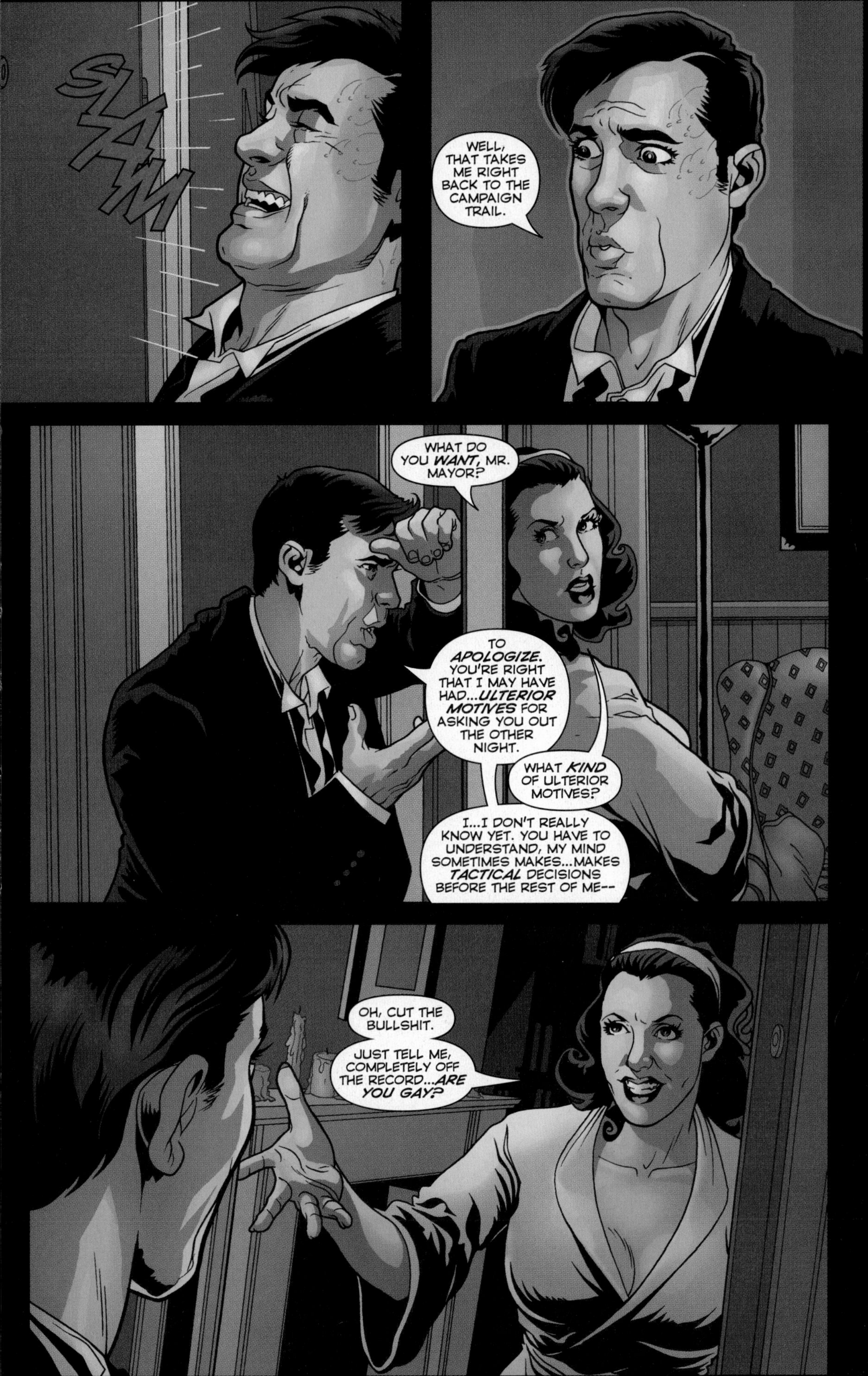
SLAM
WELL, THAT TAKES ME RIGHT BACK TO THE CAMPAIGN TRAIL.
WHAT DO YOU WANT, MR. MAYOR?
TO APOLOGIZE. YOU'RE RIGHT THAT I MAY HAVE HAD...ULTERIOR MOTIVES FOR ASKING YOU OUT THE OTHER NIGHT.
WHAT KIND OF ULTERIOR MOTIVES?
I...I DON'T REALLY KNOW YET. YOU HAVE TO UNDERSTAND, MY MIND SOMETIMES MAKES...MAKES TACTICAL DECISIONS BEFORE THE REST OF ME--
OH, CUT THE BULLSHIT.
JUST TELL ME, COMPLETELY OFF THE RECORD...ARE YOU GAY?

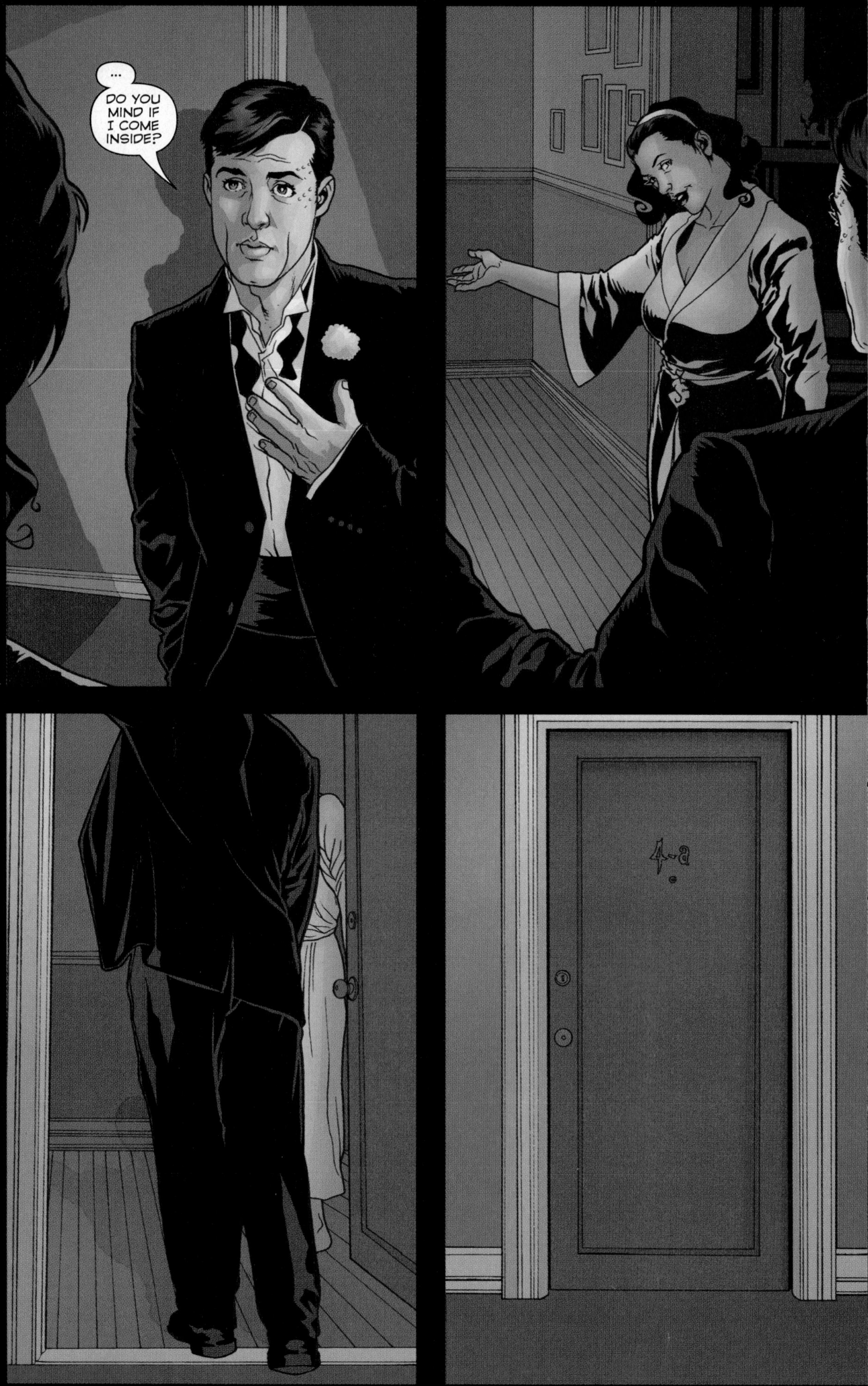
...
DO YOU MIND IF I COME INSIDE?
4-a

SKETCHBOOK

sketch
1

BY TONY HARRIS

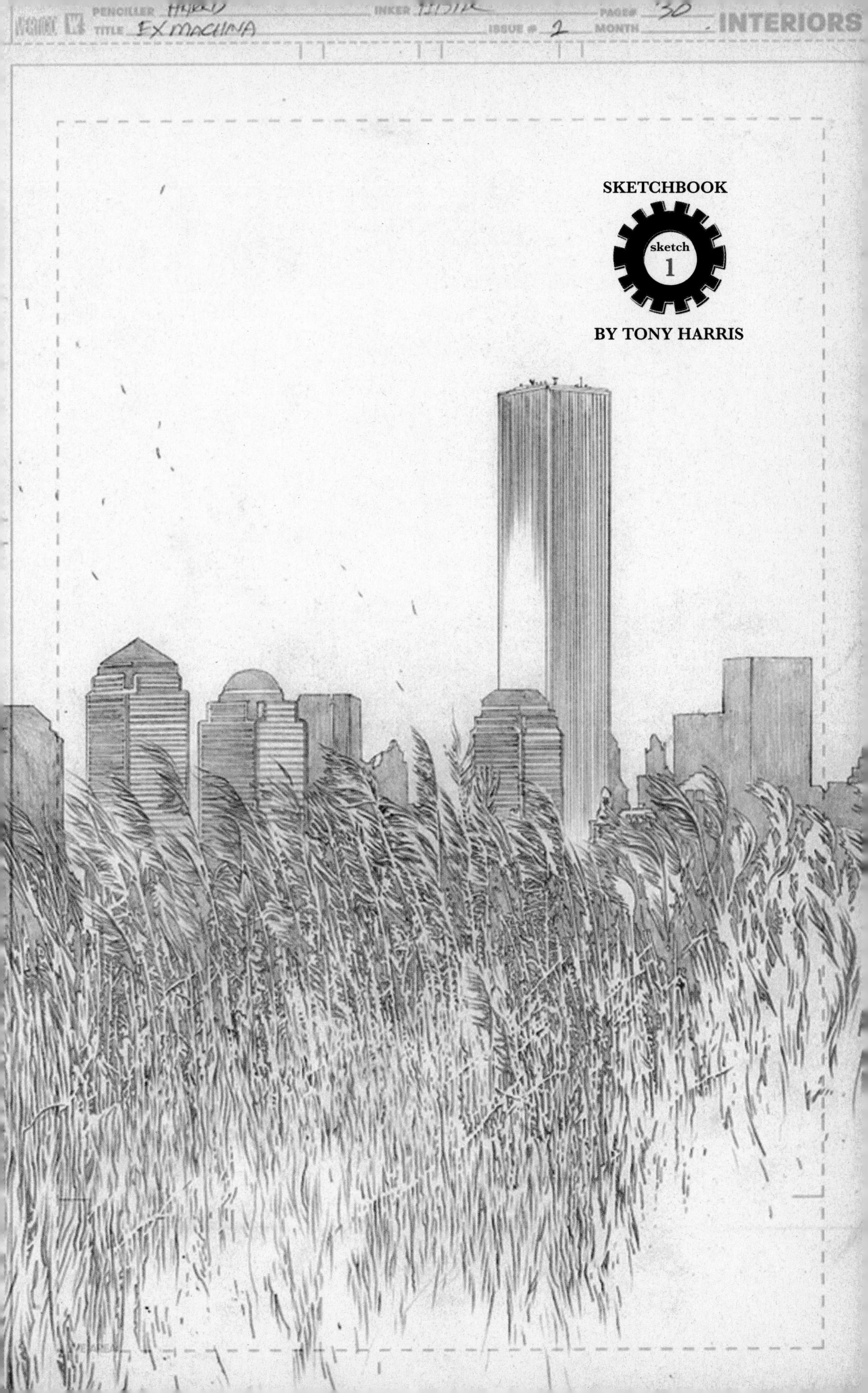
PENCILLER
INKER
PAGE# 30
TITLE EX MACHINA
ISSUE # 2
MONTH
INTERIORS

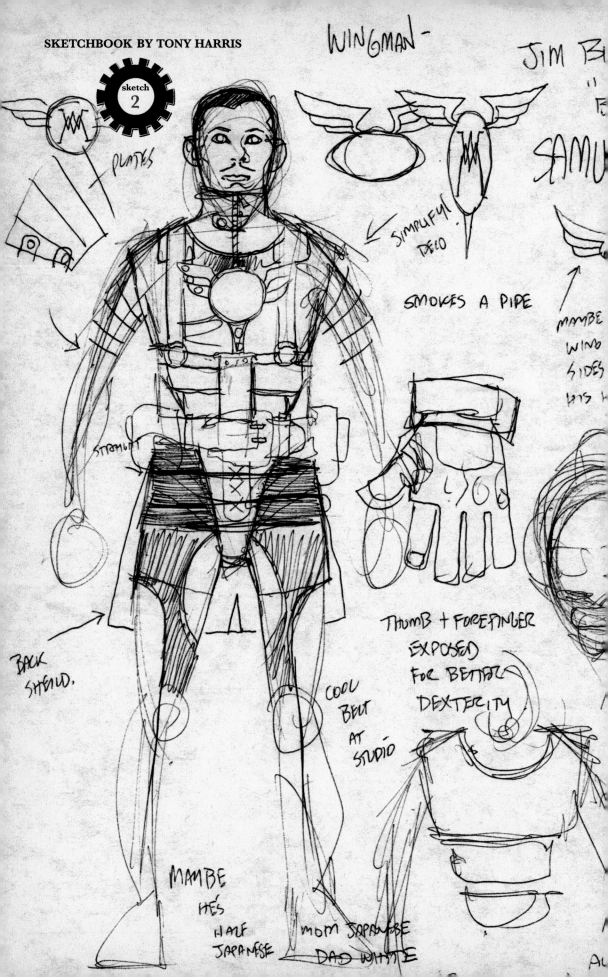

SKETCHBOOK BY TONY HARRIS

sketch 2

WINGMAN—

JIM B

SAMU

PLATES

SIMPLIFY DECO

SMOKES A PIPE

MAMBE
WING
SIDES

STRAMBT

BACK
SHIELD.

THUMB + FOREFINGER
EXPOSED
FOR BETTER
DEXTERITY

COOL
BELT
AT
STUDIO

MAMBE
HE'S
HALF
JAPANESE

MOM JAPANESE
DAD WHITE

SKETCHBOOK sketch 3 BY TONY HARRIS

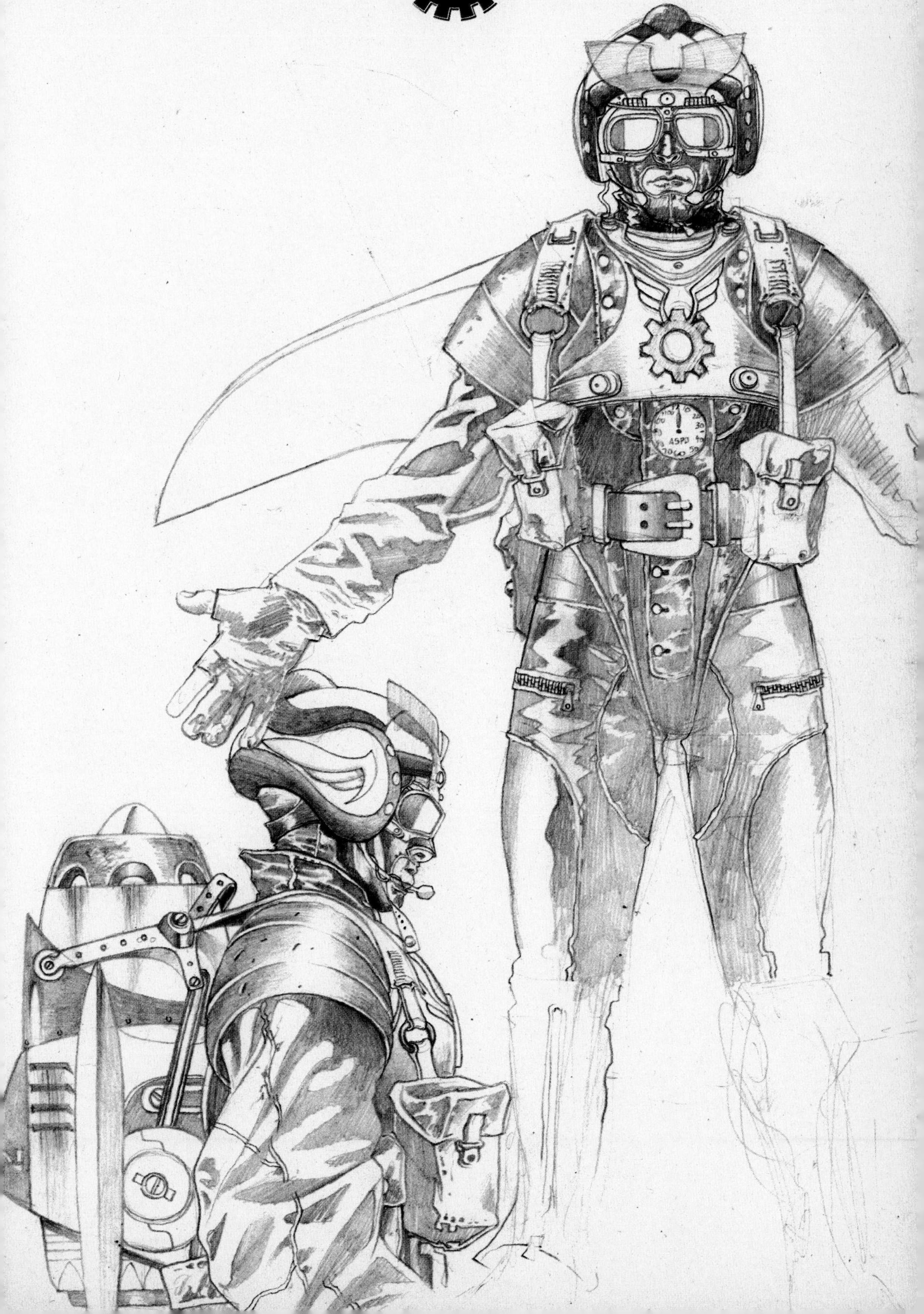

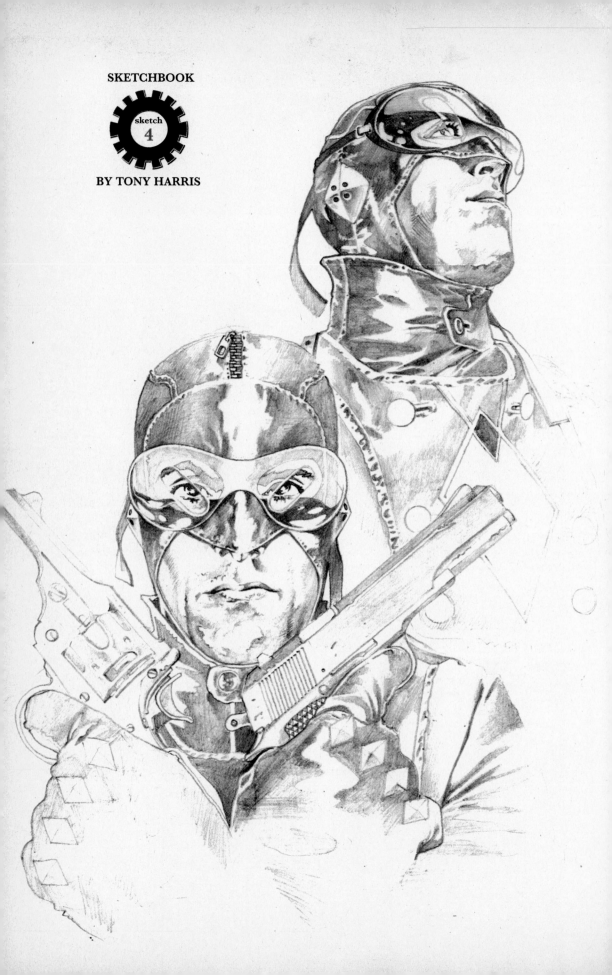

SKETCHBOOK

sketch
4

BY TONY HARRIS

**SKETCHBOOK**

sketch 5

**BY TONY HARRIS**

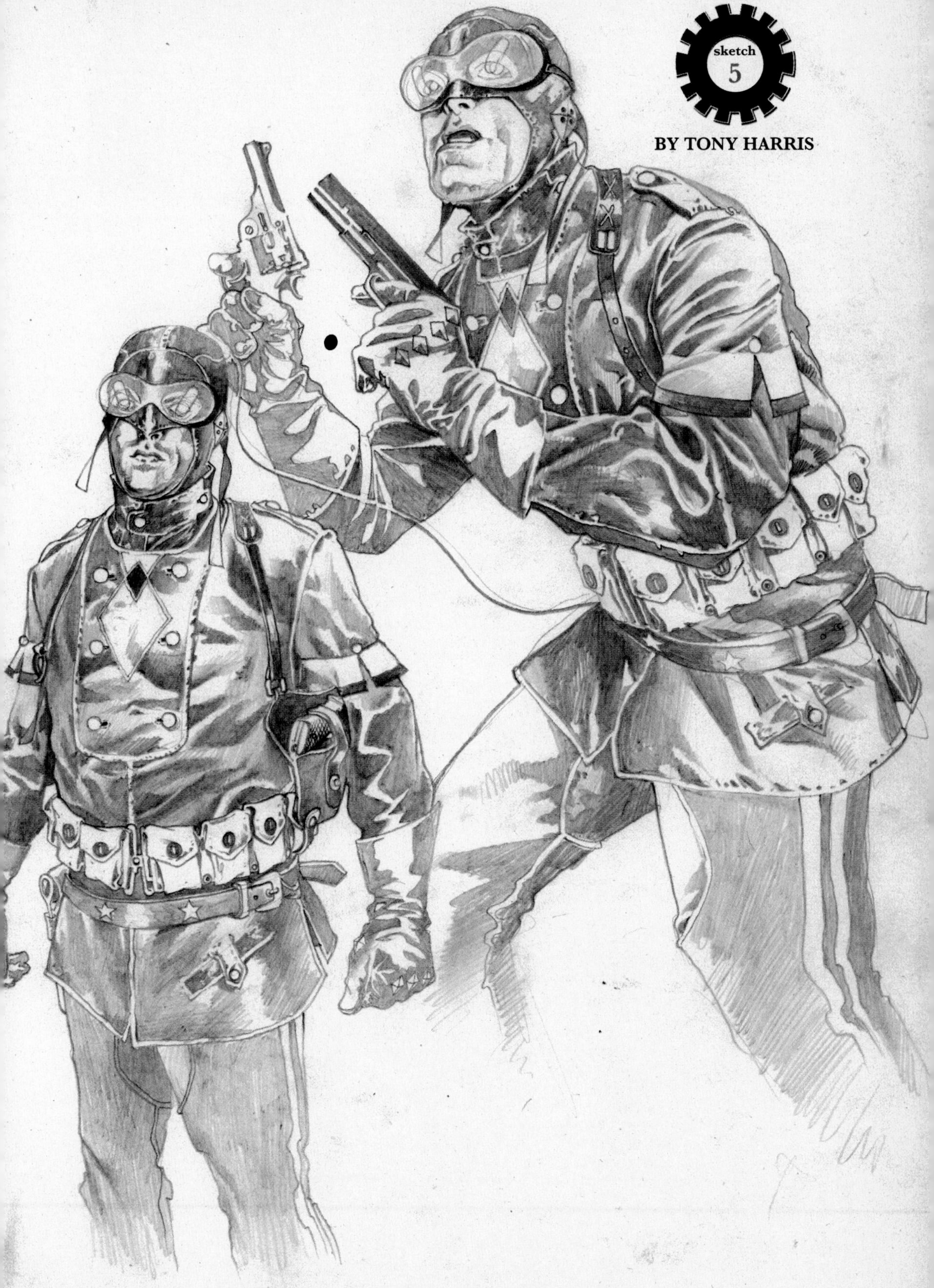

SKETCHBOOK

sketch 6

BY TONY HARRIS

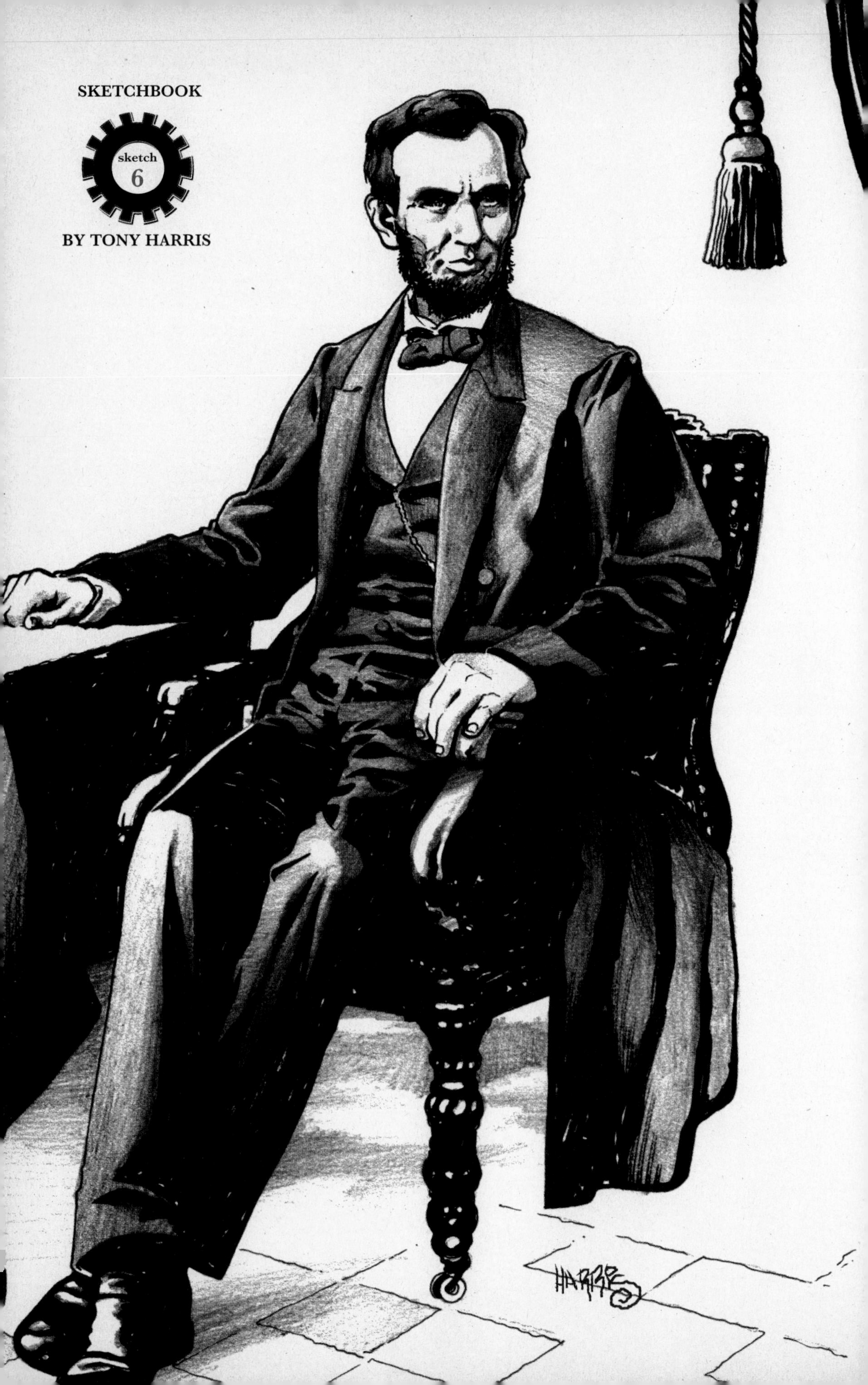
HARRIS

# BACKLIST

THE AUTHORITY
JOHN RIDLEY
BEN OLIVER
HUMAN ON THE INSIDE

THE AUTHORITY:
HUMAN ON THE INSIDE

RIDLEY/OLIVER

ALAN MOORE
KEVIN O'NEILL
The LEAGUE of EXTRAORDINARY GENTLEMEN
VOLUME II

THE LEAGUE OF
EXTRAORDINARY GENTLEMEN
VOLUMES 1 & 2

MOORE/O'NEILL

ALAN MOORE
Book Four of the Transcendent New Series
PROMETHEA
AMERICA'S BEST COMICS
AMERICA'S BEST COMICS
J.H. WILLIAMS III
MICK GRAY
JEROMY COX

PROMETHEA
BOOKS 1–5

MOORE/WILLIAMS III/GRAY

sleeper
a crooked line
ed brubaker sean phillips

SLEEPER
BOOKS 1–3

BRUBAKER/PHILLIPS

**Search the Graphic Novels section of wildstorm.com for art and info on every one of our hundreds of books!**

TO FIND MORE COLLECTED EDITIONS AND MONTHLY COMIC BOOKS FROM WILDSTORM AND DC COMICS, CALL 1-888-COMIC BOOK FOR THE NEAREST COMICS SHOP OR GO TO YOUR LOCAL BOOK STORE.

# BACKLIST

VERTIGO
BOOK 4
"Has steadily proved to be one of the best examples of its art form... Fascinating."
— The Chicago Tribune
"Complete and utter comic gold."
— Publishers Weekly (starred review)
Vaughan Guerra Parlov Marzán, Jr.
THE LAST MAN
Safeword

**Y: THE LAST MAN**
**BOOKS 1–5**

**VAUGHAN/GUERRA/VARIOUS**

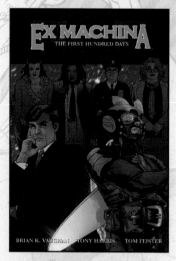

EX MACHINA
THE FIRST HUNDRED DAYS
BRIAN K. VAUGHAN TONY HARRIS TOM FEISTER

**EX MACHINA:**
**THE FIRST HUNDRED DAYS**

**VAUGHAN/HARRIS/FEISTER**

JSA
THE LIBERTY FILES
JOLLEY
HARRIS
SNYDER

**JSA:**
**THE LIBERTY FILES**

**JOLLEY/HARRIS/SNYDER**

STARMAN
James Robinson • Peter Snejbjerg
GRAND
GUIGNOL

**STARMAN**
**BOOKS 1–10**

**ROBINSON/HARRIS/VARIOUS**